# Fundamentals of Microcomputer Programming, Including Pascal

# Fundamentals of Microcomputer Programming, Including Pascal

DANIEL R. McGLYNN

A Wiley-Interscience Publication

**JOHN WILEY & SONS**

New York   Chichester   Brisbane   Toronto   Singapore

**Library of Congress Cataloging in Publication Data:**

McGlynn, Daniel R.
  Fundamentals of microcomputer programming, including Pascal.

  "A Wiley-Interscience publication."
  Bibliography: p.
  Includes indexes.
    1. Microcomputers—Programming.    2. Pascal (Computer
program language)   I. Title.

QA76.6.M4     1982     001.64′2     82-8645
ISBN 0-471-08769-6     AACR2
ISBN 0-471-08769-6 (pbk)

Printed in the United States of America

10  9  8  7  6  5  4  3  2  1

# Preface

This book is an introduction to some of the fundamental concepts in computer programming languages, in particular, the language Pascal, for microcomputers. In the last decade, advances in semiconductor technology have reduced the size and cost of computers to the point where desktop units are now readily accessible to consumers, small businesses, and educational institutions. Although the available computer hardware offers a wide variety of capabilities for all applications, the software—or computer programs—for such microcomputers remains a major hurdle for many users.

One relatively new language that offers considerable potential for a wide variety of microcomputer users is Pascal. It is widely used in colleges and universities for teaching programming languages, and increasing numbers of mini- and microcomputers now offer Pascal software.

However, Pascal is a relatively sophisticated programming language and is usually learned by those who already know another programming language like BASIC or FORTRAN. There are many who argue that Pascal should be taught as the first programming language so that the user's thought processes are not affected by the "bad habits" found in languages like BASIC and FORTRAN. This book offers one approach to Pascal as a first programming language.

The teaching of computer programming and programming languages has traditionally been from an applications-oriented perspective: computer programming for business majors, computer programming for engineers, and so on. This book approaches the teaching of computer programming from a computer science perspective, that is, computer programming as it is related to computer hardware and computer linguistics.

This book is written for the person who wants a thorough understanding of modern concepts in computer programming and programming languages and wants to apply that understanding in using Pascal or other structured programming languages. Since it assumes no previous background in programming, this book is suitable for introductory courses in programming or computer science at the college level, or for professional development courses.

v

It is not, however, intended as another book in the spirit of "how to program in Pascal." The book is intended to give the reader a greater appreciation of programming and computer software and, within that context, to present the fundamentals of the Pascal programming language. It could be said that the intent of the book is analogous to a course in art appreciation rather than in painting.

A revolution is taking place in education, based partly upon the availability of inexpensive personal computers for home and classroom use, and partly upon the development and widespread acceptance of prepackaged software and simple, easy-to-learn programming languages like BASIC. It is pertinent to ask what impact these developments can have on computer education. Other academic fields have had their revolutions—consider the "new math" as a case in point. It took only a few years of instruction in abstract concepts of sets and mappings before the books entitled "Why Johnny Can't Add" began appearing in bookstores (which was, incidentally, long before the $10 electronic calculator was on the market).

It is therefore pertinent to at least pose the question about the impact of prepackaged software on the next generation of programmers. Is the specter of "Why Johnny Can't Program" a real one? In raising such a question, we are not concerned with the students who have really mastered a high-level language like Pascal and understand programming, any more than the critics of the new math were concerned with students who actually learned arithmetic, either with the assistance of, or in spite of, the new math. Instead, we are concerned that the users of microcomputers should have a greater appreciation and understanding of computer programming.

Chapter 1 gives the reader an overview of computer hardware and software from the perspective of modern mini- and microcomputers. Chapter 2 presents a summary of the field of computer linguistics, in order to give an appreciation of how computer programming languages are related to natural languages, and how the field of computer science characterizes such languages. Chapter 3 presents the different types of computer programming languages on a conceptual level—from low level to high level languages, from sequential to concurrent processing. An introduction to the important concept of data flow languages is also presented. Chapters 4 and 5 tackle the subject of programming, from problem definition to a consideration of programming costs. Chapters 6 through 8 present the Pascal language in a fairly thorough manner, while Chapter 9 contains a number of simple programs in Pascal for different applications.

As the title of this book suggests, the microcomputer implementations of Pascal are probably of most interest, particularly for the first-time programmer. Chapter 10 describes the features and differences between a number of the most popular microcomputer implementations of the language. Chapter

11 describes in detail the widespread and popular UCSD Pascal used in a number of microcomputer implementations.

Finally, since Pascal is only one step in the evolution of programming languages, Chapter 12 briefly describes two languages—Modula-2 and Ada—which are evolutionary descendants of Pascal.

The author is grateful for the assistance of the Pascal Users' Group for use of the ISO Draft Standard on Pascal, and David V. Moffat for the use of his extensive bibliography.

DANIEL R. McGLYNN

*Anaheim, California*
*September 1982*

# Contents

# Fundamentals of Microcomputer Programming, Including Pascal

# 1

# Communicating with the Microcomputer

*. . . [T]he next postindustrial revolution would be the silicon revolution of information processing and computers that would . . . change the face of the earth.*

*Jean-Jacques Servan-Schrieber,*
*Le Défi Mondial (1980)*

When the microprocessor or "computer-on-a-chip" was introduced in the early 1970s, one of the major challenges facing the prospective users was how to communicate with it. Semiconductor technology had advanced much more rapidly than computer programming and computer languages, and the full capability of the early microprocessors was not realized. Today microcomputers are accessible to consumers, small businesses, and educational institutions, and the software—though much more highly developed than in the mid-1970s—still remains a major hurdle for most users.

Microcomputer programming and programming languages are basically concerned with communicating with a microcomputer. The present-day microcomputer users are, however, different from the original users of microprocessors in the early 1970s, and even different from the computer hobbyists who assembled computer kits in the mid-1970s and "programmed" such computers by entering instructions bit by bit on front panel sense switches. The present-day microcomputer user approaches the computer from an applications perspective—thinking in concepts of storing customer names in one file, and zip codes in another file.

Although it is instructive to consider the position taken by some that computers are intended to solve real-world problems expressed by users in such an applications-oriented perspective, the fact is that programming languages are adapted to computer hardware that exists, rather than computer hardware being designed to execute specific programming languages. Until such time that special-purpose, dedicated computer hardware is designed to execute specific languages or solve specific applications, in order to understand the task of communicating with a microcomputer, one must begin with the structures and elements of the microcomputer which participate in such communication.

With such a viewpoint explicitly stated, we consider the following basic issues:

computer architecture
hardware/software interface
types of computer programs
information theory


## COMPUTER ARCHITECTURE TYPES

There are a number of different ways to classify computer architectures, depending whether one is looking at the computer from a hardware, software, or operational perspective. Since this book is concerned with computer programming and software, it is appropriate to consider a classification based upon software, or more particularly, the proximity of the user programming language and the language actually executed by the machine. The classification is:

von Neumann architecture
syntax-oriented architecture
indirect execution architecture
direct execution architecture

In studying computer programming and software, it is important that the reader keep in mind the basic relationship between the software and the type of computer architecture. The capabilities and limitations of a particular computer language, or of a particular program, are closely related to the type of computer architecture on which the language or program is implemented. Some computer languages operate much more efficiently with a given computer architecture than with others; similarly, certain programs are executed much more efficiently on certain types of computer architectures.

Since von Neumann architecture is the most commonly implemented architecture, and the typical computer programmer will rarely encounter a non-von Neumann computer, the importance of the relationship of computer language and computer architecture is not particularly relevant from an immediate, practical viewpoint. However, it must be realized that as semiconductor and microprocessor technology advances, it will become more and more feasible to implement non-von Neumann architectures, and at such time the relationship between language and architecture will take on a new relevancy.

## Microcomputer Architectures

A microcomputer is a computer that incorporates a microprocessor as the central processing unit. Since almost all commercial microprocessors are designed with a von Neumann architecture, the broad categories of computer architectures discussed previously are not as relevant as a discussion of the system architectures implemented using microprocessors. System architecture refers not to the specific operations of the memories, registers, or control units that distinguish the broad categories of computer architectures, but to the interrelation of system components such as the central processor, peripheral processors, interfaces, operating systems, and similar components.

Microcomputers can be generally categorized according to their system architectures into five distinct categories:

microcontrollers
microcomputers
micromidis
micromaxis
micromainframes

The microcontroller is a relatively simple microprocessor-based computer typically directed to routine industrial control applications. The microprocessor employed is usually a "low end" microprocessor such as the Intel 8048 or 8022, the Zilog Z8, or the Mostek 3870, or similar 8-bit microprocessors.

The microcomputer is a term for a general-purpose microprocessor-based computer system. When used in the context of system architecture classification, the term microcomputer refers to a midrange 8- or 16-bit microprocessor-based system, such as an Intel 8080 or 8085, or even the 16-bit Intel 8086 or Zilog Z8000, in simple system configurations.

The micromidi is a 16-bit microprocessor-based computer system with the characteristics of a "midicomputer," a term that refers to a computer having capabilities greater than a minicomputer but less than a maxicomputer or mainframe. An example of a midicomputer could be the IBM System/32. The type of microprocessor used to implement a micromidi would be a 16-bit microprocessor such as the Intel 8086 or Zilog Z8000 in an extended configuration. Micromidi systems are only now just becoming feasible to implement with the commercial availability of such microprocessors and peripheral processors.

The micromaxi and micromainframe are two microprocessor system architectures that are expected to be made possible with the next generation of 16-bit and 32-bit microprocessors. Such systems refer to computers having the architecture of the present-day commercially available maxicomputers or mainframe computers. The next generation of microprocessors which will make these systems possible is expected to include a pseudo-32 bit processor (i.e., 32-bit internal architecture with 16-bit external buses), as well as, eventually, actual 32-bit processors.

Associated with these levels of system architectures are corresponding levels of software. One proposed system architecture for future microcomputer systems contemplates the use of modularized programs which can be used as building blocks for more complex systems. Some of the most important modular programs to be developed are various operating system kernels. By selecting and combining appropriate operating system kernels, the user will be able to define different software levels and capabilities.

**User-Level Architecture**

The discussion of computer and microcomputer architectures in the preceding sections is, practically speaking, of little relevance to the computer user. Although a knowledge of machine architecture is useful for fully understanding the operation of the computer, as well as its capabilities and limitations, the basic machine architecture generally cannot be easily changed by the user. In many instances the particular type of machine architecture is not even important to the user's application.

However, certain aspects of machine architecture are visible and even important to the user. We call such aspects of the machine architecture which are apparent to the user or programmer the "user-level architecture." All other features of the machine—whether hardware or software—which the user is not aware of are called "transparent" features.

The concept of different levels of computer architecture will be developed in greater detail in the next two sections on the hardware/software interface, and in a discussion of technological hierarchies. It is merely important to note at this point that although two different computers may appear the same, operationally, from the perspective of the user, the machines may have completely different architectures.

User-level architecture is a relative term depending upon the particular user, rather than the particular hardware configuration. One user sitting at the console of the computer may communicate with certain features of the computer in a completely different manner than another user sitting at a remote location and communicating with the computer via a terminal. Although both users have their instructions executed by the same hardware, the nature of their interaction or "interfacing" with the computer is different. In effect, the two different users are interacting with two different user-level architectures.

The user-level architecture is principally defined by software. Although computer architecture basically describes the computer hardware, computer software is a very important component of a system's architecture. The architecture that is apparent to the user is a combination of hardware and software features that dynamically interact. The nature of this hardware/software interface and interaction, and the relationship of the user to this interface are described in the next section.


## HARDWARE/SOFTWARE INTERFACE

The preceding discussion of computer architecture focused on the hardware aspects of computer design. Another important aspect of the computer design is the role of computer software at all levels of the architectures, and the interface between such software and the computer hardware.

In order to place the hardware/software interface in perspective, we consider the following issues in the present section:

basic definitions
language levels


### Basic Definitions

Before turning to the discussion of the hardware/software interface, it is important to establish definitions for some of the terminology. Some key terms are:

programming language
grammar
language level
metalanguage
string
instruction
data

Simply defined, a programming language is the means used for communicating instructions to the computer. Computer languages will be described in much greater detail and much more precisely in the following two chapters; however, for our purposes here, such an inferential definition is adequate.

We already mentioned various programming languages such as FORTRAN, COBOL, Pascal, and ALGOL. It must be emphasized that these are programming languages employed by a programmer of a general purpose computer to communicate with it.

A grammar is a set of rules that describe or define the programming language. Grammars will also be described in greater detail in the next chapter.

The language level is an informal designation of the degree of complexity of the operations described by a single communication in a language. These levels are listed in Table 1.1.

A metalanguage is a language used to describe a programming language.

A string is an ordered sequence of characters in a programming language, and may represent a statement, a computation sequence, or a data element to be processed.

An instruction is an element of a programming language which defines a specific operation or sequence of operations to be performed.

Data is any information other than instructions or control operations handled by the processor.

## Language Levels

Just as there are different levels of architecture from user architecture to machine architecture, there are different levels of languages associated with the computer. Another way to describe a language level is as the relative degree of complexity of the operation described by a single communication at that level.

Table 1.1 lists five language levels from the simplest and most closely related to the machine hardware, to the most complex and most closely related to the user.

**TABLE 1.1**

| Level | Name | Example |
|-------|------|---------|
| 0 | microcode | test bit |
| 1 | machine instruction | ADD or XOR two bytes |
| 2 | machine instruction group; macro, or co-routine | SQUARE ROOT |
| 3 | procedures, tasks, modules, in a high level language | PROCEDURE SORT |
| 4 | language description, metalanguage | $<$digit$> ::= 0|1|2| \ldots$ etc. |

The 0 level is the microcode or primitive language level. It is associated with basic hardware operations at a bit level.

The 1 level is a more complex operation describing a sequence of machine operations to define a single arithmetic or logical concept, such as machine language instructions ADD or XOR (exclusive-OR).

The 2 level describes a sequence of 1 level instructions which define yet a higher arithmetic or logical abstraction, such as an instruction for "square root."

The 3 level defines a more complex programming language instruction which is composed of sequences of lower level instructions. Instructions in a high level language are also examples of the 3 level.

The 4 level is the metalanguage, a description of the programming language itself.

An important aspect of the hardware-software interface is the correspondence or noncorrespondence of various facilities in the high level language and in the machine. In some cases, the facilities in the language reflect that of the machine on which the language was developed; in other cases, there may be no such correspondence.

A historical example is a useful illustration. In the original FORTRAN language there were three index variables I, J, and K, which were used for indexing looping operations. It might be asked, "Why only three?" The hardware on which the language was originally developed provides the answer: the IBM 704 had only three index registers.

Of course, in many instances the language facilities are more ambitious than the machines they were implemented on. PL/I, for example, has a variable length string feature in the language which is not present on the IBM System/370, on which it was developed and implemented.

## TYPES OF COMPUTER PROGRAMS

Although most of the discussion in the previous sections has been concerned with physical units of the computer—computer hardware—the basic subject of this chapter is communicating with the computer. In this section we finally consider "how" to communicate with the computer.

The term that is generally used for communicating with the computer is "programming," and the communications are known as "computer programs." As we shall see later, in Chapter 5, the term programming encompasses a variety of tasks performed by a computer user ranging from problem definition to program maintenance, and does not focus on the issue of "communication" which we are developing in this chapter. Moreover, programming generally presumes knowledge and use of a specific computer language, which we also have not yet discussed.

In understanding how to communicate with the computer, it would be useful to temporarily forget about one's notions of computer programs, languages, or other modern concepts, and consider the basic issue of communication between person and machine.

There are three basic types of levels of communication between the user and the computer:

system level

application level

task level

Corresponding to each of these levels are computer programs or computer languages, but such further categorization is not important at this point.

System level communication enables the user to establish the basic interface to the hardware so as to provide a specific environment for various jobs and tasks to be communicated to the computer. In other words, the system configuration must be defined before specific jobs are executed on the computer. Such definition must be achieved through some type of communication with the computer.

System level communication generally takes place through a computer program known as an operating system, or an executive. Such programs are generally developed by the hardware manufacturers of the computer equipment, and enable the user to communicate with the hardware concerning the basic computer configuration and system resource allocation. The user communicates through a special-purpose computer language by using "system commands."

Application level communication enables the user to perform specific applications on the hardware. Such communication takes place through an application program, which is designed to run on the specific hardware in question. These application programs may be developed by the hardware manufacturers, but are typically developed by systems houses which sell them to the user separately from the computer hardware.

Finally, task level communication takes place while the computer is executing a specific job or program for the user, and enables the user to interact with the operation of the computer in order to more precisely define the computer operations. Task level communication takes place through some simple question/answer facilities which are provided as part of the application program. Of course, the ultimate end user is not concerned with such a task-oriented language; the task language is designed for the actual user of the computer equipment in its operating environment.

These three levels of communication are generally performed by different personnel in operating a computer system. The system level communication is generally performed by "system programmers." The system programmers have a knowledge of the hardware—such as the peripheral equipment—and the capabilities and limitations of such hardware. These system programmers then configure the appropriate system resources to meet the expected demands of the application. In other words, the system programmer handles resource management, and ensures that the system is capable of handling the jobs and tasks that make up the intended application.

Application level communication is generally performed by personnel known as applications programmers. Applications programmers have a greater knowledge of the intended application—the parameters, algorithms, and data flow—than of the specific issues of implementing that application on the hardware.

Task level communication is performed by the ultimate computer user— the person who sits at the terminal and "talks" to the computer for solving a specific problem. Such a person may not be classified as a "programmer" at all, but as a computer operator, order entry clerk, or other position title. Such a user does communicate with the computer in a certain language, and receives responses from the computer in that language.

## INFORMATION THEORY

The concept of information was originally developed by C. S. Shannon in the context of communication. Information is represented in an electronic system as a signal having certain voltage or current characteristics. Information is represented by the capability of distinguishing one choice among alternatives. In a digital system, information is represented by a single binary digit (bit), or one choice between two alternatives (the possible bits 0 and 1).

In an analog system, the signal may represent magnitude over a predetermined range. In comparison to a digital system, such an analog signal may represent as many as 12 or 16 bits of information.

The fundamental limitation in communication is noise, which produces a distortion in the signal, be it digital or analog. The two key variables in a communication system are the power of information-containing signals, and the power of the noise. The parameter that is used as the criteria for measuring the effectiveness of the communication channel established is the probability of error over a predetermined period of time.

Shannon's theorem relates the maximum rate at which information can be transferred without error to the signal power $P$ and the noise power $N$ as follows:

$$C = B \log_2 \left( \frac{P + N}{N} \right)$$

where $B$ is the bandwidth of the communication channel.

The maximum rate at which information can be transferred without error is known as the channel capacity and is represented by $C$ in the above equation. The above equation (which is more properly known as the Shannon–Hartley theorem) assumes a band-limited gaussian channel in the presence of white noise. A channel is called gaussian if the amplitude distribution function of the noise in the channel is described by a gaussian probability distribution.

One of the important consequences of the above theorem is that for a given channel there is a trade-off between the signal to noise ratio and bandwidth. Information theory is therefore of particular interest in the design of communications systems implying bandwidth-limited channels in the presence of noise.

Another conclusion which can be drawn from information theory is that in order to increase the efficiency of a communiations channel some form of coding may be necessary in order to approach the maximum channel capacity $C$ while minimizing errors. The simplest example of coding is the addition of additional bits (called parity bits or check bits) to the message which increases the redundancy of the message but minimizes the likelihood of error.

## REFERENCES

A. V. Aho and J. D. Ullman, *The Theory of Parsing, Translation and Compiling*, Prentice-Hall, Englewood Cliffs, NJ, 1972.

G. A. Anderson and E. D. Jensen, Computer Inter-connection: Taxonomy, Characteristics, and Examples, *ACM Computing Surveys* **7**(4) (December 1975).

C. G. Bell and A. Newell, *Computer Structures: Readings and Examples*, McGraw-Hill, New York, 1971.

E. G. Coffman, Jr., M. J. Elphick, and A. Shoshani, System Deadlocks, *ACM Computing Surveys* **3**(2) (June 1971).

P. H. Enslow, Jr., Ed., *Multiprocessors and Parallel Processing*, Wiley, New York, 1974.

Caxton C. Foster, *Computer Architecture*, Van Nostrand Reinhold, New York, 1970.

R. E. Griswold and M. T. Griswold, *A SNOBOL 4 Primer*, Prentice-Hall, Englewood Cliffs, NJ, 1973.

J. E. Hopcroft and J. D. Ullman, *Formal Languages and their Relation to Automata*, Addison-Wesley, Reading, Mass., 1969.

E. C. Joseph, Innovations in Heterogeneous and Homogeneous Distributed Function Architectures, *IEEE Computer Magazine* (March 1974).

R. R. Korfphage, *Discrete Computation Structures*, Academic Press, New York, 1974.

P. M. Lewis, II, D. J. Rosenkrantz, and R. E. Stearns, *Compiler Design Theory*, Addison-Wesley, Reading, Mass., 1976.

P. M. Lewis, II, and R. E. Stearns, Syntax Directed Transduction, *JACM* **15**(3), 465–488 (July 1968).

D. M. Ritchie and K. Thompson, The UNIX Time-Sharing System, *Communications of the ACM*, 365–375 (July 1974). K. Thompson and D. M. Ritchie, The UNIX Time-Sharing System, *Bell System Technical Journal*, 1905–1930 (July-August 1978).

B. W. Kernighan and P. J. Plauger, *Software Tools*, Addison-Wesley, Reading, MA, 1976.

R. W. Hamming, *Coding and Information Theory*, Prentice-Hall, Englewood Cliffs, NJ, 1980.

C. E. Shannon, A Mathematical Theory of Communication, *BSTJ* **27**, 10 (1949).

C. E. Shannon, Communication in the Presence of Noise, *Proc. IRE* **37**, 10 (1949).

A. Viterbi, *Principles of Coherent Communications*, McGraw-Hill, New York, 1966.

# 2

# Computer Linguistics

*Perhaps of all the creations of man language is the most astonishing.*

Lytton Strachey, Words and Poetry

In studying computer programming languages, it is appropriate to begin by placing programming languages into the context of natural languages (i.e., languages actually spoken by people), and to try to characterize the features and properties of programming languages in terms of the features and properties of the more familiar natural languages. In order to do this in a systematic way, the present chapter considers the following topics:

language and linguistics
formal language theory
automata theory
artificial intelligence
computational complexity

## LANGUAGE AND LINGUISTICS

Language is defined as a body of sounds or words and the method of combining such sounds or words so as to be intelligible to a certain group. Linguistics is the term for the scientific study of language and languages.

The term "language," as defined broadly above, includes communications not only between persons (natural languages), but also between animals and

12

between man and machine. The study of man-machine languages is generally called computer linguistics.

Computer linguistics, as we use it here, is therefore the study of communication between man and machine—the way it is done, the theoretical capabilities of such communication, the role of languages, and the effect of such communication on both man and machine. (The word "man" is used generically here.)

Computer linguistics must not, incidentally, be confused with *computational* linguistics. Computational linguistics is a well-established term for the use of computers in linguistic research and applications, such as in the analysis of natural languages or language translation by machine. Computational linguistics will be discussed later in this chapter.

First, we must consider the function of language. Language primarily permits communication between members of a group. However, language also provides a framework for thoughts or other mental activity. A person who speaks two or more languages may frequently "think" in one language while speaking in another. Language provides an organization, a structure, upon which one can develop ideas. This organizational function of language is particularly important in considering computer languages.

A computer language is not only concerned with man-machine communication, but with how a computer "thinks." We do not want to probe this question too deeply, raising issues of whether a computer "understands" what it is thinking, or whether such "thinking" can be regarded as "intelligent" behavior. Such questions are equally semantical as they are philosophical. Our point here is that the computer language provides a framework or organization for basic computer processes.

Thus we attempt to approach the machine, the computer, in operation—lights blinking, a tape or disk drive spinning—and try to communicate with it, much with the same trepidation we might approach an alien beast.

A basic question presents itself: is man going to learn the language of the beast, or will the beast be taught to speak English?

Well, in spite of the many multicolored marketing broachures that proclaims ". . . communicates in a language a businessman speaks—English," computers do not yet communicate in the English language. Of course they may output certain phrase-book homilies like

HELLO. MY NAME IS ELIZA. WHAT'S YOURS?

and may even seemingly "converse" with the user in apparently perfect, grammatically correct English. Yet computers do not really understand English in the same way that they understand their own language. In the above example, if the response was relatively unusual, for example,

## NAPOLEON BONAPARTE

the computer might not respond in the same manner as a human. A computer does however "understand" its own language. If it is looking for a response of 001, 010, or 100, and the input data is

111

then the computer will respond differently than if it had received a correct response. In effect, the computer "understands" that 111 is incorrect or inappropriate, just like the human "understands" that "NAPOLEON BONAPARTE" is an incorrect or invalid name of a computer user.

A programming error or failure of man-machine communication takes place when:

1. The machine did not "understand" the human language.
2. The human did not speak the correct machine language.

Since the human does not speak (or fully "understand") the language of 1's and 0's spoken by the computer, and the computer does not understand human language, a compromise must be made. The machine must be made to accept something closely related to its language, and the human must learn to communicate in this new intermediate language. This new intermediate language—a programming language—is now the vehicle of communication between man and machine.

Again, a coding error or failure of man-machine communication takes place when:

1. The machine did not comply with the programming language.
2. The human did not use the programming language correctly.

There is a major difference under this situation compared with that suggested previously. Before, the human language and the machine language were relatively independent of one another. If something was expressed in one language that could not be translated in the other language, a failure of communication took place. (The natural languages have many words that express abstract aspects of human experience that cannot be easily translated from one language to another. Consider the English word *wistful*, the French *déspoir*, or the German *gemütlich*.)

Now the medium of communication is the programming language. The machine is assumed to understand the programming language, as is the human. It is as if a native English speaker was communicating with a native Chinese speaker by using French, the only language they both mutually understood.

In the study of programming languages it is very important to realize that the "programming language" is not really the language of the computer, no matter how remote it seems from natural English. The programming language is only an intermediary between the computer and the human to establish communication.

The limitations of programming languages are essentially due to a mismatch between the facilities of the computer and the capabilities as expressed in the computer programming language. As we pointed out in the previous chapter, such mismatch is reflected in terms of the efficiency of the operation of a computer language on a given computer. In striving toward a universal language, many of the architectural features of a computer may be overlooked and simply not provided in the language.

In approaching the study of programming languages in this book, the basic function of the programming language to bridge the gap between the logical constructs of human thought and natural languages and the artificial structures of computer architecture of machine language must always be kept in mind. The programming language—that is, the high level language like Pascal or Ada—is intended only as a compromise based upon a wide class of problems to be solved and a wide class of machines and architectures on which the problems are to be solved.

## FORMAL LANGUAGE THEORY

Formal language theory is concerned with specifying and describing the elements of a language, either a natural language or a programming language, in a rigorous mathematical (or "formal") manner. Formal language theory is therefore more closely related to automata theory than to linguistics, and its approach is more highly abstract than descriptive.

A language, from the point of view of formal language theory, is defined abstractly as a set of strings over a finite alphabet. Such a definition of a formal language is clearly directed to a *written* language (which of course computer languages are) rather than a spoken language, so that the broader issues and concepts present in natural languages cannot even be described in formal language terms.

The operations of formal language theory belong to a branch of mathematics known as group theory. A set of symbols called the "alphabet" is first defined. The elements of the alphabet can be utilized by combining (or, more accurately, concatenating) the letters of the alphabet to form words and phrases, and even sentences. These concatenated objects are called strings. Thus, as noted above, the language is defined as a set of strings over a finite alphabet.

Such an abstract definition may seem self-evident, as well as correct. English is composed of strings like *the*, *quick*, *brown*, *fox* which are combined into sets to form sentences:

The quick brown fox jumped over the lazy dogs.

The set of strings is of course formed from the alphabet:

a b c d e f g h i j k l m n o p q r s t u v w x y z

Such a definition of a language has its limitations, and is more directed to describing the structures of strings that form a sentence, rather than being a means for generating sentences, or providing a criteria for telling which strings are sentences.

With such limitations in mind, we can present the formal classification known as the Chomsky hierarchy. The four classes of languages are:

1. Recursively enumerable.
2. Context-sensitive.
3. Context-free.
4. Regular.

The four classes are listed in rank order from the broadest or most general class to the most specific. The hierarchy is organized so that each class properly contains the next class in the hierarchy.

The definition of these classes are closely related to the grammar of these languages. The word "grammar" is also used in a formal sense rather than actual or practical sense; the grammar describes the construction of every possible sentence in the language. Whether some of such sentences are empirically "grammatical" or make sense to a native speaker is a question that goes beyond the realm of mathematics and formal systems into the realm of linguistics. Thus, our formal notion of a grammar may state that the sentence

* Apple it.

is not a grammatical sentence. A higher level of analysis is required to state that

\* Green ideas sleep furiously.

is also not grammatical.

The classes of languages (and their associated grammars) listed previously are related to (and in fact equivalent to) a similarly ordered set of so-called nondeterministic machines, namely,

1. Turing machine.
2. Linear bounded automaton.
3. Pushdown store automaton.
4. Finite-state automaton.

The Turing machine is the broadest category of machine, while the finite-state automaton is the narrowest. The grammars and machines at the top of the Chomsky hierarchy were known in the 1930s and 1940s, while regular languages were not described until the 1950s. The formal proof of the equivalence of grammars and machines was achieved in 1964.

Programming languages are generally designed with features that reflect the anticipated applications or the computer hardware they are associated with. On the computer hardware level, it is noted that most digital computers are designed with Boolean logic, and constructed with electronic devices with two logical levels (0 and 1). Many of the early programming languages developed in the early 1950s therefore incorporated such Boolean operations explicitly in their instruction sets.

However, it must be realized that Boolean logic is not the only logical theory in mathematics, and is not the only type of logic upon which a computer system may be designed. Multiple valued logic systems are also possible. An $n$-valued logical algebra was first described by E. L. Post in 1921, and such algebras are now known as Post algebras.

Although the early programming languages like FORTRAN and ALGOL were based upon 2-valued logic, they did incorporate some $n$-valued logical concepts, such as an $n$-way branch. FORTRAN I, first announced in 1954, included a computed GO TO statement which branched to one of a set of program statements, depending upon the value of a certain argument. The original ALGOL, known as ALGOL 58, also included a similar branching facility.

The difficulty with the $n$-valued branch in FORTRAN and ALGOL 58 is that the programming language, as well as the underlying computer system, are not based upon $n$-valued logic but upon 2-valued logic. Thus, the $n$-valued branch cannot be directly represented, but must be implemented as a sequence of nested 2-way branches.

The difficulty with the computed GO TO statement gradually led to its replacement in ALGOL by the CASE statement, defined in ALGOL 68. More recently developed programming languages, like Pascal, also make use of the CASE statement.

The theory of formal languages is probably of more interest to mathematicians and philosophers than linguists or computer scientists. In fact, formal languages are closely related to a number of theories developed in a wide range of academic disciplines. Although it is not our purpose to explore these relationships here, it is interesting to simply list some of the related disciplines:

mathematical logic and recursive function theory

switching circuit theory and logic design

network theory and design

pattern recognition

modeling of biological systems, for example, discrete-state neural networks

modeling of self-reproducing and developmental systems

mathematical and computational linguistics: language translation

computer language theory

## AUTOMATA THEORY

Automata theory is a branch of mathematics concerned with describing a conceptual model of the operations of a digital computer, and more particularly, the capabilities and limitations of a conceptually defined computer. In describing automata theory it is important to keep in mind its definition. Automata theory is concerned with an abstract, mathematical model. It is not meant to be a descriptive analysis of the operation of a digital computer, or an analysis of a simulation of such a computer. It is concerned with the basic concepts of computer operation, not their implementation, optimization, or utilization. As a model, it is completely removed from any hardware considerations or other physical constraints.

Broadly considered, automata theory is concerned with the results of operations according to a set of rules defined by a formal system. One realization of such operations is that of a highly simplified digital computer, but it must be realized that the same results equally apply to other concepts like nerve networks, pattern recognizers, generative grammars, or other discrete-state devices.

## ARTIFICIAL INTELLIGENCE

Artificial intelligence is concerned with computer programs that are directed to problems loosely associated with "intelligent" behavior or responses. Some of these areas include:

problem solving
game playing
theorem proving
pattern recognition
concept formation
deductive question answering

Problem solving is the term generally used for programs that attempt to solve a posed problem for which there is no simple algorithm. The user constructs an approximation technique and uses it to construct tentative solutions to the problem, and repeats the technique until the "best" solution is found.

Problem solving techniques, like other areas of artificial intelligence, are seen to be routine computer programs. The "intelligent" input is not really supplied by the computer, but supplied by the programmer in defining the approximation technique and criteria for determining a suitable solution to the problem. The term "artificial" intelligence, in describing computers executing such programs, is an appropriate one.

Game playing is a very popular area of computer programming with numerous versions of checkers, chess, backgammon, and other games being available for microcomputer systems, as well as in stand-alone electronic games.

Theorem proving is an area of artificial intelligence that is primarily of academic interest in the area of computer science. There are a number of different techniques for "proving" well-defined mathematical theorems. One, called Wang's algorithm, utilizes a technique known as the falsification method. Theorem proving is concerned with the problem of determining whether a given formula is true or false. If it is true, the technique must demonstrate that it is. One utilizes lists of formulas that are already known to be either true or false, and performs various operations to relate the unknown formula with the known formulas.

Pattern recognition is a form of data processing a two-dimensional image. The image may be obtained from digitizing a three-dimensional subject, or may be an original two-dimensional image. The computer then attempts to recognize a predetermined object or pattern by comparing templates with the digitized pattern. A series of characterizers or feature detectors operate upon portions of the pattern, and decisions are made based upon the number and types of correspondences that are found.

Concept formation is concerned with simulating the process of formulation of "concepts" based upon various attributes (color, size, shape, position, etc.), and the interpretation of new objects from an inherent "understanding" of the concepts learned from other objects. Variations of concept formation are concerned with the simulation of learning and forgetting due to the interference of later learning.

Finally, deductive question answering is concerned with the ability of a computer to receive certain stated facts, and then respond to questions concerning the stated facts in a deductive fashion.

## COMPUTATIONAL COMPLEXITY

Computational complexity is basically concerned with describing and measuring the relative difficulty (or "complexity") in computing a given function or performing a given algorithm. More specifically, it is concerned with the study of the types of problems or functions that are "computable," and the nature and efficiency of the various possible algorithms that may be used to solve the problem posed.

In describing computational complexity two types of measures may be defined: *static* and *dynamic*. A static measure is some gross structural parameter descriptive of some program feature such as size or number of elements. A dynamic measure is descriptive of some run time feature of a program, such as the number and nature of the instructions executed. Another measure is the amount of resources (e.g., memory) used in the computation.

In addition to these measures, computational complexity theory attempts to establish some upper bound on the time required to solve a given problem.

## REFERENCES

E. L. Post, Introduction to a General Theory of Elementary Propositions, *Am. J. Math.* **43**, 163–185 (1921).

Programming Research Group, IBM, *Preliminary Report, Specifications for the IBM Mathematical FORmula TRANslating System, FORTRAN*, November 10, 1954.

J. W. Backus, ALGOL 58, *The Syntax and Semantics of the Proposed International Algebraic Language of the Zurich ACM-GAMM Conference*, IBM, New York, May 1958.

J. W. Dijkstra, GO TO Statement Considered Harmful, *Comm. ACM* **11**, 147–148 (1968).

A. V. Wijngaarden (ed.), Report on the Algorithmic Language ALGOL 68, *Numerische Mathematik* **14**, 79–218 (1969).

## Artificial Intelligence

C. L. Chang and R. C. T. Lee, *Symbolic Logic and Mechanical Theorem Proving*, Academic Press, New York, 1973.

E. B. Hunt, *Artificial Intelligence*, Academic Press, New York, 1975.

N. Nilsson, *Problem Solving Methods in Artificial Intelligence*, McGraw-Hill, New York, 1971.

J. R. Slagle, *Artificial Intelligence: The Heuristic Problem Approach*, McGraw-Hill, New York, 1971.

P. H. Winston, *Artificial Intelligence*, Addison-Wesley, Reading, Mass., 1977.

# 3

# Computer Languages

*Language serves not only to express thoughts, but to make possible thoughts which could not exist without it. . . . Language, once evolved, acquires a kind of autonomy: we can know, especially in mathematics, that a sentence asserts something true, although what it asserts is too complex to be apprehended even by the best minds.*

*Bertrand Russell,*
Human Knowledge: Its Scope and Limits

A computer programming language may be broadly defined as a set of abstractions and operations which enable a user to communicate with a computer. More specifically, the abstractions may consist of data, and the operations may be instructions from a well-defined instruction set. The present chapter considers the various types of computer programming languages, and discusses some of their key features:

low level/high level languages
language characteristics
microprogramming and nanoprogramming
concurrent and higher order languages
data flow languages

## LOW LEVEL/HIGH LEVEL LANGUAGES

The most basic classification of computer programming languages is as low level or high level languages, where the term "level" refers to the degree of

22

abstraction or representation of machine operations. Low level languages are those most closely related to basic machine operations, while high level languages are more related to user applications, and the expression of operations or instructions associated with such applications.

Machine language is generally considered the "lowest" of the low level languages. Machine language is simply sequences of binary numbers. Some computers are actually programmed by the user in machine language: these computers have "front panels" with 8 or 16 data switches, which the user sets to indicate a binary 1 or 0. Of course, such programming directly in machine language is tedious and prone to error, and is generally only done for special purposes, such as loading, testing, or during hardware development.

The next higher level—but still a "low level" language—is assembly language. Assembly language is based upon machine language instructions but represents the instructions in mnemonics. For example,

LDA 3

ADD 2

is a sequence of two instructions which tells the computer to first load the value 3 into the A register, and then add 2 to that value. The characters LDA is a mnemonic for "load into the A register," while ADD is a mnemonic for "add to the value in the A register." The mnemonics are simply symbols used to represent the actual machine language instruction so that the programmer can write programs using easy to remember codes for specific computer operations.

Assembly language is translated by a program known as an assembler into the actual machine language of the computer. A program that is written by the user is known as a "source program," while the program that is actually run on the computer (i.e., the machine language program) is known as the "object program." Thus, the assembler translates the source program into an object program.

One extension of assembly language is the inclusion of a facility known as a *macro*. A macro is a single, user defined instruction which replaces a predetermined sequence of regular assembly language instructions. The macro facility is a capability of the assembler program. Upon reading a macro statement in the source code, the assembler will translate it into the defined sequence of machine instructions automatically. Such automatic translation greatly simplifies the user's programming task, and reduces the chance of error.

High level languages are those that use greater abstractions to represent machine operations. To take the example given previously of adding two numbers together, a high level language would merely express the desired operation as

$$3 + 2$$

The expression of "three plus two" is the user's conception of the problem, not the computer's. A high level language therefore permits the expression of the user's conception in symbolic form, rather than the eventual interpretation of this expression by the computer.

A high level language also attempts to "speak" the user's language, rather than the computer's. For example, the same problem of adding 3 and 2 may be expressed as:

$$A = 3 + 2$$
$$\text{PRINT A}$$

Here the high level language instruction "PRINT A" tells the computer, in English, to print the value of the variable A. It is assumed that an output printer is attached to the computer, and that the computer will respond to the instruction by outputting the value A on the printer.

### High Level Languages

High level languages are the most important type of computer languages, and are most frequently the language that the user or programmer encounters. High level languages basically have the advantage in that they permit the user to write code in English-like statements (even if the user's native language is not English). Such statements enable the programmer to "structure" the program into something that is visibly and logically meaningful to a human reader, rather than something that is particularly meaningful to a computer. Since the program statements utilize easily recognizable words (such as **program, procedure, begin, end**), efficient software design is facilitated, and the program may be easily transferred from computer to computer with minor changes. Moreover, the program structure and language allows debugging, testing, and validation to take place with comparative ease.

One of the earliest high level languages was FORTRAN, an acronym for *for*mula *tran*slation. As the name implies, the language was based upon converting mathematics formulas and notation into a computer language. FORTRAN proved to be a highly successful language, and the latest version, known as FORTRAN IV, is widely used for scientific and engineering computation. Because FORTRAN is basically concerned with algebraic manipulation and calculation, it is sometimes referred to as an algebraic language.

After the introduction of FORTRAN, an effort to develop a more comprehensive language was undertaken, principally with international, and particularly European backing. The language that emerged was called ALGOL, for *algo*rithmic *l*anguage. Although ALGOL proved popular in Europe, it did not catch on strongly in the United States.

For business applications, the high level language COBOL, for *co*mmon *b*usiness *o*riented *l*anguage, was developed. COBOL has also proved to be highly successful, and is typically used on large scale, commercial data processing systems.

For personal computers, the BASIC language has emerged as the most popular. BASIC, an acronym for beginner's all-purpose symbolic instruction code, was developed in the early 1960s at Dartmouth College as an interactive language for time-sharing on a large university computer by students. Because of the simplicity of the language, it proved to be highly appealing to the computer hobbyist or personal computer enthusiast whose computational requirements typically did not exceed the capabilities of either the microcomputer or the language.

High level languages are translated into machine language by a program known as a compiler or an interpreter. A compiler operates by translating the entire source program into an object program. After the compilation is completed, the compiled object program is then executed by the computer. An interpreter, on the other hand, translates the source program line by line, and executes the object program line by line. Thus the interpreter must be present in the computer while the object program is being run. Interpreters are more frequently associated with time-sharing systems or interactive systems where the user requires immediate response from the computer.

**High Level Language Classification**

High level languages are usually categorized according to their intended application, which is usually determined by the special features incorporated in the language. A broad categorization is as follows:

algebraic languages
special-purpose languages
all-purpose languages
extendable languages

Algebraic languages are those that are principally concerned with the manipulation of algebraic symbols and the execution of mathematical operations. The typical structures found in algebraic languages are vectors and arrays, as well as facilities for performing algorithms using vectors or arrays. Examples of algebraic languages are FORTRAN and ALGOL.

Special-purpose languages are those that have been designed to handle specific types of data objects, or to perform a certain type of operation on such data objects. Two good examples of special-purpose languages are LISP and SNOBOL. LISP was developed by John McCarthy in 1959 and implemented at M.I.T. in 1960. LISP is directed to the special application of list processing, and features a binary tree as an important data structure. It is widely used for artificial intelligence projects. SNOBOL was developed at Bell Telephone Laboratories in 1962 and was designed for the special application of manipulating character strings. The key data structure in SNOBOL is therefore the character string, and the language includes powerful commands for manipulating such strings.

An "all-purpose" language is one that contains a wide variety of features and is intended for general-purpose use, including mathematical and scientific calculation, and commercial data processing, as well as for special-purpose applications. The premier all-purpose language is PL/1, developed by a committee of IBM users together with IBM researchers, which possesses many of the features of FORTRAN, ALGOL, and COBOL combined.

Finally, the extendable language is one that incorporates a small set of primitive operations, together with a mechanism for defining new operations in terms of the set of primitives. Thus, the user can "extend" the language by defining new features that are specially adapted for the intended application.

### High Level Languages and Microcomputers

In the early 1970s when microprocessors were first introduced, high level languages were not available for them. Microprocessors were viewed as semiconductor circuits—building blocks for use by digital design engineers in constructing a digital circuit heretofore constructed from random logic. Microprocessors were produced by semiconductor manufacturers, many of whom did not have the capabilities or inclination to enter the systems business, or to develop or support a high level language.

The applications of microprocessors in the early 1970s primarily consisted of the replacement of smaller scale integrated chips in a digital system. The hardware designers who employed such products did not need the relatively sophisticated capabilities of high level languages to develop the typical control programs necessary for the average microprocessor application. Although some of the microprocessor manufacturers did develop a high level language compiler based upon a subset of the all-purpose language PL/1, most digital designers were totally unfamiliar with PL/1, and the use of languages like Intel's PL/M did not seem to offer that much advantage.

Indeed, many of the early compilers for such microcomputer high level languages were relatively inefficient: the amount of machine code generated from such compilers far exceeded that developed from assembly language. At a time when semiconductor memory was relatively expensive, it was frequently more advantageous to expend an extra effort in assembly language programming to reduce the size of the control program stored in ROM, and thus perhaps save one or more ROM chips in final system hardware.

During the second half of the decade, the widespread acquisition of microcomputer systems by persons familiar with high level languages and compiler writing led to the development of interpreters and compilers for such languages as BASIC and FORTRAN for microprocessors such as the Intel 8080 and Motorola 6800. The development of such software, and the rise of the "personal computer" were largely ignored by the semiconductor manufacturers, who again deliberately avoided the "systems" business. Only one or two semiconductor manufacturers—like Rockwell with its AIM microcomputer-on-a-board with integral keyboard and printer, or Texas Instruments with its personal computer 99/4—ventured into the new marketplace of computer hobbyists or small computer enthusiasts.

Moreover, the rapidly decreasing prices of semiconductor memory made larger and larger memory systems practical for the same price, thus encouraging the use of larger interpreters and operating systems.


## LANGUAGE CHARACTERISTICS

In considering computer languages, it is important to discuss their key features and characteristics. We begin by defining two different classes of characteristics—functional and technical. Functional characteristics are concerned with how the language is defined and used. Technical characteristics are concerned with the technical features of the language itself.


### Functional Characteristics

We consider four different functional characteristics of computer programming languages:

objectives
compatibility
standardization
availability

*Objectives*

The first and most basic characteristic of any computer programming language is its objectives. There are hundreds of different programming languages, and more are continuing to be defined and implemented each year. In approaching any one language, the first question to ask is: what is the purpose of the language?

Computer programming languages are written for a wide variety of different purposes: to solve a particular type of problem; to be used by a particular type of programmer; to be used with particular hardware or in a particular environment. Some languages are intended to be special-purpose, with only one or two applications, while other languages are intended to be general-purpose and capable of handling a large category of applications.

In comparing and evaluating different computer programming languages, the objectives of such languages must be kept in mind. A language may seem deficient for certain applications the user might have in mind, and for that reason the user might dismiss that language from consideration. Another user with the same applications may try to extend the language with new instructions or other facilities to handle the application more effectively.

In the case of many computer programming languages, the objectives of the language are sometimes only stated informally. In many cases, the authors of such languages might not have even started with certain objectives in developing the language, but just let it develop and evolve. When presented with the query "why doesn't the language have —," the missing feature is added to the language.

On the other hand, other languages like Ada have started out from formally defined technical requirements and objectives. These technical requirements include such matters as:

general design criteria

general syntax

types

expressions

constants, variables, and scope

classical control structures

functions and procedures

input/output, formatting, and configuration control

parallel processing

exception handling

representation and other translation time facilities

translation and library facilities

support for the language

The detailed requirements for Ada are presented in the "Steelman" document in Appendix D. Further discussion of the Ada language is presented in Chapter 12.

## *Compatibility*

Another important functional feature of a programming language is its compatibility among different computer systems (often called "implementations"). As we point out in the previous section, some computer programming languages have been developed for particular hardware or a particular environment (e.g., multiuser time-sharing). In many cases, the technical features of a programming language are so appealing that users may desire to implement the language in a different environment or on different hardware to satisfy their own applications. The result may be incompatible versions of the same programming language—two different versions of the language in which programs written in the language are not directly transferrable from one environment to another.

One approach to achieving compatibility is through the use of an intermediate language. UCSD Pascal is an example of an implementation of a programming language that has as its objective compatibility among a wide class of microcomputers. In order to achieve this compatibility, the UCSD Pascal code is compiled into an intermediate language called p-code. The p-code has characteristics that are common in the instruction sets of many microprocessors, and therefore it is relatively easy to translate a p-code representation into the code for any particular microprocessor through the use of an interpreter program.

Another aspect of language compatibility that must be discussed is dialectization. A dialect of a computer language, like a dialect of a natural language, is a slight variation of the original language. Dialects of computer languages are really extensions or modifications of the originally defined language. The terminology that is frequently used for one class of dialects is to state that language L is a "subset" of language M. Alternatively, one might state that language M is a "superset" of language L. The "set" terminology refers to some language feature, such as the number and type of instructions, or the nature of the data the language can handle. An example is that a language only with integer capability may be considered a subset of another version of the same language with both integer and real capability.

*Standardization*

Standardization refers to the establishment of a formal technical standard for a programming language. A standard is a widely recognized document that specifies various operating characteristics of a product or procedure. Industry standards are developed by a wide variety of different parties, including trade associations, departments of government, national standards organizations, and international standards organizations. In the United States the compliance with standards is usually voluntary, although the economic advantages of interchangeability of parts from different manufacturers conforming to the same standard often justify the adoption of a standard, particularly for items which are mass produced or for which there is a large market using an adopted or defacto standard.

An example of a standard for a programming language is the first ISO draft proposal for the language Pascal, which is presented in Chapter 8.

*Availability*

Another important factor in considering the selection of a programming language is the availability of the language on a particular computer, that is, whether the language has been implemented on that computer. In addition to the existence of a compiler for the language, the user may also be concerned with the availability of utilities such as editing and debugging facilities while utilizing the language. In the case of a popular language, like Pascal, the user has the choice of a number of different compilers and operating systems that are capable of handling Pascal for the same microcomputer.

**Technical Characteristics**

The technical characteristics of a programming language are the basic internal features of the language. In the present section we consider the following features as a way of introduction to the structural composition of a programming language:

notational features
basic elements
syntax and semantics
data
executable statements
nonexecutable statements

*Notational Features*

By notational features we refer to the character set of a programming language, and the different meaning given to such characters when used in different contexts. Notation features are actually part of the syntax of a language, but because such features are often part of a particular hardware representation, it is useful to consider them separately.

Some programming languages have an extended character set to represent certain control functions or operators, and some software systems utilize distinctions between upper and lower case, or use the keyboard's control key plus a character to provide certain functions. Even a programming language like FORTRAN utilized a distinction between certain letters of the alphabet to designate the type of the variable: any identifier beginning with the letters I, J, K, L, M, or N denoted an *integer* type, whereas others were of *real* type.

*Basic Elements*

The basic elements of a programming language are called *tokens* and are analogous to words in a natural language. These elements are manipulated by the user to construct a computer program, similar to the way a speaker of a language uses words to construct sentences and thereby convey information.

Tokens are either system defined or user defined. By system defined, we mean that the token is defined by the language specification in which it is used, or is defined by the system operating software which utilizes the token. A user defined token, as the name implies, is a token that the user creates and utilizes in a particular program, and has no independent meaning outside of that particular program or application. The best examples of user defined tokens are identifiers which are used to refer to program variables and constants.

The basic elements or tokens in Pascal are:

special symbols
identifiers
directives
numbers
labels
character strings

Further discussion of these tokens will be found in Chapter 7.

*Syntax and Semantics*

The syntax of a programming language defines the form of the expressions that are to be considered grammatical within the programming language. Semantics refers to the rules for interpreting the meaning of the statements written in the language according to the syntactical rules.

The technical specification of the syntax and semantics form a large part of the language standard. As an example, the ISO draft standard for Pascal considers the following syntax specifications:

blocks and scope

constant definitions

type definitions

declarations and denotations of variables

procedure and function declarations

expressions

statements

input and output

The following sections discuss the issues of data, executable statements, and nonexecutable statements (declarations) in more detail.

One way in which syntax may be used to distinguish computer programming languages is the relationship between the operators (the specific instruction or the command) and the operands (the data or the object upon which the operator effects). There are essentially four different methods of relating the operators and the operands:

1.  The conventional method in which an operator has associated with it an address which designates the operand, and from which address the operand is fetched for execution by the processor.
2.  The data flow method in which the operand has associated with it the address of the operator associated with it.
3.  The ring distribution method, as typified by the lambda calculus and the LISP programming language.
4.  The tree distribution method.

*Data*

A computer program operates on data, and therefore one of the principal technical characteristics of a computer programming language is the type of data that the language is capable of operating upon. The subject of data types will be discussed in greater detail in subsequent chapters. However, at this point it can simply be observed that data variables can be classified into distinct categories, such as:

character
integer
real
complex
string
and so on

Each distinct data type admits different grouping or structuring methods (for example, forming a vector or matrix with the data as components), and different operations or computations that can be performed on the data.

### Executable Statements

The executable statements of a programming language are analogous to the verbs in a natural language—they define the actions or operations to be performed upon the data. Different programming languages have different classes of executable statements, as well as different sets of executable statements within each class.

The classes of executable statements comprise:

assignment
sequence control
input/output

Assignment is the designation of a name for the result of some calculation or operation. Some languages use the equals sign ("=") for the assignment operation, but more modern languages have trended away from such usage, since the assignment statement

$$I = I + 1$$

(which means that the current value of I is set equal to the old value of I, plus 1) may be syntactically correct in a programming language, but does not appear to be good mathematics if one casually thinks of the "=" designation as a mathematical equals sign. Pascal, for example, uses the ":=" symbol as the assignment symbol.

Sequence control is the ability to alter the sequence of operations in a program depending upon the results of some computation. Examples include control structures such as the statements

$$\textbf{while } i < 1000 \textbf{ do } \text{----}$$

or

$$\textbf{repeat } \text{----} \textbf{ until } i > 1000$$

The above two statements indicate that a certain operation (which we merely signify by dashes ----) is treated by the program while a certain condition is still valid, namely the value of the parameter i is less than 1000. It is assumed that the operation changes the value of i until some time when the value of i exceeds 1000, after which the program will progress to the next statement in its sequence. Of course, if the value of i does not change during the operation, or does not change to a point at which it exceeds 1000, the program will continue executing that operation indefinitely, and there may be an error in the program.

Input/output is the final category of executable statements which we consider. Generally, such statements provide the means for communicating between the operating program and the external system environment. The statements may also reference other programs or utilities of the system, and not just provide user input/output.

### Nonexecutable Statements

The nonexecutable statements of a programming language fall into one or more of the following categories;

data declarations
system configuration
formatting
comments

Data declarations are those statements in which the user tells the program the specific data type and scope of the variables appearing within the program.

System configuration instructions are those statements in which the user structures the system environment (either hardware or software facilities) for the particular program being executed.

Formatting refers to the particular format or organization of the input or output data that is handled by the computer program. A format statement would instruct the computer to provide data in exponential notation, for example, or to provide real data only to three decimal places.

Comments are those statements which form part of the documentation of a computer program and which are merely inserted by the programmer into the text of the program as an aid in reading the text. Comment statements are automatically disregarded by the compiler in producing object code.

## MICROPROGRAMMING AND NANOPROGRAMMING

### Microprogramming

Another type of computer programming language is that associated with microprogramming. Microprogramming is not so much a type of programming as it is a computer design technique. A microprogrammed system is one in which the control signals for the various elements of the computer are generated from data stored in a memory, rather than generated by random logic (arrays of gates and flip-flop circuits). Although the concept of microprogramming was proposed in 1951, it was not until the development of suitable read-only memories that implementation of microprogramming techniques became practical.

A microprogrammed computer features a sequence of microinstructions which are used to control various machine functions. The microinstructions are similar to machine language instructions, and may therefore also be considered a low level language. However, the microinstruction differs from the machine language instruction in that in addition to defining the operations to be carried out, it also defines the address of the next microinstruction to be executed.

The set of microinstructions, or the microprogram, essentially defines the external architecture of the machine, including the external instruction set that the machine is capable of executing. One of the earliest uses of microprogramming was as a tool of the computer designer in order to achieve compatibility between different machines with slightly different hardware. The architecture of one computer (called the "target machine") could be emulated in another computer (called the "host machine") by a microprogram by automatically converting the instructions of the target machine to those of the host machine through a microprogram. These host machines are said to be "internally microprogrammed."

In addition to the internally microprogrammed computers, there are a number of computer systems, particularly minicomputers, which are user microprogrammable. The user microprogrammable computers enable the user to customize the instruction set of a computer for a particular application, or to operate in a particular environment with other computers which are then the user's target machines.

In addition to microprogrammable minicomputer systems, the bit-slice microprocessors available from a number of semiconductor manufacturers enable the user/computer designer to customize both the hardware and the software of a computer system through the use of such digital building blocks.

Microprogrammable computer systems provide one level of control below the conventional machine language instruction set of the computer, that is, a "micro" level below the conventional instruction set. It must be realized that it is also possible to have more than one level of control below the instruction set level, that is, a "nano" control structure as well as a "micro" control structure. The Nanodata QM-1 minicomputer is the unique example of a "nanoprogrammable" machine which executes nanoprograms to define the micro level machine in the same manner in which the microprogram defines the macro level machine.

### Microprogramming Applications

In the typical application, a first digital computer, called the target computer, is assumed to have an architecture that includes a certain number of functions to be performed using a particular set of target instructions. Another digital computer, called a host computer, is provided with an architecture that is designed to be compatible with the target computer. In order to achieve software compatibility, the host computer must emulate the target computer, that is, perform the same functions as the target computer by executing programs written using the target instruction set.

The motivation for using a host computer to emulate a target computer is that because the host computer can be designed with more advanced semiconductor components, it may operate with better performance than the typically older target computer. Such a host computer may also cost less than the target computer to manufacture and maintain.

The IBM System/370 computers are frequently the target computers that emulate so-called "plug-compatible" host computers. A plug-compatible host computer that emulates a System/370 computer is able to perform previously written System/370 target programs without requiring reprogramming.

Most host digital computers have been designed using microinstruction control. Such host digital computers operate under microinstruction control to execute each target instruction. More specifically, the execution of a target instruction in a host computer typically requires the execution of a sequence of microinstructions in the host computer. When the sequence of microinstructions is executed, the result is execution of the target instruction.

The performance of the host computer in executing the target instruction is determined in part by the architecture of the host computer. In general, the host computer operates to fetch each target instruction. The operation code (Op Code) from the target instruction is employed by the host computer to develop a sequencing path to the microinstructions necessary to execute the target instruction. The necessary microinstructions are generally stored in a number of subroutines, each subroutine including a series of microinstructions. These subroutines must be accessed and executed to cause execution of the target instruction.

One way of accessing the microinstruction subroutines in the host computer is by accessing a series of subroutine calls from a series of indirect addresses stored in the low order locations of a microstore. The Op Code from the target instruction to be executed is used to address the low order locations of the microstore. The low-order locations of the microstore are preloaded with indirect addresses to provide jumps to call subroutines. Each indirect address specifies the location of a call subroutine unique to a particular target instruction. The call subroutine in turn contains a series of subroutine addresses which are accessed in sequence to call the subroutines necessary for executing the target instruction. In such an indirect address implementation, the number of microinstructions necessary to execute each target instruction is excessive because of the necessity of obtaining first the indirect address and thereafter the subroutine call addresses.

Another way of accessing the microinstruction subroutines in the host computer is to employ a separate addressable storage unit as a hardware jump table. The jump table provides a microaddress for addressing the microstore. The Op Code from the target instruction addresses the jump table to obtain the microaddress of a calling subroutine. That microaddress is used directly to address the microstore to access the call subroutine. The call subroutine in turn contains a series of subroutine microaddresses which are accessed in sequence to call the subroutines necessary to execute the target instruction. The use of a hardware jump table avoids the need for an additional indirect address cycle, and thereby saves at least one cycle of the host computer for each execution of a target instruction.

Although the use of a hardware jump table eliminates one cycle of the host computer for each target instruction execution, the hardware jump table still requires execution of a call subroutine. For each call subroutine, the host computer normally must execute at least one call microinstruction which undesirably requires at least one cycle of the host computer. Such host computer cycles allocated to call subroutines necessarily degrade performance of the host computer in the execution of target instructions.

Yet another approach for processing target instructions makes use of a stack. In this approach, the processor unit is operated under the control of microinstructions. A sequencer generates sequences of microinstructions which are executed by the processor to effect execution of each target instruction.

The processor unit stores the microinstructions in a microstore. Sequences of microinstructions are accessed from the microstore under control of sequences of microaddresses. The sequences of microaddresses are generated by a microaddress generator that includes a plurality of microaddress sources. One of the sources of microaddresses is a stack unit.

The stack unit includes a stack memory, a link memory, and a stack control unit. The stack control unit controls the selection of microaddresses from the stack memory and from the link memory.

The link memory is employed when the processor operates as a host computer for executing target instructions. Target instructions are executed as a result of executing a plurality of microinstructions within the host computer. Each target instruction requires execution of a different sequence of microinstructions.

The sequence of microinstructions is determined, at least in part, for each target instruction by unique entries for each target instruction in the link memory. The link memory includes several unique locations for each of the target instructions which is executable by the host computer. Whenever a target instruction is to be executed, the target instruction is employed to address its own unique location in the link memory to provide one or more microaddresses. Those microaddresses from the link memory address subroutines of microinstructions in the microstore which must be executed in order to cause execution of the target instruction.

The microaddresses required in connection with the execution of any particular subroutine are loadable and retrievable from the stack memory within the stack unit or are otherwise available from other sources forming part of the microaddress generator. Whenever the stack memory is empty, the next link memory location associated with the particular target instruction being executed is accessed. The function of the link memory is to link the microinstruction subroutines for each target instruction without the need in many instances for use of a call subroutine. The link memory within the microaddress generator thus enhances the performance of the host computer in executing target instructions.

The stack unit may also include, in addition to the stack memory and link memory, other sources of microaddresses. In one example, an implicit address register may be employed to provide microaddresses from the control bus when the available microaddresses from the link memory have been exhausted.

. The microaddress generator may also include other sources for providing microaddresses to the microstore. These other sources could include a register, an adder, an indirect address register, and an external address register. A register may also be provided for selecting the next microaddress explicitly from the current microinstruction and an adder may also be provided for incrementing each current microaddress by one to obtain the next sequential address for storage in a next sequential register. An indirect address register provides microaddresses indirectly from other parts of the processor unit. An external address register provides microaddresses externally from the processing unit.

## CONCURRENT AND HIGHER ORDER LANGUAGES

The discussion of computer languages and linguistics up until now has been concerned with conventional programming languages in which a single process or procedure is executed by a computer. Such languages are analogous to natural languages in which a single speaker is talking. However, such simple communication procedures are not the only ones possible, in both natural languages as well as computer languages. In the natural language realm, interpersonal communication does not always consist of one person talking to one listener. Consider for example a group of four persons: sometimes one person talks, sometimes two people talk; sometimes what is said is directed specifically at one individual, sometimes to the whole group; sometimes a person simultaneously listens while speaking.

Until fairly recently, the study of computer languages and programming has been concerned with those languages and language implementations analogous to the situation in which a single person talks. These conventional programming languages can be referred to as *sequential* languages with *static* data and operational structures.

Research in computer languages and linguistics has pretty much been concerned with variations and advances in such sequential languages. One can trace, for example, the evolution of a high level language like ALGOL from ALGOL 60 to ALGOL W and ALGOL 68, and finally the development of Pascal.

The reason for such research direction was that most computer activity and communication took place with a single computer in a sequential fashion. Although multiprocessor configurations did exist, they were used for special purposes and the presently existing sequential programming languages were adequate to manage such applications.

Concurrent computer programs are those that are executed simultaneously. More particularly, the programs work together in the solution of a common problem and cooperate with each other by sharing and exchanging data through the use of shared variables. A concurrent language is one that enables the programmer to write a program in which several independent processes are able to be executed simultaneously.

Concurrent Pascal is a language that was developed by Per Brinch Hansen at the California Institute of Technology in the early 1970s, and originally implemented on the PDP 11/45. Concurrent Pascal is an extension of standard sequential Pascal defining the use of concurrent processes and monitors.

A process is a portion of a program which may be executed simultaneously with other processes. Various processes relate to each other through input and output buffers. A process also has *access rights* to other system components, which are called the *parameters* of that process. A process also has *private variables* which are not accessible by other processes.

A monitor defines a set of shared variables, and also functions to control the execution of various processes to sequence and time the interaction between processes.

## DATA FLOW ARCHITECTURE AND LANGUAGES

The standard type of computer architecture known in most commercial systems is the single instruction stream–single data stream (SISD) computer represented in Figure 3.1. Such a computer operates with a sequence of instructions (called a "computer program") being applied to a central processing unit, which is generally called an arithmetic logic unit. Each of the instructions or operators has associated with it an operand which is represented by the corresponding data elements shown in the figure. The corresponding data element may reside in a random access memory, or in an associated register. The instruction operand may transfer the data element from one memory position or register to another in the computer, or compute an arithmetic or logical operation upon one or more of the data elements. Such a computer architecture is essentially "control flow" architecture because the entity that "flows" through the system is instructions.

**FIGURE 3.1.**   Single instruction stream, single data stream computer.

**FIGURE 3.2.**    Single data stream (data flow) computer.

In contrast to the "control flow" computer architecture is the "data flow" computer architecture in which the control operators are fixed and through which variable data flow. A highly simplified representation of a data flow computer is shown in Figure 3.2.

To illustrate the operation of a data flow computer, we consider a very simple program containing an arithmetic operation which is repeatedly performed on an incoming data stream. The program as expressed in an ALGOL-like notation is shown in Figure 3.3.

The operation of the program is to accept two input variables, w and x, perform a calculation, and output the result y. The particular calculation in the present example involves a loop in which the looping parameter t varies from 0 to the value of the input parameter w. The calculation is performed on the input variable x which is now given the assigned name of y. If y is greater than 1, the computer divides y by 2. If the value of y is equal or less than 1, calculation is made of three times y. The process is continued until t equals the predetermined value of w.

The elementary data flow program equivalent to the above program is shown in Figure 3.4. It is noted that the data flow program is essentially a direct graph having two types of nodes, one type called a link, the other type called an actor. The links are shown in Figure 3.5a and the various types of actors are shown in Figure 3.5b. The data flow essentially takes place through channels from actor to actor by way of the links.

In the figure x and w are input links, while y is the output link.

The execution of the data flow program is performed by a sequence of operations of both the links and the actors. Execution may be described by a

```
INPUT (w, x)
    y := x; t := 0;
    WHILE t ≠ w DO
    BEGIN
        IF y > 1 THEN y := y ÷ 2
                 ELSE y := y × 3;
        t := t + 1;
    END
    OUTPUT y
```

**FIGURE 3.3.**    Sample program for illustrating data flow implementation.

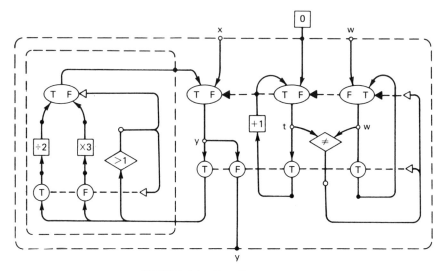

**FIGURE 3.4.** Data flow program.

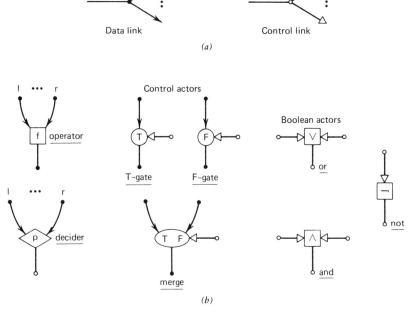

**FIGURE 3.5.** Node types for data flow programs. (*a*) Links. (*b*) Actors.

42

Data link                    Control link

**FIGURE 3.6.**  Firing rules for link nodes.

sequence of "snapshots" in which each "snapshot shows the data flow program with a data token and an associated value placed on a predetermined arc of the graph of the program. Such data tokens may be generalized to n-bit words so that each token may represent a sequence of n-consecutive bubbles in the propagation path representing a predetermined binary value.

In the case of the control arcs, associated values are either "true" or "false," that is, switch closed, or switch opened. For data arcs the values may represent integer, real, or string values as represented by the associated binary word.

The execution of a data flow program advances from one snapshot to the next through the firing of some link or an actor that is enabled by the earlier snap shot. The rules governing the enabling and the firing of the link nodes are shown in Figure 3.6, and rules for the actors are shown in Figures 3.7 and 3.8. The node prior to firing is shown on the left while the node after firing is shown on the right.

One of the most important conditions for implementing the data flow architecture is that an appropriate number of token positions be provided between each of the actors in the architecture so that the data flow is represented by the relative position of the words throughout the architecture rather than the specific timing of advancing the tokens from one position to another as required by the architecture. The firing of a node absorbs the tokens associated with the word from the input arc and places the tokens on

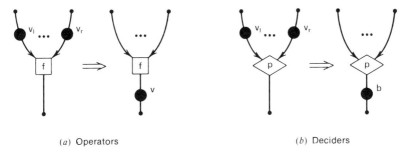

(a) Operators                    (b) Deciders

**FIGURE 3.7.**  Firing rules.

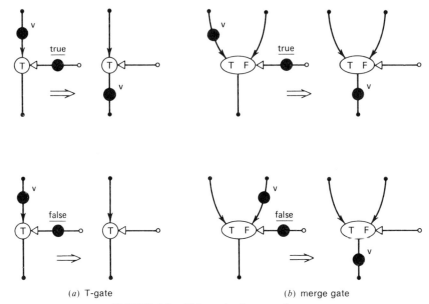

(a) T-gate                    (b) merge gate

**FIGURE 3.8.**    Firing rules for control actors.

the output arc. Firing an operator applies the function denoted by the symbol written in the operator to the set of values associated with the tokens on the input arc and associates the resulting values with the tokens placed on the output arcs.

Firing of a decider has a similar effect, but the function in the decider denotes a predicate P and results in a control value B associated with the output token. Of course, implementation of such a predicate is a matter of the particular design of the gate for performing the desired function. Boolean actors OR, AND, and NOT act with respect to the control values just as an operator acts with respect to the data values for the T gate, merge gate, and F gate, respectively.

## REFERENCES

M. Joseph, Towards More General Implementation Languages for Operating Systems, *Proc. 2nd International Symposium on Operating Systems, IRIA, France, 2–5 October 1978.*

M. Joseph, V. R. Prasad, K. T. Narayena, I. V. Ramakrishanan, and S. Desai, Language and Structure in an Operating System, *Proc. 2nd International Symposium on Operating Systems, IRIA, France, 2–5 October 1978.*

## Concurrent and Higher Order Languages

J. Backus, Can Programming Be Liberated from the von Neumann Style? A Functional Style and Its Algebra of Program, *Comm. ACM* **21**(8), 613–641 (1978).

K. Berkling, Reduction Languages for Reduction Machines, *Proc. Second Ann. Symp. Computer Architecture*, January 1975, pp. 133–140.

R. E. Bryant, and J. B. Dennis, *Concurrent Programming*, Computation Structures Group (Memo 148-2), Laboratory for Computer Science, MIT, Cambridge, Massachusetts, July 1978.

## Data Flow Architecture and Languages

Arvind and K. P. Gostelow, *Dataflow Computer Architecture: Research and Goals*, Department of Information and Computer Science (TR 113), University of California—Irvine, Irvine, California, February 1978.

J. B. Dennis, First Version of a Data Flow Procedure Language, *Programming Symposium: Proceedings, Colloque sur la Programmation*, B. Robinet, Ed., *Lecture Notes in Computer Science*, Vol. 19, 362–376, 1974.

J. B. Dennis, and D. P. Misunas, Data Processing Apparatus for Highly Parallel Execution of Stored Programs, U.S. Patent 3,962,706, issued June 8, 1976.

J. B. Dennis, and D. P. Misunas, *The Design of a Highly Parallel Computer for Signal Processing Applications*, Computation Structures Group (Memo 101), Laboratory for Computer Science, MIT, Cambridge, Massachusetts, August 1974.

J. B. Dennis, and D. P. Misunas, A Preliminary Architecture for a Basic Data-Flow Processor, *The Second Annual Symposium on Computer Architecture: Conference Proceedings*, January 1975, pp. 126–132.

C. L. Hankin, P. E. Osmon, and J. A. Sharp, *A Data Flow Model of Computation*, Department of Computer Science, Westfield College, Hampstead, London, 1978.

P. R. Kosinski, *A Data Flow Programming Language*, IBM T. J. Watson Research Center (RC 4264), Yorktown Heights, New York, March 1973.

R. E. Miller, and J. Cocke, Configurable Computers: A New Class of General Purpose Machines, *International Symposium on Theoretical Programming*, A. Ershov, and V. A. Nepomniashy, Eds., *Lecture Notes in Computer Science*, Vol. 5, 1972, pp. 285–298.

D. P. Misunas, *A Computer Architecture for Data-Flow Computation*, Laboratory for Computer Science (TM-100), MIT, Cambridge, Massachusetts, March 1978.

# 4

# Microcomputer Programming

*I view a programming language primarily as a vehicle for the description of (potentially highly sophisticated) abstract mechanisms.*

*E. W. Dijkstra*

Programming is the use of a computer programming language to solve a given problem on a computer. Broadly defined, it is concerned with conceptualizing the problem, utilizing the facilities in the language to represent the problem, and testing and maintaining the resulting program. The present chapter considers:

problem definition
architectural design
algorithm development
coding
debugging
testing and validation
documentation and maintenance

## PROBLEM DEFINITION

The first task of the programmer is to analyze the problem presented, and to recast the problem in a form in which it is capable of computer solution. In

46

order to do this, the programmer must first have a knowledge of the type of operations that can be performed by the computer, and relate the solution of the problem in terms of such operations.

It is possible to classify the types of problems to which computers are applied into five distinct categories:

data acquisition
data storage and management
data processing
data output and report generation
inquiry/response

Data acquisition is concerned with the problem of receiving a data input from one or more sources, analyzing the nature of the data according to predetermined criteria, and utilizing it in some particular manner. For example, a data acquisition routine may monitor several CRT display terminals, receive data from one or more of them, analyze the data from each terminal, and route the data to another terminal or to computer storage depending upon the particular program specification.

Data storage and management is concerned with the filing and classification of data so that it may be accessed and retrieved according to one or more keys associated with each filed data item. The data "management" facility is concerned with updating or deletion of file information.

Data processing is probably the most common computer application. As the name implies, data processing concerns the manipulation of data by the computer—using the data to perform arithmetic or logical calculations, or the transfer of data from one location to another.

Data output and report generation is the utilization of the computer to select particular data items stored by the computer, and present them in the form of a report. Such a function is an extension of capabilities of data storage and data processing discussed previously.

Inquiry/response is a mode of operation of a computer system to obtain data stored therein, or processed, in an interactive fashion.

Any "problem" for solution by the computer falls into one or more of these categories: using the computer for acquiring data, storing or processing data, or outputting data. Once the programmer fully has characterized the problem as a data handling problem, the next task is to identify the types of operations that can be performed by the computer.

The operations performed by the computer are known as instructions. In order to understand the nature of the computer problem, the programmer must be aware of the capabilities and limitations of the instruction set of the computer, or of the high level language being used. Some types of problems may not be able to be solved because the computer's internal word length is not long enough to handle the number of digits being contemplated. Other types of problems may not be capable of solution because of limitations in the high level language: for example, the inability to handle arrays of a certain size. In answering such questions, the programmer is concerned with questions of practicality, rather than theoretical feasibility. Although it may be possible, through complex programming, to handle a certain problem, it may not be easily programmed, or practical to execute on a particular computer. We are not concerned here with the more difficult questions of problems that are "ill-posed," or with noncomputable functions, just the simple question—can this computer, using this programming language, solve this problem?

If the answer to this "existence question" is "yes," then we can next concern ourselves with how to define the problem so that the computer is able to find the solution. If the answer to the question is "no," then we must concern ourselves with deeper questions of computability theory and the limitations of computer architecture and programming languages, which go beyond the scope of this book. The question of noncomputable functions, or of computable functions that cannot be calculated with present computers and programming languages, are nontrivial problems that merit further study in the future.

Assuming, once again, that the computer is capable of solving the problem, the programmer must break the problem into subproblems that can be solved sequentially. The importance and relevance of sequential solution is that most computers operate sequentially. (If of course one had a computer capable of parallel processing, and the problem presented a parallel data input stream, then the solution of the problem would be described in terms of that particular computer architecture and data input.)

As we pointed out above, the first task of the programmer is then to recast the problem in a form that is capable of being handled by the computer being used. In the typical case, this means to recast the problem into a sequence of suboperations or tasks which when performed sequentially define the solution of the problem.

The recasting of the problem into a form that is more readily relatable to the computer operations can be called the architectural design of the program. The specific sequence of computer operations which provides the solution to the problem is called the algorithm.

Although the relationship between data, the algorithm, and other program elements will be considered in greater detail in the next chapter, the basics of architectural design and algorithm development are presented in the immediately following sections.

## ARCHITECTURAL DESIGN

Just like an architect planning the design of a building, the programmer planning the structure of a program to solve a particular problem must view the subject from different perspectives. What are the overall objectives? What types of materials does the designer have to work with?

One design approach is to consider the operations that must be performed sequentially, and break the entire effort into a sequence of sequential subproblems. In the case of a building, the designer would consider such tasks as excavation, pile driving, laying a foundation, and so on. Similarly, the program designer would consider receiving data input, performing sequential operations on that input, and producing an output.

Another approach is to consider the entire project broken into functional submodules. In the case of a building, the designer would separately consider such submodules as a garage, landscaping, interior layout, and so on, in addition to the building proper. Similarly the program designer can break the entire program into functional modules such as data description, subroutines, and input/output modules.

In the present section we consider three approaches toward the architectural design of programs:

control flow
data flow
functional modules

It should be emphasized that each of these approaches is not exclusive, and any program designer may use one or more of the approaches in the design of any particular program. Just like the architect who must conceptualize building subcomponents or modules, as well as schedule subcontractors (control flow) and material deliveries (data flow), the programmmer is in fact involved with all three approaches to architectural design. The point is that not all programmers explicitly utilize such considerations in the design process, particularly for smaller scale software projects. The purpose of the present section is to make the programmer aware of the possibility of using such approaches in the future.

### Control Flow Design

The first and most common method of the architectural design of computer programs is control flow design—or more popularly, flowcharting. Control flow design is concerned with considering the program as a sequence of distinct operations, with the sequencing from one operation to another being descriptive of the control operation of the program.

The formal sequence of operations is described by a diagram known as a flowchart, and the overall solution of the problem or control flow described by the flowcart is known as an algorithm.

A flowchart is a diagram representing the sequence of steps or operations used in solving a given problem. each element of the diagram represents one type of operation performed—an input, a calculation, a decision made to do one thing or another, and so forth. The various types of operations are represented by different symbols of the flowchart, as shown in Figure 4.1. A simple flowchart, for a problem concerning polling a sequence of terminals, is shown in Figure 4.2.

In solving a problem, it is generally useful to begin with the broadest statement of the problem and to flowchart that operation first. In the example shown in Figure 4.2, very general statements such as "accept data from

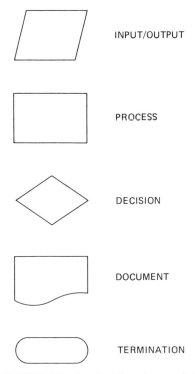

FIGURE 4.1.   Standard flowchart symbols.

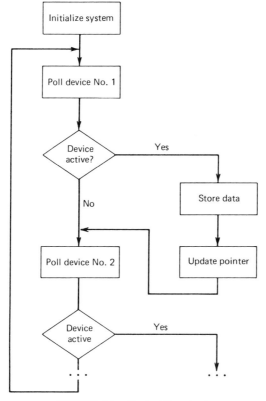

**FIGURE 4.2.**  Typical flowchart.

terminal" or "process data" are used. In actual practice, each of these elements may represent a lengthy series of operations. However, at first analysis, the representation of the program in terms of these broad, general statements is most practical. After such a functional flowchart is made, the
programmer may turn to each step and refine it further, filling in the details.

It is therefore possible to say that there are two types or levels of flowcharts—the functional flowchart and the detailed flowchart. The functional
flowchart is the broadest specification of the program, while the detailed
flowchart provides more step-by-step details of the sequence of instructions
to be performed. A functional flowchart may be language independent, while
a detailed flowchart may make explicit reference to facilities in a given programming language.

## Data Flow Design

Another method of architectural design of computer programs is data flow design. Data flow design is concerned with the program as a sequence of operations on a given item of data, with the sequencing from one operation to another being the sequence of operations on that data. The subject of data flow architecture has already been discussed at length in the previous chapter, so there is no necessity of repeating it here.

## Functional Modules

The third and final approach to architectural design is that of functional modules. In the previous chapter we have seen that the technical characteristics of a programming language include distinct elements such as nonexecutable statements, executable statements, and data. One approach to the architectural design of a program utilizes these distinct elements as individual design components which we call blocks or modules.

Some programming languages are adapted to block structuring more than others. ALGOL was the first language to really implement block structuring as part of the syntax of the language. The syntax provided that data indicated by an identifier declared within a block structure was *local* to that block structure, that is, the identifier had no meaning outside of the block. Global variables are those that are defined only in the outermost block.

## ALGORITHM DEVELOPMENT

After the programmer has defined the architectural design of the program, the next major step is algorithm development. An algorithm is simply a set of well-defined rules for the solution of a problem. When applied to information processing, an algorithm is a sequence of instructions on the computer for implementing the solution of the problem. The word "algorithm" itself is derived from the name of al-Khowârizmî, the ninth-century Persian author of the book *Kitab al jabr w'al-muqabala*, from which the word "algebra" is derived.

There may be many different algorithms to solve a given problem. The calculation of the discrete Fourier transform, for example, may be done directly, but it would require the calculation of $N^2$ multiplications, where $N$ is the number of terms in the series. On the other hand, one could use the

Cooley–Tukey algorithm* and solve the same problem with only $N \ln N$ multiplications. Clearly the choice of the algorithm is critical in the solution of computation-intense problems.

Since problems themselves fall into many different categories, there are also a wide variety of different classes of algorithms. Donald E. Knuth's book, *The Art of Computer Programming*,† suggests the following classes:

fundamental algorithms
seminumerical algorithms
    random numbers
    arithmetic
sorting and searching
combinatorial algorithms
    combinatorial searching
    recursion
syntactical algorithms
    lexical scanning
    parsing techniques

## CODING

Coding is the task of translating the blocks or modules in the flowchart or block diagram into instructions in the language being used. The instructions are called "code," or more specifically "source code." The term source code is used to distinguish the instructions written by the user in a high level language from the "object code" or machine language instructions (in 0's and 1's representation) which are produced by the compiler or interpreter.

## DEBUGGING

Debugging is the process of finding and correcting errors (or "bugs") in a program. Before considering the process of debugging itself, the first question that must be posed is: how does the user know that an error has occurred? There are generally five approaches:

* J. W. Cooley and J. W. Tukey, *Math. Comput.* **19**, 297 (1965).
† D. E. Knuth, *The Art of Computer Programming*, Addison-Wesley, Reading, Mass., 1973.

error detection during compilation

error detection during execution

failure to execute, or to terminate execution

evidentially incorrect output

detection by use of a test program

**Error Detection During Compilation**

The first opportunity for error detection arises during the process of compilation, or converting the user's source code into machine language. Most modern compilers provide as part of their utility programs a debugging facility which detects violations of language syntax or semantics. Such error checking is directed to program validity— is the programmer's code a valid expression in the programming language.

Such debugging facilities advise the user of the nature of the error by providing an error message statement, either explicitly naming the type of error and the line number where it was detected, or providing an error number that corresponds to a table of error messages. An example of the Texas Instruments Pascal (TIP) error messages is provided in Table 4.1.

For certain obvious typographical errors (such as the failure to provide a right-hand parenthesis, or a semicolon at the end of a line), the compiler may be able to automatically correct the error. Some program statements may appear to be incorrect, although no technical syntax violation has occurred; in such cases the user is provided with a "warning" to double-check the statement cited. Finally, the compiler tags a certain number of errors as "fatal" errors, which if executed would be invalid, and which clearly violate the syntax of the language.

It must be pointed out that compile time error checking will be able to determine if the statements actually will perform the desired operations to solve the problem: such issues refer to program correctness and ability to be implemented, not syntactic validity.

**Error Detection During Execution**

Assuming that no errors were detected during compilation, the user executes the program. Many operating systems have facilities for error checking during execution. Like the facilities provided during compilation, these facilities explicitly describe the type of error detected, and the point of the program where it has been encountered. An example of the Texas Instruments Pascal (TIP) error messages during program execution is provided in Table 4.2.

## Failure to Execute or Terminate Execution

If the operating system debugging facilities do not detect an error, the user may still have an opportunity to note that an error has occurred. One of the most obvious events that is indicative of program error is the failure to execute, that is, to provide an output in accordance with the intention of the program. In short, the program fails to reach that portion of the program proscribing an output, and stops. A variation of the above is the case in which the program continues to execute indefinitely without reaching the proscribed output, such as the case when the program is in an infinite loop.

Although the user may be aware that an error has occurred when such events take place, such events do not provide the location or source of the error.

## Evidentially Incorrect Output

If the debugging facilities do not detect an error, and the program executes, the user may yet have another opportunity to detect an error. This is the situation in which the user has knowledge of the "correct" results, either from experience, another implementation of the program, or even from hand calculations. If the computer provides output which in view of the user's experience is evidentially incorrect, the user could justifiably conclude that an undetected error has occurred.

## Detection by Use of a Test Program

If all of the previous approaches fail to detect an error, the user still has one more alternative—the use of test programs. The subject of test programs is more properly part of the larger area of testing and validation, which is covered in the next section.

## TESTING AND VALIDATION

Another important aspect of programming is testing and validation. If no errors are detected by usual debugging programs, and the output data appears to be correct, what is the justification for software testing? Software testing, like any other aspect of product development, is generally justified by simple economics: does the potential cost of failing to detect a program error out-weigh the cost of an extensive program of software testing?

**TABLE 4.1.** Error Messages

## Compiler Error Messages

This paragraph lists the error messages issued by the TIP compiler. The error number is shown, followed by a letter and the error message text. The letter is either W, E, or F. A warning message is identified by a W; an E identifies a message describing an error that the compiler may be able to correct; an F identifies a message describing a fatal error. The messages are:

| | | |
|---|---|---|
| 1 | E | ERROR IN SIMPLE TYPE |
| 2 | E | IDENTIFIER EXPECTED |
| 3 | E | 'PROGRAM' EXPECTED |
| 4 | E | ')' EXPECTED |
| 5 | E | ':' EXPECTED |
| 6 | E | ILLEGAL SYMBOL |
| 7 | E | PARAMETER EXPECTED |
| 8 | E | 'OF' EXPECTED |
| 9 | E | '(' EXPECTED |
| 10 | E | ERROR IN TYPE |
| 11 | E | '(.' EXPECTED |
| 12 | E | '.)' EXPECTED |
| 13 | E | 'END' EXPECTED |
| 14 | E | ';' EXPECTED |
| 15 | E | INTEGER EXPECTED |
| 16 | E | '=' EXPECTED |
| 17 | E | 'BEGIN' EXPECTED |
| 18 | E | ERROR IN DECLARATION SECTION |
| 19 | E | ERROR IN FIELD LIST |
| 20 | E | ',' EXPECTED |
| 22 | E | '..' EXPECTED |
| 23 | E | '.' EXPECTED |
| 24 | E | ':' NOT ALLOWED |
| 40 | E | ILLEGAL PARAMETER TYPE |
| 42 | E | STATEMENT TERMINATOR EXPECTED |
| 43 | E | STATEMENT EXPECTED |
| 45 | W | 'EXTERNAL FORTRAN' EXPECTED |
| 49 | E | 'ARRAY' EXPECTED |
| 50 | E | CONSTANT EXPECTED |
| 51 | E | ':=' EXPECTED |
| 52 | E | 'THEN' EXPECTED |
| 53 | E | 'UNTIL' EXPECTED |
| 54 | E | 'DO' EXPECTED |
| 55 | E | 'TO' / 'DOWNTO' EXPECTED |
| 57 | E | 'FILE' EXPECTED |
| 58 | E | ERROR IN FACTOR |
| 60 | E | 'CHAR' EXPECTED |
| 61 | E | UNARY '+' / '−' NOT ALLOWED IN TERM, OR 'NOT' IN BOOLEAN PRIMARY |

TABLE 4.1. *(Continued)*

| 62 | E | EXPRESSION OR '.)' EXPECTED |
|---|---|---|
| 63 | E | '..' ',' OR '.)' EXPECTED |
| 64 | E | ',' OR '.)' EXPECTED |
| 65 | E | USE 'DIV' FOR INTEGER '/' |
| 66 | E | TYPE IDENTIFIER EXPECTED |
| 67 | W | QUESTION MARK UPPER BOUND EXPECTED |
| 68 | E | PROGRAM PARAMETERS NOT IMPLEMENTED |
| 80 | W | OPTION IDENTIFIER EXPECTED |
| 81 | W | ILLEGAL OPTION IDENTIFIER |
| 82 | W | PROGRAM SENSITIVE OPTION MAY NOT BE CONTROLLED HERE |
| 83 | W | STATEMENT SENSITIVE OPTION MAY NOT BE CONTROLLED HERE |
| 84 | W | NULL BODY EXPECTED |
| 101 | E | IDENTIFIER DECLARED TWICE |
| 102 | F | LOWER BOUND EXCEEDS UPPER BOUND |
| 103 | F | IDENTIFIER IS NOT OF APPROPRIATE CLASS |
| 104 | E | UNDECLARED IDENTIFIER |
| 105 | F | CLASS OF IDENTIFIER IS NOT VARIABLE |
| 107 | E | INCOMPATIBLE SUBRANGE TYPES |
| 108 | E | FILE NOT ALLOWED HERE |
| 109 | E | TYPE OF IDENTIFIER MUST BE ARRAY OR SET |
| 110 | E | TAGFIED MUST BE SCALAR OR SUBRANGE |
| 111 | E | RECORD VARIANT CONSTANT INCOMPATIBLE WITH TAGFIELD TYPE |
| 117 | E | UNSATISFIED FORWARD REFERENCE TO A TYPE IDENTIFIER OF A POINTER |
| 119 | E | ':' EXPECTED (PARAMETER LIST NOT ALLOWED) |
| 120 | E | FUNCTION RESULT MUST BE SCALAR, SUBRANGE, OR POINTER |
| 121 | E | FILE VALUE PARAMETER NOT ALLOWED |
| 122 | E | ':' EXPECTED (FUNCTION RESULT NOT ALLOWED) |
| 123 | E | FUNCTION RESULT EXPECTED |
| 126 | F | IMPROPER NUMBER OF PARAMETERS |
| 127 | F | TYPE OF ACTUAL PARAMETER DOES NOT MATCH FORMAL PARAMETER |
| 128 | E | PARAMETER INCOMPATIBLE WITH PREVIOUS PARAMETER (DYNAMIC ARGUMENT) |
| 129 | E | TYPE CONFLICT OF OPERANDS IN AN EXPRESSION |
| 130 | F | EXPRESSION IS NOT OF SET TYPE |
| 131 | W | INTEGER OPERANDS CONVERTED TO REAL FOR '/' |
| 132 | W | BASE TYPE OF SET IS LONG INTEGER |
| 133 | W | LONG INTEGER ELEMENT IN SET |
| 134 | F | ILLEGAL TYPE OF OPERANDS |

**TABLE 4.2. Typical Error Messages During Program Execution**

*Attempt to Skip Beyond EOM*

An attempt has been made to skip beyond the end-of-medium (EOM) in a call to procedure SKIPFILES. Correct the program to prevent the call. When EOF is true following execution of SKIPFILES, the file is at EOM and no further call to SKIP-FILES should be made.

*Attempt to Read Past EOF*

The program has attempted to read from a file that is positioned at EOF. The program should test for end-of-file by calling function EOF. If it is desired to read a file that follows the EOF of the same medium, call procedure SKIPFILES to position the file at the beginning of the next file.

*Cannot Load Overlay*

The library routine OVLY$ has received an error status code from the operating system when attempting a load overlay operation (supervisor call code $14_{16}$).

*Cannot Get Memory*

Memory required for the program plus the memory requested for stack and heap exceeds the amount of available memory. Try to execute the program with smaller stack and heap values.

*"CASE" Alternative Error*

The selector expression of a CASE statement has a value that is not equal to any of the CASE labels, and there is no OTHERWISE clause. The OUTPUT file message includes the statement number and the selector value.

*Code = _____ PC = _____ Stack: _____ Heap: _____*

A program using the minimal runtime library has terminated. The code value is one of the error codes. The PC value is the contents of the Program Counter when the error occurred, or zero for normal termination. The stack and heap values are hexadecimal numbers of bytes of stack and heap, respectively, used by the program.

*Divide by Zero*

An integer or fixed-point division was attempted with a divisor of zero.

*Dynamic Array Size Out of Range*

The value of the size of a dynamic array was either zero or negative when the routine that contains the array was entered.

*Error Code = _____*

An error has occurred. The value is one of the error codes.

**TABLE 4.2.** *(Continued)*

*Escape-from-Routine Error*

An ESCAPE statement that references a routine name has been executed, but the statement is not within the scope of the named routine.

*Fatal Compilation Errors*

An attempt to execute a routine that has fatal compilation errors has been made; the name of the routine follows this message.

*Field Exceeds Record Size*

The field specified for a formatted READ from or WRITE to a textfile is longer than the logical record length of the file.

*Field Width Too Large*

A parameter of a call to a WRITE procedure has a field length longer than the logical record length of the file.

*File _____ Access Name _____*

An I/O error occurred on the file the name of which follows the word FILE. The access name, if known, or the word UNKNOWN, follows the words ACCESS NAME. A message describing the nature of the problem follows.

*Floating Point Error—Illegal Instruction*

The floating point interpreter did not recognize the code of a floating point instruction. Either CODEGEN wrote bad object code or the program code areas has been modified, possibly by storing data at the wrong location. The OUTPUT file contains the bad instruction and the address following the instruction.

*Floating Point Error—Division by Zero*

The divisor of a division operation of REAL numbers was zero.

*Floating Point Error—Overflow*

A floating point operation has resulted in a value that is too large to be represented (magnitude greater than $10^{75}$). The OUTPUT file contains the instruction that produced the error and the address following the instruction.

*Floating Point Error—Relink for Extended Precision*

The runtime routines for double precision REAL values were not linked with a program that attempts to perform double precision REAL operations. Add the following to the link control file:

    INCLUDE (FL$ITD)
    INCLUDE (TEN$D)

For many applications, particularly a small number of noncritical micro-computer applications, software testing would not be justified. If an error occurs, the result of the error might not have a serious effect on life or property. The error can be corrected in due course, and suitable apologies made to those inconvenienced by the error.

On the other hand, there are many applications where a software error can have serious consequences. Software used in large scale industrial pro-cesses, or in life critical situations is expected to operate correctly. Any deviance from correct operation would pose serious threat to life or property. In such applications, software testing is justified, and the extent of the soft-ware testing would depend upon the complexity of the program and the extent of the risk incurred by incorrect operations.

Software testing may include one or more of the following techniques:

instrumentation

bebugging

diagnostics

tracers

assertion checking

auditing

Instrumentation is merely a fancy term that refers to adding executable program code to a program under test for the purpose of stimulating certain program operations or making measurements during execution. The task of "instrumenting" a program is generally referred to as *dynamic testing*, in which an instrumented program is executed and test data derived during execution. An analysis of the test data is then performed against a quality assurance or correctness criteria.

Bebugging is the technique of adding identified program bugs or errors to a program that is otherwise assumed to be correct. The program is then tested according to plan and a check is made to determine whether the previously inserted program errors are in fact detected by the test program.

In addition to providing verification of the functioning of the test pro-gram, bebugging also allows the interaction of the identified program bugs with other program elements that may constitute latent program bugs.

Diagnostics is the term referring to the output of a test program. Like any data, diagnostics must be compared to the program's expected behavior, or against a predetermined quality or correctness criteria. Diagnostics may be used to indicate which portions of a program are most frequently executed, or which portions are not executed at all (and which therefore may be untested).

Tracers are routines that exercise each possible variation of the executable statements in a program, and in doing so search for unreachable or "dead" codes.

Assertion checking is the technique of inserting statements and conditions in a program which should hold true at all times, that is, at each state of program execution.

Auditing is testing for program consistency and traceability. Consistency is checking the uniformity of identifiers for program constants and variables throughout the program, and making sure that the same identifiers are not used in program modules that refer to different logical program constructs. Some programs are in fact deliberately written by programmers taking advantage of the fact that an identifier has a particular value, or perhaps even a random value if the identifier for that variable has not been previously defined.

Traceability refers to the identification of program identifiers or symbols which permits them to be traced through the software from module to module and from one system component to another.

Robustness testing refers to testing a program at ranges of absolute value of input and output beyond the range in which the program is intended to operate. Such testing is useful to determine the extent to which a program is able to continue to execute in spite of the ranges of input or output, and to what extent such execution is "correct," based upon the actual intended algorithm using such values.

### Validation

Computer program validation is the name given to the test procedure or procedures that determine whether a particular computer code complies with certain functional or interface requirements. An example of program validation is the use of a "validation suite," applied to a Pascal program to determine whether the program code conforms to a particular standard language specification.

### Verification

Computer verification is a step-by-step procedure in which a determination is made that a program satisfies the following:

system specification

requirements

specification

code

Each of these steps must be independently verified.

## Certification

Computer program certification is the term used to describe the testing of a computer program under actual operational conditions, and the determination that the program is operationally effective and meets the requirements originally imposed on the program by the specification. Certification therefore not only evaluates the computer program itself, but whether the specification for the computer program is properly descriptive of the desired operation and results under actual operational environment.

## DOCUMENTATION AND MAINTENANCE

Documentation is a written record of how a system works, or how it was developed and implemented. Documentation is an important aspect of software development, and is a key criteria to be used in comparing and evaluating different software packages and systems.

Documentation serves the following functions:

provides user or operator instructions on how to use the system

provides a detailed specification of the system

provides a reference on development of the system for later modifications or extensions

There are of course many different kinds of documentation for different categories of persons who would use that documentation. One might consider that associated with any software package or system there would be several different types of manuals:

user's manual

operator's manual

programming manual

systems manual

development reference manual

In the following sections we will consider each of these manuals in greater detail.

## User's Manual

The user's manual and the operator's manual fulfill the first of the three functions of documentation noted above—they provide the user or operator with instructions on how to use the system. We make a distinction between user and operator, and in fact suggest that there be two different manuals for such persons, although in many cases, such as for simple software systems, such manuals may be combined into a single user/operator manual.

The user is regarded as the person responsible for specifying and implementing the system for a particular application. In some organizations such a person may have the title of data processing manager. The DP manager is interested in a broad overview of the system capabilities in order to evaluate whether it is suitable for the intended application, as well as the requirements in hardware and personnel necessary for implementing the system. The user is not concerned with technical details, which are delegated to systems analysts and programmers, or with the operational details of the system, which are delegated to the operators or actual users who work with the system at the CRT screen and keyboard.

As we have pointed out previously, for small scale software systems, particularly software packages for microcomputers, the user may be the same person as the operator, and the information provided in the documentation may therefore be provided in a single document.

## Operator's Manual

The operator's manual is intended to explain to the personnel at the CRT and keyboard how to use the system. In many cases the personnel may not be programmers, and the computer will be conducting conversations with the user through the means of prompts and multiple-choice selections. The operator's manual provides an overview of such operations for training and instructing the operators prior to hands-on contact with the system. The operator's manual also provides a reference concerning system malfunction, error messages, and the like.

## Programming Manual

The programming manual is intended to explain to applications programmers how the system software has been programmed, and how the programmer may be able to modify or extend the program to meet the needs of a specific application or operator environment. Some software systems, such as smaller software packages accompanying microcomputers, include the entire source code of the program so that the programmer may redesign the program at will. Other software systems, such as compilers, provide the programmer with the equivalent of a user/operator's manual, which describes the instruction set, editing facilities, debugging facilities, and system interfaces for implementing the programmer's applications program on the user's hardware.

## Systems Manual

The systems manual is intended to explain to systems analysts how the computer hardware should be configured in order to accommodate the software system in question. The systems manual therefore discusses the entire hardware-software system from a more technical perspective than the user's manual. Such topics as timing and memory size requirements would be covered, as well as input/output structures, alternative implementations, and test configurations. The systems manual also includes a summary of the programming manual, since the systems analyst must have a knowledge of whether the specific systems tasks needed can be implemented through the supplied software.

The systems manual also typically includes a detailed specification of the sytem for control purposes, thereby fulfilling the second of the three important functions of documentation noted previously.

## Development Reference Manual

The development reference manual is a part of the software documentation which is used by the developers of the software, not by the user or the user's organization. The development reference manual essentially provides a reference on the development of the system for use by the system designers or their successors for maintaining, modifying, and extending the system, and therefore fulfills the last of the three functions of documentation noted previously.

# REFERENCES

## Programming

N. Wirth, *Algorithms + Data Structures = Programs*, Prentice-Hall, Englewood Cliffs, NJ, 1976.

L. Kronsjö, *Algorithms: Their Efficiency and Complexity*, Wiley, New York, 1979.

## Testing

G. J. Myers, *Software Reliability: Principles and Practices*, Wiley, New York, 1976.

G. J. Myers, *The Art of Software Testing*, Wiley, New York, 1979.

R. B. Anderson, *Proving Programs Correct*, Wiley, New York, 1979.

# 5

# Program Design

*. . . [I]n existing machines the time for coding problems is comparable to the solution time . . .*

H. H. Goldstine and J. von Neumann (1946),
from J. von Neumann's Collected Works

In recent years there has been a considerable amount of attention and interest in program design and an analysis of the "structure" of programs. There are two good reasons for such interest:

1. The realization in the commercial data processing industry that the investment in software is the principal component in system cost, and that such cost is amenable to proper management.
2. The emergence of programming as an academic discipline in its own right.

In the present chapter we consider two aspects of program design:

structured programming
programming costs

## STRUCTURED PROGRAMMING

Structured programming is the general term (or, more accurately, "buzzword") for a variety of related approaches to program design which were

**66**

developed and popularized in the 1970s, primarily in circles concerned with large scale software development projects. Some of the important concepts that were developed and analyzed were:

program structure
graph theory
program correctness
content evaluation
top down design

## Program Structure

As the name implies, one of the most basic concepts in structured programming is the notion of program structure. Program structure is established at the design phase of a program—at the level of problem definition and architectural design, to use the terminology of the previous chapter. It is concerned with the organization of the basic building blocks of the program, or to again use the architectural analogy, the building components and framework that when assembled together define the architecture.

The interest in program structure has received greater attention since various studies of software failures began reporting that errors due to design flaws were more common than coding errors. Questions were asked. What was the nature of the design errors? Can such errors be detected? Can such errors be prevented?

Attention began focusing on the structure associated with program design—the components of a flowchart. Consideration was given to the various types of control structures in the flowchart, and reducing them to a few simple structures. The basic building blocks of the flowchart were therefore reduced to the three nodes shown in Figure 5.1—function nodes, predicate nodes, and collector nodes. Any computer program can be reduced to these basic building blocks.

The basic objective for introducing these building blocks is to simplify the program design process by using a small number of simple control structures as standards for program construction.

An important consequence of the building block structure is the automatic modularization of programs. In order to minimize design flaws in a program, it is appropriate to break the program into easy-to-manage modules that are relatively independent of one another. The independence of the modules is achieved by minimizing the interconnections between them, while still maintaining program cohesiveness.

Function

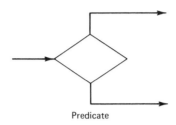

Predicate

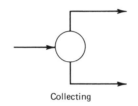

Collecting

**FIGURE 5.1.**   Flowchart building blocks.

Structured programming therefore focuses the designer's attention on the following issues:

the overall program structure
partitioning the program structure into modules
definition of modules using the basic building blocks
minimizing interconnections or dependence between modules
ensuring overall program cohesiveness

The advantages of such program design techniques is apparent from both the program testing and maintenance viewpoint. Modules are easier to test and correct than entire programs. Since the behavior of a module is easier to understand than the entire program, maintenance of the program is also simplified.

**Graph Theory**

Although programming languages may be described in terms of formal languages, and the operation of such languages on a computer modeled by automata, the issues of program structure and design are not apparent from such abstractions. It is, however, desirable to represent the structure and operation of a program in a rigorous fashion.

As we have pointed out in the previous section, the flowchart is an appropriate place to begin. The flowchart describes the dynamic operation of the computer program: the actualization and realization of the computer language, the life and movement of the static form of the program structure.

Again, an analogy with natural languages and life would offer a useful insight here. Just as a dictionary and grammar does not tell much about of the behavior of a society, knowledge of a computer programming language does not describe how it operates, its dynamic behavior. The flowchart of a computer program, however, is like a script for a play. The language is used, but more important, the spectator learns much more about the characters and the plot through watching them.

Although computer linguistics may be concerned with computer languages, just like linguistics is concerned with natural languages, there is an entirely separate field of literature concerned with the use of language in novels, poetry, drama, and so forth. Similarly, there is an entire separate field of study of the dynamic operation of computer programs as reflected in flowcharts. That field is called graph theory.

Graph theory is a highly descriptive mathematical theory with particular applications in statistical mechanics and combinatorics. Although a flowchart is a directed graph, and the flowchart can be described as a collection of a vertex set, an arc set, and an edge set, the full capabilities of graph theory are not realized in program description.

There are a number of evident reasons for this. Different flowcharts may describe the same algorithm or mathematical calculation. On the other hand, the notion of equivalence in graph theory is the concept of isomorphic graphs with a one-to-one correspondence between vertex sets, arc sets, and edge sets. Thus, although graph theory may describe the same graphs, it falls short of describing what the graphs do.

**Program Correctness**

Closely associated with the concept of structured programming is the concept of program "correctness." Simply defined, a "correct" program is one that meets certain specific "correctness" criteria. The correctness criteria are usually defined in terms of the design rules for a properly structured program, so that a program that satisfies such design rules is deemed "correct." Correctness of a program is usually demonstrated through the use assertions which are placed throughout the program. An assertion defines the relationship between certain variables of the program at a particular point in execution. If the assertion is found to be valid, then the program is proved to be "correct" with respect to the defined design rules. Correctness proofs of the type indicated is one method of program testing, as has been previously discussed in the section on program testing and validation.

## Content Evaluation

The concept of program validation and correctness is closely related to the more general problem of evaluating the content and meaning of any statement or text in a natural language. In order to appreciate some of the concepts and ramifications of validation and correctness criteria in a computer language, it would be worthwhile to consider some corresponding content evaluation criteria in a natural language context.

For our purpose here, we can consider the simple analogy of validation and correctness in a natural language by considering the possible criteria for evaluating a statement or text in English. In order to properly understand the criteria, we consider the text as a translation from a foreign language of a report of a newsmaking event. Four possible criteria are:

reliability
accuracy
validity
value

Although in common usage the meaning and interpretation of these terms may overlap, we shall give these terms special meaning in the context of content evaluation.

Reliability is concerned with whether the expression of the text, rather than the contents thereof, is fully and accurately reported. In the example of the text being a foreign language translation, reliability expresses whether the translation is an accurate one.

One way of measuring reliability is through different observers or reporters, or different translations. If the translations are consistent, it could be said that the text is a reliable one.

In the information processing context, reliability refers to the ability to perform specific functions in spite of the existence of certain hardware or software faults. In other words, a reliable program is one that will continue to function even though there may be errors in some components of the program.

In hardware terms, reliability refers to the probability that a device will continue to function over a specific time period. In such terms, the reliability of a component or a system is measured in quantitative terms as the mean time between failures (MTBF), or the failure rate (1/MTBF, which is a measure of the number of failures per unit time). Thus, in hardware terms reliability refers to absolute failures, whereas software reliability refers to a measure of error tolerance.

In a communications context, reliability refers to the bit error rate. A highly reliable transmission is one that contains very few bit errors.

Accuracy refers to how closely the content of the text reflects the reality. In the example of the text being a report of a newsmaking event, the issue of accuracy refers to whether what was reported actually corresponds to pre- cisely what occurred. The usual way of measuring accuracy is through the first-hand knowledge of different observers or reporters who witnessed the event. If such observations are consistent, it could be said that the text was an accurate one. In the information processing context, accuracy refers to whether the digital representation corresponds to reality, typically an analog reality. More particularly, accuracy is simply the number of correct digits in a multidigit computational result.

Validity refers to whether the content of the text is true and valid. The statement "two plus two equals five" may be reported reliably and accurate- ly, but it simply is not a valid statement. Validity testing goes beyond merely the content of the message and considers its meaning in the context of prior knowledge. In the information processing context, validity testing is quite frequently done in many applications programs to prevent some common errors, such as writing a check for a negative amount if a negative balance is shown on an accounts payable record.

Finally, value refers to the significance or usefulness of the statement. The statement "two plus two equals four" is not of very much value in a typical context. In the information processing context, value of a computer result must be judged against the application criteria and purpose of the com- putation.

## Top Down Design

Another feature of structure programming is the concept of top down de- sign. Top down design of a program is to consider first the broadest or most general elements of the system, and then turn to the narrow and more specific subsystems. In other words, top down programming is to structure the program task in a hierarchical manner, and to begin the design at the top of the hierarchy and work down.

The basic process of top down design is illustrated in Figure 5.2. First the operating system environment is defined. Then linkage editors are added. Finally, the main program is appended to the operating system, and various subprograms or subroutines are appended to the main program.

Such a design process is typically the opposite of how much program development is done in industry today. In bottom up programming, the smaller units or subprograms are developed first, and they in turn are integrated into higher and higher levels of the final system.

## Software Evaluation and Acceptance Criteria

The foregoing discussion of program structure, correctness, and design is of little use if it is not actually used in establishing some quality standard for software. Unlike most commodities, it is difficult to establish a quality standard for software. Yet as software becomes more and more important, and the dollar value of software development projects increase, there is an increasing effort by all segments of the computer industry to establish some useful measures of software quality. The concepts of structured programming is one approach toward this goal.

The most important application of software evaluation and acceptance criteria is in software development contracts, in which a computer user

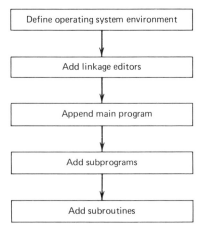

FIGURE 5.2.   Top-down program design.

contracts with a vendor to develop some well-defined programs. Although the vendor may meet the project milestones, and deliver a product that appears to work and meet the specifications, the user is often at a loss to judge the "quality" of the work.

It is of course not possible to objectively state how "good" a program is in quantitative terms. However, it is possible to say, based upon studies in structured programming, that a "good" program is one that

makes effective and efficient use of the available resources
is well documented
is easily maintained

Further criteria that could be applied judge whether the program

is portable
is adaptable

By "portable" it is meant that the software can be transferred from one computer to another, or from one operating system or environment to another, without extensive reprogramming or interfacing effort. By "adaptable" it is meant that the program can be modified or adjusted to a user's particular requirements, such as the form of the input, the format of the output, or similar features.

It is possible to summarize these criteria into four specific attributes that are indicative of a "good" program:

usefulness
human factors
documentation
error analysis

The *usefulness* of a software package refers to the technical capabilities of the package to perform the tasks required by the user for a specific application. Does the software have the capabilities to handle all the features and exceptions that may arise in the user's application? Does the package give the user the type of information necessary for the particular application? Affirmative answers to such questions are indicative of the usefulness of a software package.

The *human factors* of a software package are concerned with the ease of implementing and using the package on a particular computer or in a particular environment. Does the package interface with a widely used operating system? Is the control language of the package simple and easy to use? Can the package be used by someone without an extensive computer or programming background? Affirmative answers to such questions are indicative of the favorable human factor aspects of the package.

The *documentation* refers to the quantity and quality of the descriptive material accompanying the software which explains the implementation and use of the package.

*Error analysis* is concerned with the facilities provided within the software package itself to detect and report user errors. If the user makes an incorrect entry, a software package with little error analysis capability may simply fail to execute, leaving the user in a quandary, to wonder what is wrong. A software package with extensive error analysis capability will specifically point out that the previous entry was in error, and might even point out the nature of the error.

## PROGRAMMING COSTS

Although we have pointed out that programming has become an academic discipline and the great interest in structured program design is related to program reliability, the fact remains that most programming done in the world today is done in a commercial environment (the concept of "commercial" being broadly interpreted to include government funded and nonprofit institutions) in which the cost of programming has now become uppermost in the minds of the administrators and managers who have the responsibility of utilizing the capability of computers to solve problems in the world of business, government, and other endeavors.

In the early days of the computer industry the relative cost of software with respect to the total systems cost was relatively low, as suggested in Figure 5.1. However, as advances in the field of integrated circuits in the 1960s, and further advances in process technology in the 1960s reduced the size and cost of semiconductor components, the price of computer hardware dropped sharply. The costs of computation for different generations of computers have been estimated in Table 5.1.

TABLE 5.1.   Costs of Computation

| | |
|---|---|
| 1952 | $1.26 |
| 1958 | 0.26 |
| 1964 | 0.12 |
| 1970 | 0.05 |
| 1975 | 0.01 |

The costs of computation becomes even more striking when the change in the consumer price index (CPI) is taken into consideration.

As software became the major portion of a system's cost, increasing attention has been paid to the cost of programming and software and attempts made at estimating and quantifying such costs. A large part of the recent interest in languages like Pascal arises from the possibility of significant cost savings by using such a language. It is therefore important to appreciate some of the issues in quantifying programming costs before analyzing a new language like Pascal.

First, the large number of variables that can affect programming cost must be noted:

type of language
   high order/assembly
experience of programmers in the language
type of application
experience of programmers in the application
type of software
   batch/real-time
   application program/systems programs
hardware configuration
   single CPU/multiple CPUs
   uniprocessor/distributed processing
user environment
   single user/multiple user
   interactions between users

Once the programming manager has fully understood the specification of the programming task in terms of the application, hardware, and user environment, and has a knowledge of the experience of a programmer team in terms of similar programs for the same application, hardware, or user environment, the task of programming cost quantification can begin.

The basic approach is simply called "the experience method." The basic software development project is broken into six distinct tasks which are performed successively:

requirements analysis
architectural design
detailed description

coding and debugging
integration and test
validation testing

The portion of the total cost that is consumed by each of these individual tasks is typified by the typical programming project illustrated in Figure 5.3. Although upper management may be concerned with the overall cost of a software project, it is the project managers who are concerned with the day-to-day manpower and schedule requirements. A key objective of quantitative cost estimating is to forecast and schedule two basic management parameters—manpower and time—based upon the requirements and specification of the application.

An example of an estimate of manpower requirements over time for each of the six tasks identified in Figure 5.3 is given in Figure 5.4.

It is clear from Figure 5.4 that the manpower requirements are not constant over time. The software development project manager must schedule the manpower resources among different software projects based upon the specific task being undertaken at any one time.

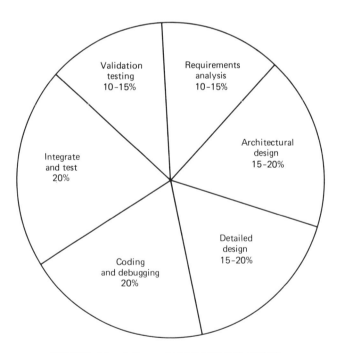

**FIGURE 5.3.**   Software development task analysis.

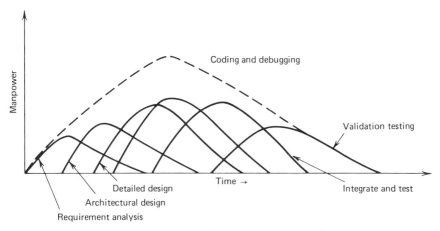

**FIGURE 5.4.** Software development manpower requirements.

## Productivity

Productivity is an important economic parameter in measuring and comparing the efficiency of a production process, be it the production of goods and services in the economy, or the production of computer software. Simply defined, productivity is the aggregate final output per unit of input. Because of the various types of outputs and inputs in any one production process, the most commonly used productivity measure (called single-factor productivity) measures the output divided by the number of person-hours of labor input used to produce this output.

In the production of software, the amount of output is relatively easy to define: it is the quantity of code (e.g., number of lines), and the amount of documentation. Such a raw productivity measurement must be tempered by at least three other considerations:

the size and complexity of the application

the correctness and efficiency of the code

the cost or resources used to produce the code

## REFERENCES

### Structured Programming

H. D. Mills, *Mathematical Foundations for Structured Programming*, FSC 72-6012 IBM Corporation, Gaithersburg, Md., February, 1972.

E. W. Dijkstra, and C. A. R. Hoare, *Structured Programming*, Academic Press, New York, 1972.

E. W. Dijkstra, GOTO Statement Considered Harmful, *Comm. ACM* **11**, 147 (1968).

N. Wirth, *Systematic Programming: An Introduction*, Prentice-Hall, Englewood Cliffs, NJ, 1973.

## Programming Cost

F. P. Brooks, *The Mythical Man Month*, Addison-Wesley, Reading, Mass. 1975.

W. F. Sharpe, *The Economics of Computers*, Columbia University Press, New York, 1969.

# 6

# Pascal: Overview

*The development of the language* Pascal *is based on two principal aims. The first is to make available a language suitable to teach programming as a systematic discipline based on certain fundamental concepts clearly and naturally reflected by the language. The second is to develop implementations of this language which are both reliable and efficient on presently available computers.*

*N. Wirth*

Pascal is a highly structured, high level language that was developed in the early 1970s by Professor Niklaus Wirth of the Federal Institute of Technology (Eidgenössiche Technische Hochschule) in Zurich, Switzerland. The language was named after the seventeenth-century French mathematician Blaise Pascal, and was originally intended as a tool for teaching programming in a systematic manner. The advantages of Pascal were soon noted in the programming community, and various implementations of the language were developed by the end of the decade, including many for microcomputers.

The present chapter provides of brief overview of Pascal, considering the following topics in particular:

organization
data structures
control structures
syntax

## ORGANIZATION

Pascal is organized as a highly structured, block structured language, written in a sequential manner with certain indentation conventions in order to be readily understood by the reader. In describing some of the important features, it is useful to present an example of a portion of a Pascal program:

```
procedure pairint (var n:integer);
    var i:integer; temp: integer; rev: boolean;
    begin rev := true;
        while rev do
        begin rev:=false;
            for i := 1 to n-1 do
            begin;
                if a(i) > a(i+1) then
                    begin rev:=true;
                        temp:= a(i);
                        a(i) := a(i+1);
                        a(i+1):=temp
                    end;
                end;
            end;
    end;
```

In the present section we analyze the notational features and program structure of a Pascal program.

### Notational Features

The notational features refer to some of the purely visual features of how a language is written, or the typography in the case of a printed version. Some of the most striking notational features can be seen in the sample program above. Before we turn to these notational features in detail, a .prefatory remark must be made on typography.

In this book, we have chosen to represent Pascal programs using boldface and italic typography. Such a representation enables the reader to first clearly distinguish a programming language statement from the remainder of the text, and secondly, to distinctly highlight the program structure. Such a convention is not novel, but is found in previous books by Niklaus Wirth.

Using such notation, the reader will be able to tell that the expression

$$a(i)$$

is a mathematical term used in the text, while the expression

$$a[i]$$

is a statement in the Pascal language.

The reader must realize that on a CRT or printer the program will appear in upper-case letters:

PROCEDURE PAIRINT (VAR N:INTEGER)
    VAR I:INTEGER;   TEMP:INTEGER;   REV:BOOLEAN;

and so on. Our aim here is not to reproduce how Pascal will eventually appear on a CRT or a printer, but to make the language easy to read and understand.

It should also be pointed out that with CRT terminals or printers having both upper- and lower-case letters, it is possible to type the keywords in upper-case, and the remaining statements in lower-case:

PROCEDURE pairint (VAR n:integer)
    VAR i:integer;   temp:integer;   rev:boolean

Such a representation enables the user the highlight the program structure on the terminal, much like the typography does in this book. In many implementations, no distinction is made between upper- and lower-case letters or words as far as the semantics and syntax of the language is concerned, so that as far as compilation of the program text is concerned, all of the following expressions are equally acceptable to the computer:

PROCEDURE PAIRINT
procedure PAIRINT
PROcedure Pairint
procEDuRe pAirInt
procedure pairint

First, we should note some of the important notational features used in writing Pascal programs. These notational features are not, strictly speaking, part the language itself, any more than a particular alphabet or script are part of a natural language, such as English. However, in learning to read English, it is important to learn first the Roman letters in the alphabet, and only then would one be able to associate a particular printed sequence of characters with an English word. Similarly, in learning to read Pascal programs, one should begin with the notational features, and then consider the semantic and syntactic features of the language.

In the printed form of the Pascal program above, we note immediately that some words (e.g., "begin," "while," "end") are printed in boldface type. These words are *keywords* which have a special meaning in a Pascal program and cannot be arbitrarily used or defined by the programmer. In typewritten or handwritten programs such words are underlined. The list of all keywords in Pascal is presented in Table 6.1.

These keywords must be used exactly as shown in Table 6.1, that is, the symbols

**downto**

or

**goto**

must be used, and not

**down to**

or

**go to**

TABLE 6.1.    Pascal Keywords

| and | function | program |
|-----|----------|---------|
| array | goto | record |
| begin | if | repeat |
| case | in | set |
| const | label | then |
| div | mod | to |
| do | nil | type |
| downto | not | until |
| else | of | var |
| end | or | while |
| file | packed | with |
| for | procedure | |

TABLE 6.2.  Pascal Special Symbols

| + | := | : | < | ( | { |
|---|----|---|---|---|---|
| – | . | ' | <= | ) | } |
| * | ' | = | >= | [ | ↑ |
| / | ; | <> | < | ] | |

Another notational feature is various special symbols such as + or *. The list of special symbols in Pascal is presented in Table 6.2.

There are also a number of symbol sequences shown in the printed text in italics, such as

$$rev := true$$

In typewritten or handwritten programs these words would simply be written in lower-case.

These symbol sequences are formed from combinations (or more accurately, concatenations) of the usual letters and digits shown in Table 6.3.

The symbol sequences may form identifiers, numbers, constants, or other entities which will be subsequently described and defined.

Another important notational feature of Pascal is the highly structured indentation conventions. The fundamental block structure of the Pascal program is highlighted by the vertical alignment of matching begin and end symbols, with each begin-end pair defining a block of operations. In order to provide clarity in reading, each begin and end statement is written on a separate line.

The purpose of the indentation is to provide a pictorial representation of the logical operation of the program. In the case of the program example given above, a nested block structure, such as suggested in Figure 6.1, is visually apparent from the four levels of indentation corresponding to four begin-end pairs.

## Program Structure: Block Organization

The basic program structure of Pascal consists of a sequence of blocks, closely reflecting the block structure notational feature of the language. A

TABLE 6.3.  Pascal Character Set

0 1 2 3 4 5 6 7 8 9
a b c d e f g h i j k l m n o p q r s t u v w x y z

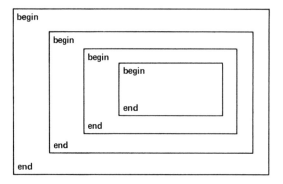

**FIGURE 6.1.** Nested block structure.

highly simplified example of the program structure of a simple Pascal program is illustrated in Figure 6.2.

The first block shown in Figure 6.2 contains the program name and various declarations. More accurately, the program name forms a heading which is above the block, while the declarations themselves form the block.

The heading gives the program a name solely for the use of the programmer or the operating system. It has no use or function within the program itself. The program name is defined by an *identifier*, a concept which is important in Pascal and which should be defined at this point. An identifier is a name given by the user to denote a constant, type, variable, procedure, or function in Pascal. It must begin with a letter and be directly followed by a number of letters or digits in any combination. Various implementations of the language only recognize the first eight or so characters as significant.

The programmer may therefore define the program name with some meaningful name, for example,

**program** *pairintegersort*

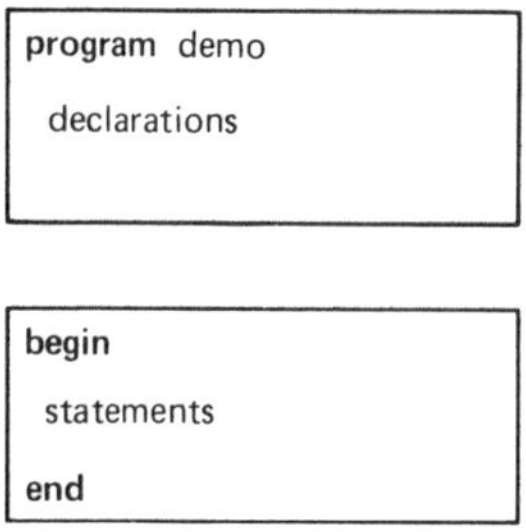

```
program demo
  declarations
```

```
begin
  statements
end
```

**FIGURE 6.2.**    Pascal program block structure.

or perhaps

**program** *pairint*

It should be noted that

**program** *pair integer sort*

is not a valid program name: no blank spaces are allowed in an identifier. It is important to be able to distinguish between valid and invalid identifiers. The following are valid identifiers:

*Z80ASSEMBLER*
*QWERTY*
*P123456789*
*ADD2AND2*

The following are invalid identifiers:

*8086ASSEMBLER*
*COLLECT$200*
*P234 OPEN*
*FUNCTION*

The first example is invalid because it does not begin with a letter. The second example is invalid because it contains a character ($) not included in the Pascal character set (see Table 6.3). The third example is invalid because it consists of a blank space. Finally, the fourth example is invalid as an identifier because it is a keyword (see Table 6.1).

The second block shown in Figure 6.2 consists of the instructions or statements that form the main body of the program. These statements are grouped into a series of blocks which have one entry point (i.e., at the "top" of the block) and one exit point (i.e, at the "bottom" of the block). One pair of keywords that define the top and bottom of a block are begin and end, and these two words are used in the example in Figure 6.2.

It is these program blocks that define the basic "structure" of a Pascal program. Since each block is associated with one set of calculations, it is far easier to design, code, and test a Pascal program block by block than to work with a less structured language. It is also far easier to read and understand the logic of a program when it is broken into blocks or modules than when it is written line by line.

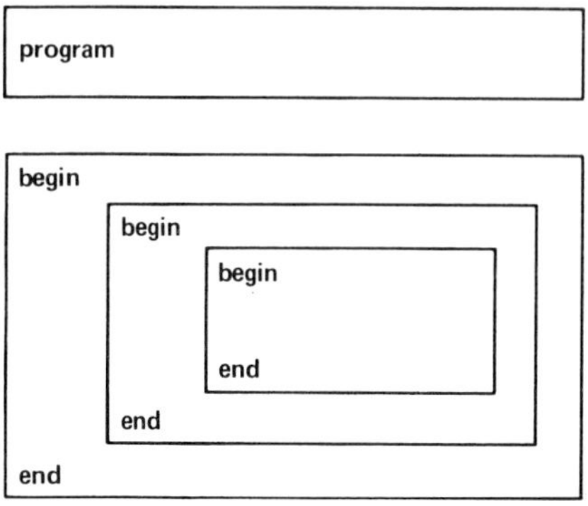

FIGURE 6.3.    Pascal program: nested blocks.

More complex block structures in a Pascal program are shown in Figures 6.3, 6.4, and 6.5. Figure 6.3 shows how blocks may be nested one inside the other. The pair integer sort program shown in the beginning of this chapter is a good example of nested blocks of begin-end statements.

Figure 6.4 shows a sequence of blocks in which each block is on the same level. Figure 6.5 shows a combination of nested blocks and a sequence of blocks.

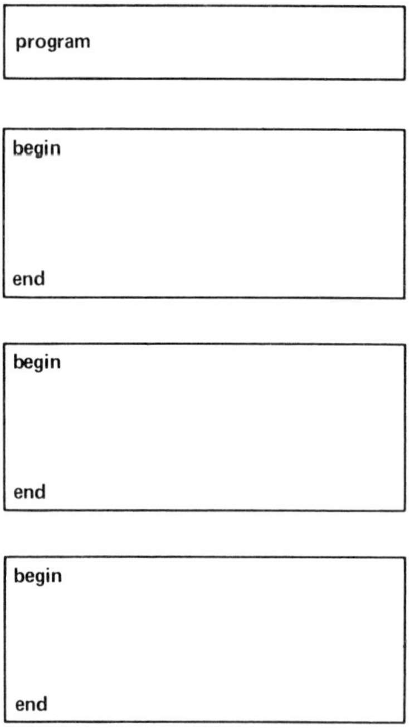

FIGURE 6.4.    Pascal program: sequential blocks.

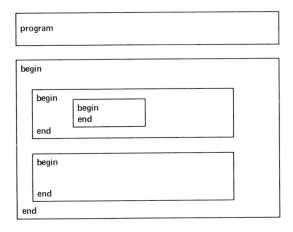

**FIGURE 6.5.** Pascal program: nested and sequential blocks.

One of the important consequences of the block structure of Pascal is that variables and other parameters may be defined solely within a particular block and all blocks nested therein. Such variables are said to be *local* variables. Variables that are not local to any particular block are called *global* variables and are defined for the entire program. The concept of local and global variables and other objects will be explored in greater detail at a later point.

## Program Structure: Abstract Organization

The program structure of Pascal reflects the modern view of programming as a construction of procedural and data abstractions. This modern view emerged in the late 1960s and early 1970s as the academic discipline of computer science gradually devolved from the fields of applied mathematics and electrical engineering into a separate academic discipline in its own right. Since the modern view represents a restatement and reclassification of programming concepts that were developed throughout the 1960s, we prefer to refer to these concepts of program structure as the neoclassical concept of programming, in order, at least, to distinguish such concepts from even more contemporary developments in the area.

The neoclassical concept of program structure views the computer program as various data structures being manipulated in certain well-defined control structures. The data structures are explicitly specified or "declared" at the beginning of the program, whereas the control structures are defined in specific procedures. The block structure of Pascal reflects the abstract organization by the content and placement of the blocks.

The abstract organization of a programming language and a computer program is based upon two concepts:

procedural abstractions

data abstractions

The procedural abstraction is concerned with the algorithm or set of instructions used to process or manipulate the data. The data abstraction is concerned with the data structures being manipulated by the procedures or algorithms. A computer program itself is defined, as Niklaus Wirth puts it, as a "concrete formulation of abstract algorithms based on particular representations and structures of data."

Although such an analysis of a computer program may be done on any type of computer program—a machine language program, a FORTRAN program, or a Pascal program—what is important to realize is that Pascal makes the realization of such abstractions more explicit and visible to the programmer.

The significance and usefulness of the abstract organization being reflected in Pascal's program structures is that greater attention may be placed on programming methodology with Pascal, since the underlying abstractions in the program are more explicit than with other programs, and therefore such abstractions are more easily designed, tested, and maintained.

In the sections that follow, we consider the abstract organization of Pascal in greater detail, in particular the data structures and control structures of the language.

## DATA STRUCTURES

In any analysis of programming languages, and in particular Pascal, it is appropriate to begin with a discussion of data structures. Before doing so, data structures must first be defined and placed into the proper context in the neoclassical concept of program structure.

Programs consist of operations or procedures applied to organized sets of data. These organized sets are known as *data structures*. A data structure consists of data objects elements (e.g., bits 0 or 1) with a well-defined structural relationship between the data elements (e.g., sequential ordering).

Data structures must be distinguished from data types. A data type is the interpretation of the type or classification of data represented by a certain data structure. Examples of data types are:

characters

integers

reals

vectors

A data structure is a more general concept than the data type. The present section focuses on data structures, while data types in Pascal will be presented in the next chapter.

An illustration of the concept of data structure would be useful here. Figure 6.6a illustrates how data is stored in a random access memory in an "unstructured" manner. Although some random access memories do organize data in some manner (e.g., individually addressable bytes), such organization is a hardware form of data structure, and is thus not intended or suggested in the unstructured presentation of Figure 6.6a.

Figure 6.6b is an illustration of perhaps the most simple data structure—the bit string. The bit string is essentially a sequential, ordered arrangement of bits. The representation shown in Figure 6.6b is the most common such representation, with the most significant bit on the left, and the least significant bit on the right. The "structural relationship" in the bit string is sequential ordering from a bit designated "most significant" to a bit designated "least significant."

The data structure of a bit string is completely independent of the data type associated with the bit string. Whether the bit string represents a sequence of bits, a sequence of binary integers, or a sequence of characters is defined at the data type level, not the data structure level.

Figure 6.6c illustrates the data structure of an array. An array is essentially a two-dimensional organization or matrix of bits.

Figure 6.6d illustrates a singly linked list data structure. Here each data element is not a single bit but a collection of bits, including a specification or identification of the identity of the collection of bits which follows the collection in list order.

Figure 6.6e illustrates a binary tree data structure. Each of the data elements contains not just one, but two or more link fields which specify the subsequent data elements on the tree, in addition to the data field.

Finally, Figure 6.6f illustrates a recursive data structure in which the path followed by linking data elements is recursive, or leads back to the original data element. It should be pointed out that such recursive data structures (also called "graphs") are found in special purpose languages like LISP.

Now that the concept of a data structure is understood, we can turn to its various implementations and classifications. The present section considers:

data structure definition

data structure classification

data structure in Pascal

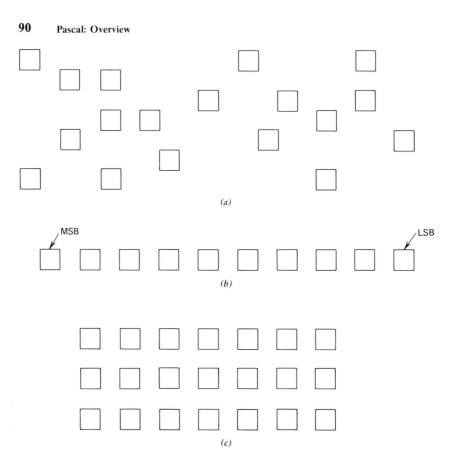

**FIGURE 6.6.** (*a*) Data structure: random bits. (*b*) Data structure: bit string. (*c*) Data structure: bit array.

## Data Structure Definition

The definition of a particular data structure can be made either by the user, by the programming language, or by the hardware or machine architecture. Such definitions include not only the general data structure, but the data type as well.

At the hardware or machine architecture level there may be provided certain hardware registers and routines that are particularly adapted to a specific data structure or control structure. In the microcomputer field, the floating point processors are examples of machine architecture that is dedicated to processing a specific data structure and type (floating point variables).

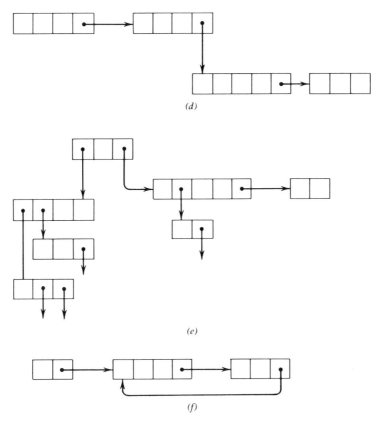

*(d)*

*(e)*

*(f)*

**FIGURE 6.6.**  (*d*) Data structure: singly linked list. (*e*) Data structure: binary tree. (*f*) Data structure: recursive list.

At the programming language level, the language syntax may define certain data structures by use of a declaration statement coupled with a keyword, like **array** or **set**. On the other hand, the syntax of the language may be limited so that declaration of a particular data structure is not possible.

Finally, the user may define specific data types that are not present in the language itself by using the facilities of the language, for example, by creating a stack or a graph.

Figure 6.7 illustrates how the data structure may be broken into several segments: a segmentation on an application level and a language level, and a segmentation between users. The figure shows that user 1 defines a tree and a graph as data structures, while user 2 defines two sets and a file, and user 3

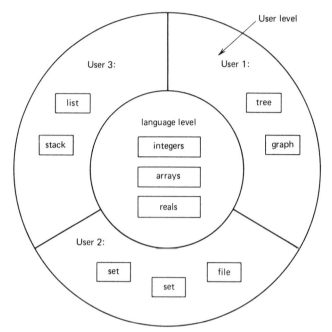

FIGURE 6.7.  Data structure: segmentation between users.

defines a list and a stack. Such data structure definitions take place on the application level. On the language level, the data structures that are present are integers, arrays, and reals.

Thus, although a language may not provide facilities for complex data structures, the user may define complex data structures and use such data structures at the application level.

**Data Structure Classification**

Data structures can be classified into three distinct categories:

basic types
composite types
abstractions

The basic types of data structures include the various representations of numbers or characters, or various types of bit fields.

The composite types of data structures include structured arrangements or composites of the basic types of data structures. For example, using integers as the basic types, a structured arrangement can be made to form a vector, and array, or a higher dimensional structure having integers as components.

The abstractions refer to those data structures that utilize data to represent certain abstract programming concepts. Examples of abstractions include a type definition, in which the programmer defines a data type by specifying the components, and the pointer, which is used to "point" to other data.

The data structures of basic types, composite types, and abstractions will be discussed in greater detail in the next chapter, in the discussion of data types.

## Data Structure in Pascal

Data structure in Pascal generally falls into the three categories considered in the previous section, although slightly different nomenclature is used. The basic types are called "simple" and consist of an ordinal quantity, like numbers or characters. The composite types are called "structured" types, while the abstractions are simply called "pointer" type. Type definition is usually classified as a simple type.

## CONTROL STRUCTURES

The control structures of a programming language define the various types of operations or procedures that are applied to the data structures. Like data structures, the control structures are defined by certain keywords, like **do**, **else**, **for**, and so on, in an operative combination with specific data structures.

Before examining the control structures in detail, it is important to emphasize the relationship between the control structures, the data structures, and the program. As we pointed out above, the neoclassical concept of a program views it as an interaction of control structures with data structures. In any given program there are a number of control structures, and a number of data structures. How these control and data structures relate to one another is one of the most important aspects of program structure, called program organization, which will be considered in more detail in the last section of this chapter.

For now, let us assume that the control structure of a program can be represented by algorithms

$$a_1 \quad a_2 \quad a_3 \quad a_4$$

and the data structure by data structures

$$d_1 \quad d_2 \quad d_3 \quad d_4$$

The program is defined as the abstract combination of these algorithms and data structure. For short, simple programs, program organization is generally not a problem. However, for long programs, the specification of a suitable combination of algorithms and data structures becomes a task in itself.

The issue is how to combine the algorithms with the data structures to produce the program. Does one associate all of the data structures with each algorithm:

$$a_1(d_1 d_2 d_3) + a_2(d_1 d_2 d_3) + \cdots$$

or all of the algorithms with each data structure:

$$d_1(a_1 a_2 a_3) + d_2(a_1 a_2 a_3) + \cdots$$

or some combination of the two?

Such a question cannot be answered categorically. The relationship between the data structures and the control structures is a complex one which defines the fabric of the program. Although it would be very simple to associate a given control structure with a data structure, as:

$$a_1 d_1 + a_2 d_2 + a_3 d_3 + \cdots$$

such simple representations are not possible for all programs. Later in this section we will tabulate some analogous control and data structures, but it must be realized that the programmer has considerable flexibility in defining appropriate control and data structures to suit the particular application requirements.

In the present section we consider:

control structure definition
control structure classification
control structures and data structures
control structures in Pascal

## Control Structure Definition

Like data structures, control structures can be defined by the user, by the programming language, or by the machine architecture. The typical case is that the user will define the control structure by making use of the facilities found in the language.

Control structure definition takes place through the use of symbols and statements in the programming language. For example,

$$x := 1$$

is an assignment statement that sets the variable $x$ equal to 1 (it is assumed that the variable $x$ has been declared with the appropriate data type to make such an assignment valid).

Similarly, the use of keyword pairs like **begin** . . . **end** or **if** . . . **then** are further examples of control structure definition.

## Control Structure Classification

Control structures can be classified in three categories:

basic types
composite types
abstractions

### *Basic Types*

There are two basic types of control structures in Pascal:

assignment
procedure calls

The assignment statement provides a means of assigning the value of a newly computed expression to a variable. For example,

$$x := 1$$

sets the value of $x$ equal to 1. Similarly,

$$x := x + 1$$

adds 1 to the current value of $x$, and then redefines $x$ to be equal to the newly computed value.

The expression on the right-hand side of the assignment symbol may be more complicated than those suggested above, for example,

$$y := (alpha + beta) * sin(x)$$

The assignment statement is a good example to use to signify the relationship between the data structure and the control structure of a program. The assignment statement may be applied to variables of any data type, such as integers,

$$x := 1$$

reals,

$$y := 1.5$$

characters

$$grade := b$$

or any other data type except files. (Data types in Pascal will be described in detail in the next chapter.)

However, each of the variables in the expression in the assignment statement must be of the same type. Thus

$$z := x + y$$

where $x$ is an integer, and $y$ a real, as defined above, is not a valid assignment statement.

Moreover, the variable on the left-hand side of the assignment symbol must be of the identical type as well. Thus if

$$z := y$$

then $z$ must be a real data type.

There is one exception to this general rule: if the type of the expression is an integer, then the type of the variable may be either an integer or real. Thus if $z$ is of real data type,

$$z := x$$

is also valid, since the expression $x$ is of integer data type. However, if $w$ is of integer data type,

$$w := y$$

would not be a valid assignment.

## Composite Types

The composite types of control structure are those that are formed as a composite of keyword pairs or tuples, for example

**begin . . . end**

**if . . . then . . . else . . .**

Composite types can be classified into three general categories:

sequential
selective
iterative

These categories are illustrated in Figures 6.8*a*, 6.8*b*, and 6.8*c*, respectively.

The sequential control structure shown in Figure 6.8*a* simply represents a sequence of operations or instructions. In a programming language, the sequential control structure is represented as an ordered sequence of statements that are to be executed in the order in which they are written.

Since most programming languages are sequential programming languages in any event, sequential control structures are not difficult to represent: the statements are just listed, separated by some predetermined symbol such as a semicolon ";".

Since Pascal is a block structured language, some of the block structuring features of the languge are reflected in the sequential control structure: the keywords **begin** and **end** are used as statement brackets so as to separate different blocks of statements. For example, the simple addition operation

$$result := 2 + 2$$

is an assignment statement that performs the addition. However, such an assignment statement must be embedded in a control structure to form part of a true Pascal program. Thus,

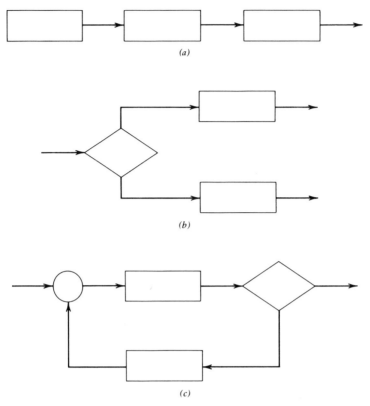

**FIGURE 6.8.** Control structure; (a) sequential; (b) selective; (c) iterative.

> **begin**
> *result := 2 + 2;*
> **end.**

is the proper way of expressing the assignment statement within a control structure.

A sequence of blocks of **begin** . . . **end** pairs, to be executed sequentially, is a typical implementation of the sequential control structure.

> **begin**
> . . .
> **end;**

**begin**

. . .

**end**;
**begin**

. . .

**end**;

The selective control structure, shown in Figure 6.8*b*, represents a selection of one of two possible paths, depending upon some predetermined criteria. The keyword tuples that may be used to express such a control structure are **if** . . . **then** . . . **else**.

Finally, the iterative control structure, shown in Figure 6.8*c*, respresents the repetition of a particular operation or instruction. The keyword pair that may be used to express such a control structure is **while** . . . **do**.

*Abstractions*

The last type of control structure is one that does not fit into any of the previous two categories, and may simply be referred to as abstractions. An example of one such control structure is the **goto** statement.

**Control Structures and Data Structures**

There are close relationships between certain control structures and data structures which reflect similar methods for structuring data as well as processing that data. These correspondences between control and data structures are shown in Table 6.4.

The analysis of data and control structures involves the following considerations:

static properties
dynamic properties
representations
storage allocation
implementation (creation, accessing, modification, and deletion)

We will not analyze these considerations here, but simply note that these are important considerations that must be understood after one has a basic knowledge of the types and uses of the various data and control structures.

TABLE 6.4.   Analogous Control and Data Structures

| Control Structure | Data Structure |
| --- | --- |
| compound statement | Cartesian product |
| conditional statement | type union |
| (if . . . then . . . else) | |
| (case . . . of . . .) | |
| bounded iterative statement | array or set |
| (for . . . do) | |
| unbounded iterative statement | sequence |
| (while . . . do) | |
| (do . . . until) | |
| procedure abstraction | data abstraction |
| (procedure . . .) | |
| recursive procedures | recursive data types |
| goto statement | pointer |

In many instances, such considerations go beyond the high level language into areas of compiler structure, operating systems, or implementations.

**Control Structures in Pascal**

The two basic types of control structures in Pascal, as we pointed out previously are

assignment
procedure calls

The composite types are

sequential

> **begin . . . end**

selective

> **while . . . do**
> **for . . . to . . . do**
> **repeat . . . until**

iterative

> **if . . . then . . . (else . . .)**
> **case . . . of . . . end**

Finally, the only abstract control structure in Pascal is

goto . . .

The detailed description of these control structures will be presented in Chapter 8.


## SYNTAX

In the following chapters, the basic specification of the Pascal language will be given. Language specification is performed by giving the *syntax* of the language. Syntax may be described by one or more of the following methods:

Backus–Naur form
extended Backus–Naur form
syntax diagram

The Backus–Naur form was named after John Backus and Peter Naur and was used in the original definition of ALGOL. An example of Backus–Naur form is illustrated by the definition of a digit:

$$< \text{digit} > :: = 0|1|2|3|4$$

The entity within the brackets is the defined object. A "digit" is then defined as any one of the "tokens" 0, 1, 2, 3, 4, and so on. The vertical lines signify alternation.


TABLE 6.5.   Extended Backus–Naur Form
Metalanguage Symbols

| Metasymbol | Meaning |
| --- | --- |
| = | is defined to be |
| | | alternatively |
| . | end of definition |
| $[x]$ | 0 or 1 instance of $x$ |
| $\{x\}$ | 0 or more repetitions of $x$ |
| $(x|y|\cdot\cdot|z)$ | grouping: any one of $x, y, \ldots, z$ |
| "$xyz$" | the terminal symbol $xyz$ |
| lower-case name | a nonterminal symbol |

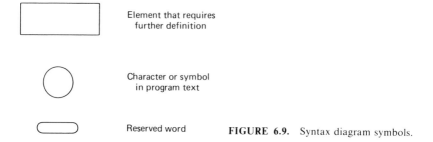

Element that requires
further definition

Character or symbol
in program text

Reserved word

**FIGURE 6.9.** Syntax diagram symbols.

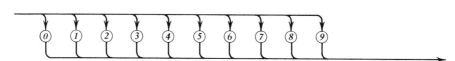

**FIGURE 6.10.** Syntax diagram: digits.

LETTER

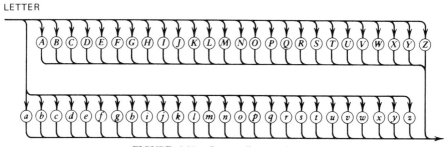

**FIGURE 6.11.** Syntax diagram: letters.

IDENTIFIER

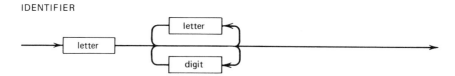

**FIGURE 6.12.** Syntax diagram: identifier.

Extended Backus–Naur form will be used in the following chapters, along with syntax diagrams. The descriptive symbols used in the description of syntax are called the metalanguage symbols, since the syntax is analogous to a "metalanguage" describing the language Pascal. The metalanguage symbols of extended Backus–Naur form are shown in Table 6.5.

A syntax diagram is a graphical means of expressing the syntax of a language. The symbols used in the syntax diagram are shown in Figure 6.9, while simple examples of how a digit or a letter is represented is shown in Figures 6.10 and 6.11, respectively. How an identifier is represented is shown in Figure 6.12.

# 7

# Pascal:
# Basic Specification

In this chapter, we present a more detailed analysis of the specification of the Pascal language. In particular, we consider the following topics:

basic elements
basic program structure
scope
data types
data types in Pascal
constants and variables
control structures

The chapter concludes with a step-by-step analysis of basic elements of the Pascal language beginning with the simple data types. Such analysis and discussion is presented in outline form for ready reference.

## BASIC ELEMENTS

In the previous chapter we presented the keywords, special symbols, and character set in Pascal. In order to complete the discussion of the basic elements or tokens in Pascal, we will consider the following remaining elements:

identifiers
directives
numbers
labels
character strings
comments (or token separators)

The following sections provide a brief definition of the elements, while a more formal presentation will be found in the Pascal draft standard in the next chapter.

## Identifiers

An identifier is used to denote a constant, variables, functions, procedures, types, parameters, and other quantities.

### *Syntactical Definition*

identifier = letter {(letter|digit)}

### *Syntax Diagram*

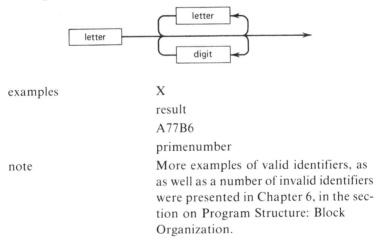

| | |
|---|---|
| examples | X |
| | result |
| | A77B6 |
| | primenumber |
| note | More examples of valid identifiers, as as well as a number of invalid identifiers were presented in Chapter 6, in the section on Program Structure: Block Organization. |

## Directives

A directive is a name that replaces a procedure block or a function block.

## Numbers

Numbers are either signed or unsigned integers or reals.

*Syntax Diagram*

UNSIGNED INTEGER

UNSIGNED REAL

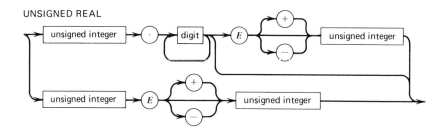

## Labels

Labels are digit sequences which are used to prefix certain statements in the statement part of a program. Labels are used in conjunction with a goto statement to indicate at which point further processing of a program is to continue.

example     *10*     *I := 0*

. . .

. . .

**goto** *10*

## Character Strings

A character string is a constant of char-type. (Char-type is a data type consisting of characters, and will be defined in the next section.) Character strings are usually employed by the programmer to output information in the user's own natural language (English, French, German, etc.) concerning the result of the computation or the state of the program. A character string is simply defined by writing the characters within two apostrophes.

example          **writeln** (*'program aborted'*)
                 would be executed by the printer or CRT
                 outputting the following:
                 program aborted

                 Similarly, the statement
                 **writeln** (*'enthalten'*)
                 might be used by a German programmer.

**Comments (or Token Separators)**

For documentation purposes, the programmer may use curly brackets to
enclose a comment.

example          *I := 0* { sets index equal to 0 }
                 The phrase inside the curly brackets is used by the
                 programmer to give the reader of the program the
                 meaning or function of the statement that the com-
                 ment is adjacent to.

## BASIC PROGRAM STRUCTURE

The basic structure of a Pascal program is shown in Figure 7.1. It consists of
the program heading, followed by the data definitions or declarations, and
then finally the program body. More particularly, a Pascal program is com-

```
Program heading
```

```
Data definition
```

```
Program body
```

**FIGURE 7.1.**    Pascal program structure, highly
simplified.

```
program  < identifier > ( input, output, < file list > ) ;
```

```
const < identifier > = < constant > ;
type < identifier > = < type > ;
var < identifier > = < type > ;
procedure < identifier > ( < parameters > ) ;
        < block >
function < identifier > ( < parameter > ) : < result type > ;
        < block >
```

```
begin
        < statement > ; < statement > ; . . .

               . . .
        < statement > ; < statement > ; . . . < statement >
end.
```

FIGURE 7.2.  Pascal program structure.

posed of the elements shown in Figure 7.2, in which specific keywords have been used as they are used in a Pascal program.

The first element, the program heading, provides an opportunity for the programmer to name the program. Some examples of program names are suggested from the following examples:

> **program** *textedit*
> **program** *demo*
> **program** *propertyanalysis*

It should be noted that the syntax of Pascal requires the program name to be a single identifier, and although the user might like to call the program

> *property analysis*

such a string is not an identifier, and cannot be used in Pascal. The user is therefore forced to inelegantly string distinct words together to form a valid identifier:

> *propertyanalysis*

Some implementations of Pascal remedy this deficiency by including the underscore symbol"_" as a member of the character set of the language. In such implementations (Hewlett Packard's Pascal 1000 is one example), the following would be a valid identifier:

*property_ analysis*

The Ada programming language specifically permits underscores to be incorporated into the definition of an identifier.

Programs are given a name so that they may be filed and accessed under that name when such programs are stored on an external data storage device, such as a disk.

It must also be noted that the name of the program is followed by the names of certains files, including typically *input* and *output*. If a program is to receive input during the course of its execution, most implementations of Pascal require that "input" be indicated after the identifier. Similarly, if the program is to provide an output, then "output" must be indicated as well. *Input* and *output* are standard files. If the program is to use any other external files, they must also be indicated after the identifier giving the program name. For example,

**program** *mailinglist (input, output, update)*

indicates that the program named "mailinglist" utilizes the external file named "update."

The standard files *input* and *output* are actually textfiles. They input or output text on a single line. (A line is defined by a certain amount of memory until an "end of line" character is reached. In physical terms, a line is simply a line on a CRT or printer which the user is utilizing to communicate with the program.) Further details on input and output in Pascal will be presented in a later section on input and output.

### Definitions and Declarations

The next element of the program is the declaration portion. Several different components of the program are declared or defined:

| | |
|---|---|
| constants | (represented by the keyword **const**) |
| types | (represented by the keyword **type**) |
| variables | (represented by the keyword **var**) |
| procedures | (represented by the keyword **procedure**) |
| functions | (represented by the keyword **function**) |

The purpose of the declaration portion of the program is to define and uniquely identify the constants, types, variables, procedures, and functions that are utilized in the program body.

The declaration of variables should be particularly noted. Each variable in the program must be "declared" to be of a particular data type. In Pascal, the data type of a variable remains the same throughout the program. Thus, if an expression or program operation changes the data type of a variable, a program error would be indicated. Because the data type of a variable is rigidly enforced by the Pascal syntax, Pascal is said to be a strongly typed language.

An example of a variable declaration is:

> **var**
>
> $temperature$ = real;
> $valve1$ = ($closed, half, open$);
>
> . . .

The variable $temperature$ has been declared to be of real type; the variable $valve1$ is declared to be of the enumerated type, and can take the values $closed, half$, or $open$. (The different data types in Pascal will be described in detail in a subsequent section; the examples here merely illustrate the declaration portion of the program.)

In addition to the standard types $integer, real, boolean$, and $char$, the programmer is able to define new types by means of the **type** declaration. The introduction of new types is motivated by the desire to express the variables in the language more clearly.

As an example, if the program had a number of variables

> $valve1$
> $valve2$
> $valve3$
> and so on

rather than repeat the values

> ($closed, half, open$)

for each variable, it is possible to define a new type as follows:

> **type**
> $position$ = ($closed, half, open$);

With such a definition made, the variables can then be declared in terms of this new type:

> **var**
> *valve1* = *position*;
> *valve2* = *position*;
> *valve3* = *position*;
> . . .

## Program Body

The program body contains a sequence of statements that constitute the algorithm for solving the problem posed by the user. Statements can be categorized as follows:

| Name | Example |
| --- | --- |
| assignment | *x* := 1.5; |
| procedure | *checksum* |
| goto | goto 15 |
| compound | **begin** |
|  |    *x* := 1.5; |
|  |    *y*: = *x*/2.3 |
|  | **end** |
| conditional | *if x ≠ y then y = 100*; |
| repetitive | *for i :=1 to 10 do k :=k + 1*; |
| with | *with date do* |

Figure 7.2 shows the statements to be confined within a single block bounded by begin and end pairs. As was pointed out in the previous chapter, the structure of a Pascal program may be defined by the user more generally, and include sequential blocks of begin-end pairs, as well as nested blocks. A distinct definition and declaration program portion may be defined for each block, associating specific variable definitions with the variables in that respective block. Further details on these "scope" rules for multiple block programs will be presented in the next section.

The block structure of a program is more evident from the syntax diagram representing a program, which specifically defines the program in terms of a "block." The syntax diagram for a program, as well as the syntactical definition of a block, and the syntax diagram for a block conclude this section on basic program structure.

*Syntax Diagram*

PROGRAM

*Syntactical Definition*

block = label-declaration-part
       constant-definition-part
       type-definition-part
       variable-declaration-part
       procedure-and-function-declaration-part
       statement-part .

label-declaration-part = ["label" label {"," label} ";"] .

constant-definition-part = ["const" constant-definition ";"
                           {constant-definition ";"}] .

type-definition-part = ["type" type-definition ";"
                       {type-definition ";"}] .

variable-declaration-part = ["var" variable-declaration ";"
                            {variable-declaration ";"}] .

procedure-and-function-declaration-part = {(procedure-declaration |
                           function-declaration) ";"} .

statement-part = compound-statement .

*Syntax Diagram*

(See p. 113.)

SCOPE

Scope refers to the range of validity of a particular identifier within a program. Scope is one of the consequences of the block structure of a programming language, which defines a hierarchy of blocks or program portions shown in diagrammatic form in Figure 7.3.

The scope of an identifier consists of those blocks in which the identifier can be accessed and used in a computation. We recall that each block of a

BLOCK

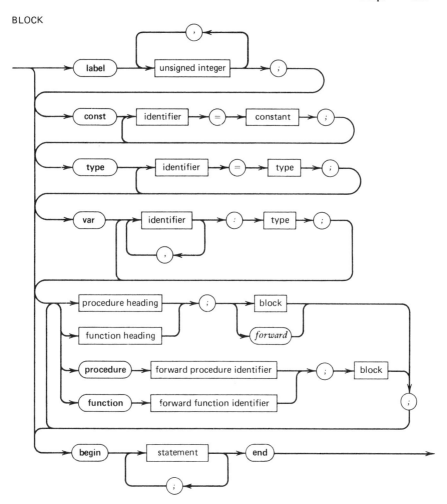

program includes a declaration portion in which the variables to be used in that block are defined. An identifer defined in a block B is said to be "local" to block B, for example, $x$ is a "local variable."

An example of the scope of various declarations is presented in Figure 7.4.

A nonlocal identifier may or may not be redefined in a lower level block. Thus $x$ may be redefined in block B1 to have a meaning different from that in block B. For example, $x$ may be of data type integer within B, and real within B1. In the same example, $y$ is defined in block B but not in block B1. The identifier $y$ is said to be local to block B, and global to block B1. The scope

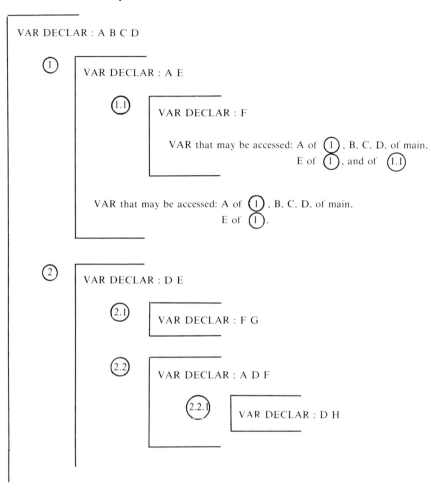

**FIGURE 7.3.** Scope: nested block structure.

of identifier $y$ is both blocks B and B1. The scope of identifier $x$, on the other hand, is limited to the block where it was defined.

## DATA TYPES

A data type is the interpretation of a collection of data objects. The most common data objects found in programming languages are bits or bit strings,

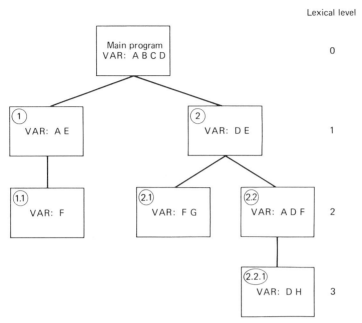

Lexical level

**FIGURE 7.4.** Scope: lexical hierarchy.

and the data type of a particular collection of bits or a bit string defines the data as a character, an integer, a complex number, or some other element of a program. The specification of a programming language defines the data types that are permitted in that language, and how such types are represented.

Data types are one of the most basic features of a programming language. In addition to the number and definition of the data types, the following syntax related issues must also be noted:

strength of type checking

type conversions

type extensions

constraints

### Strength of Type Checking

A programmer determines the data type of each variable by defining or declaring the data type explicitly in a statement that forms a part of the program. Whether or not the syntax of the language permits the program to deviate from this initial definition depends on the strength of the type checking of the language.

Type checking is a form of error checking. The more strongly typed a language is, the less likely that there is an error associated with the use of a variable in the language. Strong type checking is therefore of particular interest for novice programmers who would be likely to make errors in data types. On the other hand, strong type checking is merely a restriction which more experienced programmers feel is unnecessary. Pascal is a strongly typed language, while the programming language C is less strongly typed.

### Type Conversions

Type conversions refer to the capability in a language to convert a variable from one type to another by means of a program statement. The typical example is the conversion from an interger to a real; more complex type conversions include conversion from real to integer, or Boolean to integer. The ability to perform type conversions is an advantage to the sophisticated programmer because of the flexibility in using variables. On the other hand, by allowing conversions, the language loses some of its error checking capability.

### Type Extensions

Type extensions refer to the ability to define new data types in a program. The ability to define new data types enables the programmer to more effectively use the capabilities of data type checking and data type operations to refer to entities more closely related to the user's application than the standard data types such as characters, integers, arrays, sets, and so on.

### Constraints

In addition to the constraint on a variable imposed by the data type definition, it is also possible to provide further constraints, such as range, precision, scale, index ranges, or user defined constraints.

## DATA TYPES IN PASCAL

The use of data types in Pascal or any other high level language is intended to free the programmer from the details of the representations of various categories of data in order to concentrate on the variables themselves. Data types may be categorized into two basic categories—scalar types and structured types. The scalar types include integers, reals, Boolean, and pointers. The structured types include collections of data items of the same or different data types.

The original standard for Pascal (often referred to as Jensen-Wirth) classified the data types in Pascal as either scalar types, subranges of an already defined scalar type, or structured types. The ISO proposed standard, to be presented in the next chapter, classifies the data types as simple, structured, or pointer type. The data types in Pascal are summarized in Figure 7.5, and in the following sections.

### Overview

### *Simple Types*

The simple types in Pascal are categorized by the standard into two categories:

ordinal type
real type

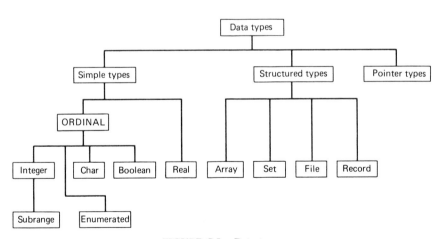

**FIGURE 7.5.** Data types.

The ordinal types, as the name implies, represent data types whose members are ordered in some way. The various categories are:

enumerated
subrange
integer
Boolean
char (for character)
ordinal-type-identifer

The real type simply consists of the real numbers, or more accurately a subset of the real numbers depending upon the implementation.

### Structured Types

The structured types fall into the following categories:

array
set
file
record

It is possible to economize on the use of storage in the computer by preceding the specific structured type with the reserve word "packed."

### Pointer Type

A pointer type is associated with a dynamic variable in a program. Dynamic variables are typically associated with dynamic data structures, the simplest example of which is the linked list. A variable of pointer type represents not the value of a variable, but the location of that variable in memory.

### Syntactical Definition

```
type-definition = identifier "=" type-denoter .
type-denoter = type-identifier | new-type .
new-type = simple-type | structured-type | pointer-type .
```

simple-type-identifier = type-identifier .
structured-type-identifier = type-identifier .
pointer-type-identifier = type-identifier .
type-identifier = identifier .

## *Syntax Diagram*

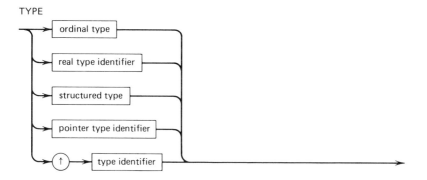

## *Syntactical Definition: Simple Data Types*

simple-type = ordinal-type | real-type .
ordinal-type = enumerated-type | subrange-type |
              integer-type | Boolean-type | char-type |
              ordinal-type-identifier .

enumerated-type = "(" identifier-list ")" .
identifier-list = identifier { "," identifier } .

subrange-type = constant ". ." constant .

*Syntax Diagram*

ORDINAL TYPE

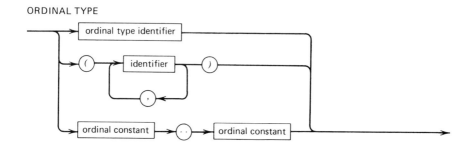

*Syntactical Definition: Structural Data Types*

    structured-type = ["packed"] unpacked-structured-type |
                      structured-type-identifier .
    unpacked-structured-type = array-type | record-type | set-type |
                      file-type .

    array-type = "array" "[" index-type { "," index-type } "]" "of"
                      component-type .
    index-type = ordinal-type .
    component-type = type-denoter .

    record-type = "record" [field-list [";"]] "end" .
    field-list = fixed-part [ ";" variant-part ] | variant-part .
    fixed-part = record-section { ";" record-section } .
    record-section = identifier-list ":" type-denoter .
    variant-part = "case" variant-sector "of"
                      variant { ";" variant } .
    variant-selector = [tag-field ":"] tag-type .
    tag-field = identifier .
    variant = case-constant-list ":" "(" [ field-list [";"] ] ")" .
    tag-type = ordinal-type-identifier .
    case-constant-list = case-constant { "," case-constant } .
    case-constant = constant .

## Syntax Diagram

STRUCTURED TYPE

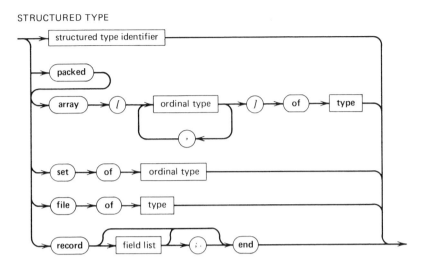

FIELD LIST

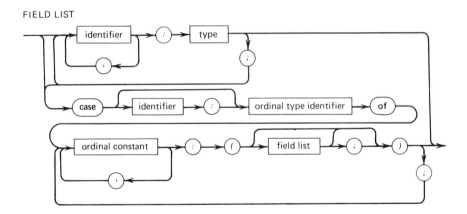

## CONSTANTS AND VARIABLES

A constant is a quantity that does not vary during the course of a program. A constant definition introduces an identifier that is used during the program to denote a constant. It is frequently easier to use the identifier rather than the constant itself, since by changing the constant definition, one is able to redefine the constant throughout the entire program, whereas if the constant was not represented by an identifier, the programmer would have to change the constant throughout the program, which could result in an error if one of the constants was overlooked.

A variable is a quantity to which a current value may be assigned, and thus may vary throughout the course of the program.

### Syntactical Definition

constant-definition = identifier "=" constant .
constant = [sign] (unsigned-number | constant-identifier)
| character-string .
constant-identifier = identifier .

### Syntax Diagram

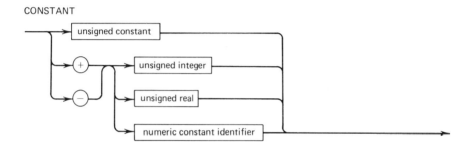

CONSTANT

UNSIGNED CONSTANT

ORDINAL CONSTANT

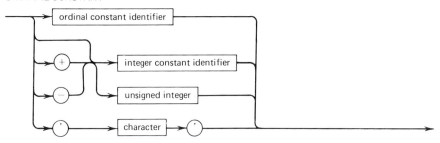

VARIABLE

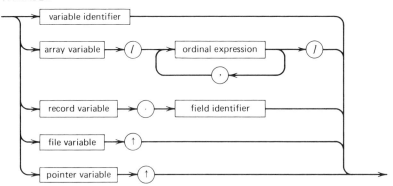

ACTUAL PARAMETERS

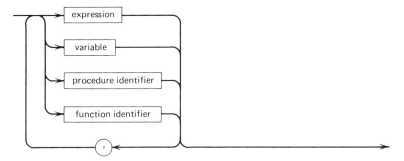

123

## CONTROL STRUCTURES IN PASCAL

The control structures in Pascal can be categorized as follows:

expressions and statements
procedures and functions .
input/output

### Expressions

There are three elements that when used in a program can possess a value:

constants
variables
expressions

Constants and variables have been considered in the previous section. An expression is a quantity which also possesses a value but which is composed of typically more than one element, such as including an operator.

### *Syntactical Definition*

```
unsigned-constant  =  unsigned-number | character-string |
                      constant-identifier | "nil" .
factor  =  variable-access | unsigned-constant | bound-identifier |
          function-designator | set-constructor |
          "(" expression ")" | "not" factor .
set-constructor  =  "[" [ member-designator
          { "," member-designator } ] "]" .
member-designator  =  expression [ ". ." expression ] .
term  =  factor { multiplying-operator factor } .
simple-expression  =  [ sign ] term { adding-operator term } .
expression  =
          simple-expression [ relational-operator simple-expression ] .
```

## Syntax Diagram

EXPRESSION

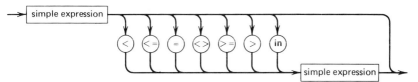

SIMPLE EXPRESSION

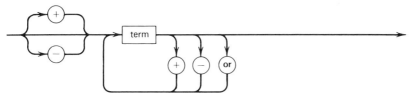

TERM

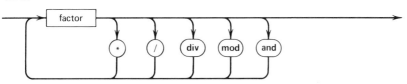

FACTOR

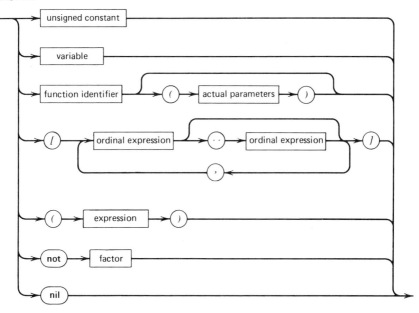

## Statements

Statements are the basic control or operational elements of a programming language, and are divided into two categories:

simple statements
structured statements

### Simple Statements

The simple statements are

assignment
procedure
goto

The assignment statement assigns a value to the variable on the left-hand side of the statement.

$$\text{Examples} \qquad x := y + z$$
$$p := (1 <= i)\, and\, (i < 100)$$

The procedure statement activates a procedure denoted by the procedure identifier.

$$\text{Examples} \qquad checksum$$
$$printoutput$$

The goto statement indicates that processing is to continue at the place indicted by the label.

Example        **goto** *15*

### Structured Statements

The structured statements are categorized:

compound
conditional
repetitive
with

Compound statements are those that are to be executed in sequential order. They are bracketed by **begin** and **end** pairs of keywords. Conditional statements include if statements and case statements. Repetitive statements include the following:

> **repeat . . . until**
> **while . . . do . . .**
> **for . . . := . . . do**

Finally, the with statement is as follows:

> **with . . . do**

## Syntactical Definitions

statement = [ label ":" ] ( simple-statement | structured-statement ) .

simple-statement = empty-statement | assignment-statement | procedure-statement | goto-statement .
empty-statement = .

assignment-statement = ( variable-access | function-identifier ) ":=" expression .

structured-statement = compound-statement | conditional-statement | repetitive-statement | with-statement .

compound-statement = "begin" statement-sequence "end" .
statement-sequence = statement { ";" statement } .
Example:   begin z := x ; x := y; y := z end

conditional-statement = if-statement | case-statement .

repetitive-statement = repeat-statement | while-statement | for-statement .

### Repeat-statements

repeat-statement = "repeat" statement-sequence "until" Boolean-expression .

### While-statements

while-statement = "while" Boolean-expression "do" statement .

## For-statements

for-statement = "for" control-variable ":=" initial-value
( "to" | "downto" ) final-value "do" statement .
control-variable = entire-variable .
initial-value = expression .
final-value = expression .

## With-statements

with-statement = "with" record-variable-list "do" statement .
record-variable-list = record-variable { "," record-variable } .

## *Syntax Diagram*

(See p. 129.)

## Procedures and Functions

Procedures and functions are portions of a program with which the programmer associates a name, and which are executed when that name appears within the body of a program. The difference between a procedure and a function is that a function returns a value to a particular expression (e.g., $\sin(x)$ returns a value for a given input $x$, the value returned is equal to the sine of $x$), while a procedure represents a group of statements that can be called (e.g., procedure alarm being executed may result in the execution of several statements).

## *Syntactical Definition*

procedure-heading = "procedure" identifier [ formal-parameter-list ] .
procedure-identification = "procedure" procedure-identifier .
procedure-identifier = identifier .
procedure-block = block .

procedure-declaration = procedure-heading ";" directive |
                        procedure-identification ";" procedure-block |
                        procedure-heading ";" procedure block .

formal-parameter-list = "(" formal-parameter-section
                        {";" formal-parameter-section} ")" .

STATEMENT

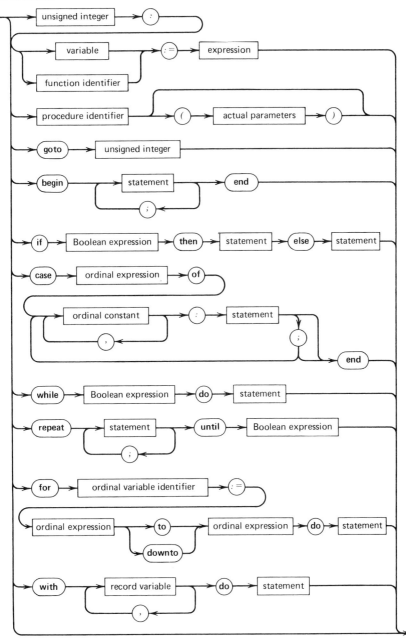

129

formal-parameter-section = value-parameter-specification |
                          variable-parameter-specification |
                          procedural-parameter-specification |
                          functional-parameter-specification .
value-parameter-specification = identifier-list ";" type-identifier .
variable-parameter-specification = "var" identifier-list ":"
                          (type-identifier |
                          conformant-array-schema) .
conformant-array-schema = "array" "[" index-type-specification
                       { ";" index-type-specification } "]"
                       "of" (type-identifier |
                       conformant-array-schema ) .
index-type-specification = identifier ". ." identifier ":"
                       ordinal-type-identifier .
bound-identifer = identifier .
procedural-parameter-specification = procedure-heading .
functional-parameter-specification = function-heading .

procedure-statement = procedure-identifier [ actual-parameter-list ] .

         Examples:      printheading
                        transpose(a,n,m)
                        bisect(fct,−1.0,−1.0,x)

## *Syntax Diagram*

PROCEDURE HEADING

FORMAL PARAMETERS

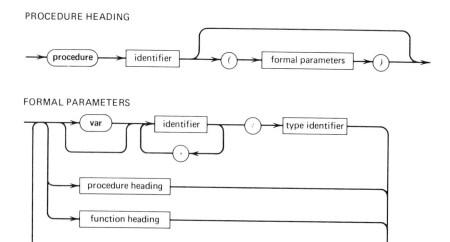

*Syntactical Definition: Functions*

> *function-designator* = function-identifier
>         [actual-parameter-list ] .
> actual-parameter-list =
>   "(" actual-parameter { "," actual-parameter } ")" .
> actual-parameter = expression | variable-access |
>         procedure-identifier |
>         function-identifier .

> function-declaration =
>   function-heading ";" directive |
>   function-identification ";" function-block |
>   function-heading ";" function-block .
> function-heading =
>   "function" identifier [[formal-parameter-list]
>     ":" result-type] .
> function-identification =
>   "function" function-identifier .
> function-identifier = identifier .
> result-type = simple-type-identifier |
>      pointer-type-identifier .
> function-block = block.

*Syntax Diagram*

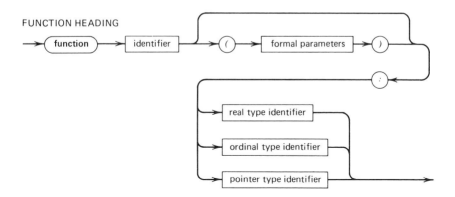

## Input and Output

Input and output in Pascal is implemented using the following statements:

**read**
**readln**
**write**
**writeln**

The above statements are actually procedures, and in fact are standard procedures defined by the language syntax that operates upon textfiles. The textfiles are called "input" and "output." These two standard textfiles are not declared explicitly, but they are listed in the program heading as parameters. The title of a program that only reads data would be:

**program** *sample* (*input*)

The title of a program that only writes data, but does not read data, would be

**program** *sample* (*output*)

while a program that both reads and writes data would be

**program** *sample* (*input, output*)

## Detailed Analysis of the Pascal Specification

The present section presents a detailed description and analysis of the key elements and features of the Pascal language. The presentation, in outline form, covers the following features:

data types
   integer
   real
   Boolean
   char
   enumerated
   subrange

*Integer*

| | |
|---|---|
| syntactic usage | data type |
| formal classification | simple type |
| formal subclassifications | standard simple type |
| | ordinal type |
| reserved words | not applicable |
| standard identifier | *integer* |
| predefined constant identifier | *maxint* |
| syntactic definition | unsigned-integer = digit-sequence |
| semantic definition | The integer data type consists of positive integers. In practice, since the amount of storage on any machine is finite, only a subset of the integers can be represented, and the permissible values for the integers range from |

$$-N \quad to \quad N$$

where N is the maximum integer that can be represented on the machine.

| | |
|---|---|
| examples | 15 |
| | 0 |
| | −100 |
| | 32749 |
| invalid example | 35000 |
| | (outside range of 16-bit computer) |
| declaration format | **var** |
| | < identifier > = *integer*; |
| declaration example | **var** |
| | *linenumber* = *integer*; |
| arithmetic operators (monadic) | The following arithmetic operators are applicable to an operand of integer type: |
| | +    (identity) |
| | −    (sign inversion) |
| arithmetic operators (dyadic) | The following arithmetic operators are applicable to operands of integer type: |

|  | + | (addition) |
|---|---|---|
|  | − | (subtraction) |
|  | * | (multiplication) |
|  | / | (division) |
|  | div | (division with truncation) |
|  | mod | (modulo) |

use of operators

2 + 2   = 4
2 − 2   = 0
2 * 3   = 6
2 DIV 2   = 1
2 DIV 3   = 0
2 MOD 2 = 0
3 MOD 2 = 1

implicit type conversion

. . .

*force = mass * acceleration'*

. . .

Although both variables *mass* and *acceleration* have been declared as integer type, setting their product equal to a variable that has been declared as real type performs an implicit type conversion.

arithmetic functions

The following arithmetic functions are applicable to integer arguments:
abs(x)
sqr(x)
sin(x)
cos(x)
exp(x)
ln(x)
sqrt(x)
arctan(x)
The following functions yield an integer value if the argument is an integer, and a real if the argument is real:
abs(x)
sqr(x)
The following functions yield a real value regardless of whether the

|  | argument is an integer or real: |
|---|---|
|  | sin(x) |
|  | cos(x) |
|  | exp(x) |
|  | ln(x) |
|  | sqrt(x) |
|  | arctan(x) |
| examples | abs(5) = 5 |
|  | abs(−15) = 15 |
|  | sqr(5) = 25 |
|  | sqr(−5) = 25 |
| ordinal functions | The following ordinal functions are applicable to integer arguments: |
|  | ord(x) |
|  | chr(x) |
|  | succ(x) |
|  | pred(x) |
| examples | ord(0) = 0 |
|  | ord(1) = 1 |
|  | succ(0) = 1 |
|  | succ(−1) = 0 |
|  | pred(0) = −1 |
|  | pred(10) = 9 |
| Boolean functions | The following Boolean function is applicable to integer arguments: |
|  | odd(x) |
| examples | odd(2) = false |
|  | odd(3) = true |
|  | odd(4) = false |
| relational operators | The following relational operators are applicable to integer arguments: |

$<$        (less than)
$<=$       (less than or equal to)
$=$        (equal to)
$<>$       (not equal to)
$>=$       (greater than or equal to)
$>$        (greater than)

The application of the above operators yields Boolean values.

examples

| | |
|---|---|
| 1 < 2 | true |
| 2 < 1 | false |
| 1 < = 2 | true |
| 1 < = 1 | true |
| 2 = 3 | false |
| 2 <> 2 | false |
| 3 > = 4 | false |
| 3 > 2 | true |

## *Real*

| | |
|---|---|
| syntactic usage | data type |
| formal classification | simple type |
| formal subclassification | standard simple type |
| reserved words | not applicable |
| standard identifier | *real* |
| syntactic definition | unsigned-real = unsigned-integer "." |
| semantic definition | The real data type is used to represent real valued variables. In practice, any specific computer is capable of representing only a subset of the real numbers, limited by a certain range and precision. One microcomputer is capable of representing real numbers between |

$$2.93873588 \cdot 10^{-39}$$

and

$$1.70141183 \cdot 10^{38}$$

to nine digits of accuracy. The tenth digit is rounded.

| | |
|---|---|
| declaration format | **var** < identifier >: *real*; |
| declaration example | **var** *mass* : *real*; |
| examples | −0.01 3.14159265 |
| arithmetic operators (monadic) | The following arithmetic operators are applicable to a real operand: |

|                              |                                                                    |
| ---------------------------- | ------------------------------------------------------------------ |
|                              | +    (identity)                                                    |
|                              | −    (sign inversion)                                              |
| arithmetic operators (dyadic) | The following arithmetic operators are applicable to real operands: |
|                              | +    (addition)                                                    |
|                              | −    (subtraction)                                                 |
|                              | *    (multiplication)                                             |
|                              | /    (division)                                                   |
| examples                     | 2 + 2.0   = 4.0                                                    |
|                              | 2.0 − 2   = 0.0                                                   |
|                              | 2 * 3.0   = 6.0                                                    |
|                              | 2 / 3    = 0.66666667                                             |
| arithmetic functions         | The following arithmetic functions are applicable to real arguments: |
|                              | abs(x)      (absolute value)                                      |
|                              | sqr(x)      (square)                                              |
|                              | sin(x)      (sine)                                                |
|                              | cos(x)      (cosine)                                              |
|                              | exp(x)      (exponential)                                         |
|                              | ln(x)       (natural logarithm)                                   |
|                              | sqrt(x)     (square root)                                         |
|                              | arctan(x)   (arctangent)                                          |
| examples                     | abs(5.5)   = 5.5                                                   |
|                              | abs(−15.5) = 15.5                                                 |
|                              | sqr(5.0)   = 25.0                                                  |
| transfer functions           | The following "transfer" functions are applicable to real arguments and return integer values: |
|                              | trunc(x)    (truncation)                                          |
|                              | round(x)    (rounding)                                            |
| examples                     | trunc(2.7)  = 2                                                    |
|                              | trunc(−2.7) = −2                                                  |
|                              | round(2.7)  = 3                                                    |
|                              | round(2.2)  = 2                                                    |
|                              | round(−2.7) = −3                                                  |

### Boolean

|                       |             |
| --------------------- | ----------- |
| syntactic usage       | data type   |
| formal classification | simple type |

| | |
|---|---|
| formal subclassifications | standard simple type<br>ordinal type |
| reserved words | not applicable |
| standard identifier | *Boolean* |
| predefined constant<br>identifiers | *false*<br>*true* |
| semantic definition | The Boolean data type is used to represent variables which may have one of two possible values. The two values are represented by the predefined constant identifiers *false* and *true*. |
| declaration format | **var**<br>    < identifier > = *boolean*; |
| declaration example | **var**<br>    *answer* = *boolean*; |
| ordering of values | *false* is the predecessor of *true* |
| Boolean operators | The following Boolean operators are applicable to operands of Boolean type:<br>or    (logical or)<br>and    (logical and)<br>not    (logical negation) |
| examples | answer 1 or answer 2 has a Boolean value determined by the truth table: |

| A | B | A or B |
|---|---|---|
| true | true | true |
| true | false | true |
| false | true | true |
| false | false | false |

| | |
|---|---|
| relational operators | The following relational operators are applicable to operands of Boolean type:<br>$<$    (less than)<br>$<=$    (less than or equal to)<br>$=$    (equal to)<br>$<>$    (not equal to)<br>$>=$    (greater than or equal to)<br>$>$    (greater than) |

The application of the above operators yields Boolean values. It must be recalled that the value *false* is a predecessor of the value *true*.

examples

false < true      true
true < false      false
false <= true      true
false = true      false

ordinal functions

The following ordinal functions are applicable to Boolean arguments:
ord(x)
succ(x)
pred(x)

examples

ord(false) = 0
ord(true) = 1
succ(false) = true
pred(true) = false
succ(true) = ERROR
pred(false) = ERROR

## Character

| | |
|---|---|
| syntactic usage | data type |
| formal classification | simple type |
| formal subclassifications | standard simple type |
| | ordinal type |
| reserved words | not applicable |
| standard identifier | *char* |
| syntactic definition | character-string = "'" string |

                                    element
      { string element } "'"
string-element = apostrophe-image
                  | string character .
apostrophe-image = "''"
string-character =
     one-of-a-set-of-implementa-
     tion-defined-characters

| | |
|---|---|
| semantic definition | A value of char-type is denoted by a character string containg a single string element. If the string of characters contains an apostrophe, the apostrophe is denoted by an apostrophe-image, "''". Each string-character is one character from the set of implementation-defined characters. |
| examples | 'a', 'b', 'c'<br>'747 Third Avenue' |
| declaration format | **var**<br>< identifier > = char; |
| declaration example | **var**<br>*textdata* = *char*; |
| ordering of values | The ordinal numbers of the character values are implementation-defined values of integer type. In most implementations<br>'a' < 'b' < 'c' < . . . < 'z'<br>and<br>'0' < '1' < '2' < . . . '9' |
| relational operators | The following relational operators are applicable to operands of char type:<br>< (less than)<br><= (less than or equal to)<br>= (equal to)<br><> (not equal to)<br>>= (greater than or equal to)<br>> (greater than)<br>The application of the above operators yields Boolean values. |
| examples | '1' < '2'    true<br>'2' < '1'    false<br>'1' <= '3'    true |
| ordinal functions | The following ordinal functions are applicable to char arguments:<br>ord(x)<br>succ(x) |

|  |  |
|---|---|
| examples | pred(x)<br>ord('0') is not necessarily 0,<br>succ('a') is not always 'b' |

## Enumerated

| | |
|---|---|
| syntactic usage | data type |
| formal classification | simple type |
| formal subclassification | ordinal type |
| reserved words | not applicable |
| standard identifier | not applicable |
| syntactic definition | enumerated-type = "(" identifer-<br>list ")"<br>identifier-list = identifer { ","<br>identifier } |
| semantic definition | The enumerated data type consists of an ordered set of values denoted by a sequential list of identifiers. |
| examples | (red, yellow, green, blue)<br>(alpha, beta, gamma, delta)<br>(third, lexington, park, madison, fifth) |
| declaration format | **var**<br>  < identifier > = (<identifier>,<br>        . . .<br>        <identifier>) |
| declaration example | **var**<br>  color = (red, yellow, green, blue)<br>**var**<br>  avenue = (third, lexington, park, madison, fifth) |
| ordering of values | The sequence of identifiers in the identifier list are mapped into the integers 0,1,2,3, . . . etc., which represents the ordinal number of the respective identifier. |
| ordinal functions | The following ordinal functions are applicable to arguments of an |

|  |  |
|---|---|
|  | ordinal type: |
|  | ord(x) |
|  | succ(x) |
|  | pred(x) |
| examples | ord(red) = 0 |
|  | ord(lexington) = 1 |
|  | succ(green) = blue |
|  | pred(fifth) = madison |
| relational operators | The following relational operators are applicable to ordinal arguments: |

< (less than)
< = (less than or equal to)
= (equal to)
< > (not equal to)
> = (greater than or equal to)
> (greater than)

The application of the above operators yields Boolean values.

| examples | red < green        true |
|---|---|
|  | beta < = alpha    false |

## Subrange

| syntactic usage | data type |
|---|---|
| formal classification | simple type |
| formal subclassification | ordinal type |
| standard identifier | not applicable |
| syntactic definition | subrange-type = constant " . . " |
|  | constant |
| semantic definition | The subrange data type is an ordered set of values which is a subrange of an ordinal type, and is specified by the smallest and the largest value in the subrange. |
| examples | 1 . . 100 |
|  | alpha . . gamma |
|  | lexington . . madison |
| declaration format | **var** |
|  | <type identifier> = |
|  | <constant> . . <constant> |

declaration example

**var**
  age = 1 .. 100
**var**
  route = lexington .. madison

ordinal functions

The following ordinal functions are applicable to arguments of an ordinal type:
ord(x)
succ(x)
pred(x)

# 8

# Pascal: The ISO
# Draft Standard

One basic defining document of the Pascal programming language at the present time is considered to be the ISO (International Standards Organization) Draft Proposal, which was first published for circulation in 1980 and is reprinted in the present chapter. The syntax of the ISO Draft Standard is summarized in Appendix E, and an index to the various terms in the standard, both in terms of paragraph number and page number of this text, is presented at the end of the book.

The ISO Draft Standard is as follows*:

## DP7185 SPECIFICATION FOR THE COMPUTER PROGAMMING LANGUAGE PASCAL

### CONTENTS

---

* Reprinted with the permission of the Pascal User's Group. The version presented is known as the ISO/DIS 7185 draft. The draft proposed American standard, known as BSR X3.97-198X being developed by the ANSI X3J9 technical committee, is essentially the same as level 0 of ISO/DIS 7185. The British standard BSI 6192 is identical to ISO/DIS 7185.

**FOREWORD**

The language Pascal was designed by Professor Niklaus Wirth to satisfy two principal aims:

(a)   to make available a language suitable for teaching progamming as a systematic discipline based on certain fundamental concepts clearly and naturally reflected by the language.

(b)   to define a language whose implementations could be both reliable and efficient on then available computers.

However, it has become apparent that Pascal has attributes which go far beyond these original goals. It is now being increasingly used commercially in the writing of both system and application software. This standard is primarily a consequence of the growing commercial interest in Pascal and the need to promote the portability of Pascal programs between data processing systems.

In drafting this standard the continued stability of Pascal has been a prime objective. However, apart from changes to clarify the specification, two major changes have been introduced:

(a)    the syntax used to specify procedural and functional parameters has been changed to require the use of a procedure or function heading, as appropriate (see 6.6.3.1). This change was introduced to overcome a language insecurity;

(b)    a fifth kind of parameter, the conformant array parameter, has been introduced (see 6.6.3.7). With this kind of parameter, the required bounds of the index-type of an actual parameter are not fixed, but are restricted to a specified range of values.

## 0.  INTRODUCTION

The appendices are included for the convenience of the reader of this standard. They do not form a part of the requirements of this standard.

## 1.  SCOPE OF THIS STANDARD

**1.1.**    This standard specifies the semantics and syntax of the computer programming language Pascal by specifying requirements for a processor and for a conforming program. Two levels of compliance are defined for both processors and programs.

**1.2.**    This standard does not specify

(a)    the size or complexity of a program and its data that will exceed the capacity of any specific data processing system or the capacity of a particular processor;

(b)    the minimal requirements of a data processing system that is capable of supporting an implementation of a processor for Pascal;

(c)    the method of activating the program-block or the set of commands used to control the environment in which a Pascal program is transformed and executed;

(d)    the mechanism by which programs written in Pascal are transformed for use by a data processing system:

(e)    the method for reporting errors or warnings;

(f)    the typographical representation of a program published for human reading.

## 2.  REFERENCES

None.

## 3. DEFINITIONS

### 3.1. Error

A violation by a program of the requirements of this standard whose detection by a processor is optional.

### 3.2. Implementation-Defined

Possibly differing between processors, but defined for any particular processor.

### 3.3. Implementation-Dependent

Possibly differing between processors and not necessarily defined for any particular processor.

### 3.4. Processor

A compiler, interpreter, or other mechanism which accepts the program as input and either executes it, prepares it for execution, or both.

## 4. DEFINITIONAL CONVENTIONS

The metalanguage used in this standard to specify the syntax of the constructs is based on Backus-Naur Form. The notation has been modified from the original to permit greater convenience of description and to allow for iterative productions to replace recursive ones. Table 1 lists the meanings of the various meta-symbols. Further specification of the constructs is given by prose and, in some cases, by equivalent program fragments. Any identifier that is defined in clause 6 as the identifier of a predeclared or predefined entity shall denote that entity by its occurrence in such a program fragment. In all other respects, any such program fragment is bound by any pertinent requirement of this standard.

A meta-identifier shall be a sequence of letters and hyphens beginning with a letter.

A sequence of terminal and non-terminal symbols in a production implies the concatenation of the text that they ultimately represent. Within 6.1 this concatenation is direct; no characters may intervene. In all other parts of this standard the concatenation is in accordance with the rules set out in 6.1.

The characters required to form Pascal programs are those implicitly required to form the tokens and separators defined in 6.1.

TABLE 1.    Metalanguage Symbols

| Meta-symbol | Meaning |
|---|---|
| = | shall be defined to be |
| > | shall have as an alternative definition |
| \| | alternatively |
| . | end of definition |
| [x] | 0 or 1 instance of x |
| {x} | 0 or more instances of x |
| (x \| y) | grouping: either of x or y |
| "xyz" | the terminal symbol xyz |
| meta-identifier | a non-terminal symbol |

Use of the words of, in, containing, and closest-containing when expressing a relationship between terminal or non-terminal symbols shall have the following meanings:

the x of a y: refers to the x occurring directly in a production defining y.

the x in a y: is synonymous with "the x of a y."

a y containing an x: refers to any x directly or indirectly derived from y.

the y closest-containing an x: that y which contains an x but does not contain another y containing that x.

These syntactic conventions are used in clause 6 to specify certain syntactic requirements and also the contexts within which certain semantic specifications apply.


## 5. COMPLIANCE

NOTE. There are two levels of compliance—level 0 and level 1. Level 0 does not include conformant array parameters. Level 1 does include conformant array parameters.

### 5.1.  Processors

A processor complying with the requirements of this standard shall:

(a)  if it complies at level 0, accept all the features of the language specified in clause 6, except for 6.6.3.6(e), 6.6.3.7, and 6.6.3.8, with the meanings defined in clause 6;

(b)  if it complies at level 1, accept all the features of the language specified in clause 6 with the meanings defined in clause 6;

(c)  not require the inclusion of substitute or additional language elements in a program in order to accomplish a feature of the language that is specified in clause 6;

(d)    be accompanied by a document that provides a definition of all implementation-defined features;

(e)    detect any violation by a program of the requirements of this standard that is not designated an error;

(f)    treat each violation that is designated an error in at least one of the following ways:

   (1)    there shall be a statement in an accompanying document that the error is not reported;

   (2)    the processor shall have reported a prior warning that an occurrence of that error was possible;

   (3)    the processor shall report the error during preparation of the program for execution;

   (4)    the processor shall report the error during execution of the program, and terminal execution of the program.

(g)    be accompanied by a document that separately describes any features accepted by the processor that are not specified in clause 6. Such extensions shall be described as being 'extensions to Pascal specified by ISO7185: 198–'.

(h)    be able to process in a manner similar to that specified for errors any use of any such extension;

(i)    be able to process in a manner similar to that specified for errors any use of an implementation-dependent feature.

## 5.2.  Programs

A program complying with the requirements of this standard shall:

(a)    if it complies at level 0, use only those features of the language specified in clause 6, except for 6.6.4.6(e), 6.6.3.7, and 6.6.3.8;

(b)    if it complies at level 1, use only those features of the language specified in clause 6;

(c)    not rely on any particular interpretation of implementation-dependent features.

NOTE. The results produced by the processing of a complying program by different complying processors are not required to be the same.

## 6. REQUIREMENTS

### 6.1.  Lexical Tokens

NOTE. The syntax given in this sub-clause (6.1) describes the formation of lexical tokens from characters and the separation of these tokens, and therefore does not adhere to the same rules as the syntax in the rest of this standard.

## 6.1.1. General

The lexical tokens used to construct Pascal programs shall be classified into special-symbols, identifiers, directives, unsigned-numbers, labels and character-strings. The representation of any letter (upper-case or lower-case, differences of font, etc.) occurring anywhere outside of a character-string (see 6.1.7) shall be insignificant in that occurrence to the meaning of the program.

letter =
"a" | "b" | "c" | "d" | "e" | "f" | "g" | "h" | "i " | " j " | "k" | "l" | "m" |
"n" | "o" | "p" | "q" | "r" | "s" | "t " | "u" | "v" | "w" | "x" | "y" | " z" |
digit = "0" | "1" | "2" | "3" | "4" | "5" | "6" | "7" | "8" | "9" .

## 6.1.2. Special-Symbols

The special-symbols are tokens having special meanings and shall be used to delimit the syntactic units of the language.

special-symbol = "+" | "−" | "*" | "/" | "=" | "<" | ">" | "[" | "]" |
"." | "," | ":" | ";" | "^" | "(" | ")" |
"<>" | "<=" | ">=" | ":=" | " . . " | word-symbol.

word-symbol = "and" | "array" | "begin" | "case" | "const" | "div" |
"do" | "downto" | "else" | "end" | "file" | "for" |
"function" | "goto" | "if" | "in" | "label" | "mod" |
"nil" | "not" | "of" | "or" | "packed" | "procedure" |
"program" | "record" | "repeat" | "get" | "then" |
"to" | "type" | "until" | "var" | "while" | "with" .

## 6.1.3. Identifiers

Identifiers may be of any length. All characters of an identifier shall be significant. No identifier shall have the same spelling as any word-symbol.

identifier = letter { letter | digit } .

Examples:

X       time       readinteger       WG4       AlterHeatSetting
InquireWorkstationTransformation
InquireWorkstationIdentification

### 6.1.4. Directives

A directive shall occur only in a procedure-declaration or function-declaration. The directive forward shall be the only required directive (see 6.6.1 and 6.6.2). Other implementation-dependent directives may be provided. No directive shall have the same spelling as any word-symbol.

directive = letter { letter | digit } .

NOTE. On many processors the directive external is used to specify that the procedure-block or function-block corresponding to that procedure-heading or function-heading is external to the program-block. Usually it is in a library in a form to be input to, or that has been produced by, the processor.

### 6.1.5. Numbers

An unsigned-integer shall denote in decimal notation a value of integer-type (see 6.4.2.2). An unsigned-real shall denote in decimal notation a value of real-type (see 6.4.2.2). The letter "e" preceding a scale factor shall mean "times ten to the power of." The value denoted by an unsigned-integer shall be in the closed interval 0 to maxint (see 6.4.2.2 and 6.7.2.2).

digit-sequence = digit (digit) .
unsigned-integer = digit-sequence .
unsigned-real = unsigned-integer ". digit-sequence [ "e" scale-factor] |
        unsigned-integer "e" scale-factor .
unsigned-number = unsigned-integer | unsigned-real
scale-factor = signed-integer .
sign = "+" | "−" .
signed-integer = [sign] unsigned-integer .
signed-real = [sign] unsigned-real.
signed-number = signed-integer | signed-real .

Examples:

1e10     1     +100     −0.1     5e−3     87.35E+8

### 6.1.6. Labels

Labels shall be digit-sequences and shall be distinguished by their apparent integral values, that shall be in the closed interval 0 to 9999.

label = digit-sequence.

### 6.1.7. Character-Strings

A character-string containing a single string-element shall denote a value of char-type (see 6.4.2.2). A character-string containing more than one string-element shall denote a value of a string-type (see 6.4.3.2) with the same number of components as the character-string contains string-elements. If the string of characters is to contain an apostrophe, this apostrophe shall be denoted by an apostrophe-image. Each string-character shall denote an implementation-defined value of char-type.

```
character-string = "'" string-element { string-element } "'" .
string-element = apostrophe-image | string-character.
apostrophe-image = "''"
string-character = one-of-a-set-of-implementation-defined-characters .
```

Examples:

```
'A'      ';'      ''''
'Pascal'      'THIS IS A STRING'
```

### 6.1.8. Token Separators

The construct

> "{" any-sequence-of-characters-and-separations-of-lines-not-containing-right-brace "}"

shall be a comment if the "{" does not occur within a character-string or within a comment. The substitution of a space for a comment shall not alter the meaning of a program.

Comments, spaces (except in character-strings), and the separation of consecutive lines shall be considered to be token separators. Zero or more token separators may occur between any two consecutive tokens, or before the first token of a program text. There shall be at least one separator between any pair of consecutive tokens made up of identifiers, word-symbols, labels, or unsigned-numbers. No separators shall occur within tokens.

## 6.2. Blocks, Scope, and Activations

### 6.2.1. Block

A block closest-containing a label-declaration-part in which a label occurs shall closest-contain exactly one statement in which that label occurs. The occurrence of a label in the label-declaration-part of a block shall be its defining-point as a label for the region which is the block.

block = label-declaration-part
       constant-definition-part
       type-definition-part
       variable-declaration-part
       procedure-and-function-declaration-part
       statement-part .
label-declaration-part = ["label" label { "," label } ";"] .
constant-definition-part = ["const" constant-definition ";"
               { constant-definition ";" }] .
type-definition-part = ["type" type-definition ";" { type-definition ";" }] .
variable-declaration-part = ["var" variable-declaration ";"
                  ";" { variable-declaration ";" }] .
procedure-and-function-declaration-part = { (procedure-declaration |
                         function-declaration) ";" } .

The statement-part shall specify the algorithmic actions to be executed upon an activation of the block.

statement-part = compound-statement .

All variables contained by an activation, except for those listed as program-parameters, shall be totally-undefined at the commencement of that activation.

## *6.2.2. Scope*

*6.2.2.1.* Each identifier or label contained by the program-block shall have a defining-point.

*6.2.2.2.* Each defining-point shall have a region that is a part of the program text, and a scope that is a part or all of that region.

*6.2.2.3.* The region of each defining-point is defined elsewhere (see 6.2.1, 6.2.2.10, 6.3, 6.4.1, 6.4.2.3, 6.4.3.3, 6.5.1, 6.5.3.3, 6.6.1, 6.6.2, 6.6.3.1, 6.8.3.10).

*6.2.2.4* The scope of each defining-point shall be its region (including all regions enclosed by that region) subject to 6.2.2.5 and 6.2.2.6.

*6.2.2.5.* When an identifier or label that has a defining-point for region A has a further defining-point for some region B enclosed by A, then region B and all regions enclosed by B shall be excluded from the scope of the defining-point for region A.

*6.2.6.* The field-identifier of the field-specifier of a field-designator (see 6.5.3.3) shall be one of the field-identifiers associated with a component of the record-type possessed by the record-variable of the field-designator.

*6.2.2.7.* The scope of a defining-point of an identifier or label shall include no other defining-point of the same identifier or label.

*6.2.2.8.* Within the scope of a defining-point of an identifier or label, all occurrences of that identifier or label shall be designated applied occurrences, except for an occurrence that constituted the defining-point of that identifier or label; such an occurrence shall be designated a defining occurrence. No occurrence outside that scope shall be an applied occurrence.

*6.2.2.9.* The defining-point of an identifier or label shall precede all applied occurrences of that identifier or label contained by the program-block with one exception, namely, that a type-identifier may have an applied occurrence in the domain-type of any new-pointer-types contained by the type-definition-part that contains the defining-point of the type-identifier.

*6.2.2.10.* Identifiers that denote required constants, types, procedures and functions shall be used as if their defining-points have a region enclosing the program.

*6.2.2.11.* Whatever an identifier or label denotes at its defining-point shall be denoted at all applied occurrences of that identifier or label.

### 6.2.3. *Activations*

*6.2.3.1* A procedure-identifier or function-identifier having a defining-point for a region which is a block, within the procedure-and-function-declaration-part of that block shall be designated local to that block.

*6.2.3.2.* The activation of a block shall contain

(a) for the statement-part of the block, an algorithm, the completion of which shall terminate the activation (see also 6.8.2.4);

(b) for each label in a statement, having a defining-point in the label-declaration-part of the block, a program-point in the algorithm of the activation of that statement;

(c) for each variable-identifier having a defining-point for the region which is the block, a variable possessing the type associated with the variable-identifier;

(d) for each procedure-identifier local to the block, a procedure with the formal parameters associated with, and the procedure-block corresponding to, the procedure-identifier; and

(e) for each function-identifier local to the block, a function with the formal parameters associated with, the function-block corresponding to, and the type possessed by, the function-identifier.

*6.2.3.3.* The activation of a procedure or function shall be the activation of the block of its procedure-block or function-block, respectively, and shall be designated within:

(a)   the activation containing the procedure or function; and

(b)   all activations that that containing activation is within.

NOTE. An activation of a block B can only be within activations of blocks containing B. Thus an activation is not within another activation of the same block.

Within an activation, an applied occurrence of a label or variable-identifier, or of a procedure-identifier or function-identifier local to the block of the activation, shall denote the corresponding program-point, variable, procedure, or function, respectively, of that activation.

*6.2.3.4.* A procedure-statement or function-designator contained in the algorithm of an activation and that specifies the activation of a block shall be designated the activation-point of that activation of the block.

*6.2.3.5.* The algorithm, program-points, variables, procedures, and functions, if any, shall exist until the termination of the activation.

## 6.3.   Constant-Definitions

A constant-definition shall introduce an identifier to denote a value.

constant-definition = identifier "=" constant.
constant = [sign] (unsigned-number | constant-identifier) | character-string .
constant-identifier = identifier.

The occurrence of an identifier in a constant-definition of a constant-definition-part of a block shall constitute its defining-point for the region that is the block. The constant shall not contain an applied occurrence of the identifier in the constant-definition. Each applied occurrence of that identifier shall be a constant-identifier and shall denote the value denoted by the constant of the constant-definition. A constant-identifier in a constant containing an occurrence of a sign shall have been defined to denote a value of real-type or of integer-type.

## 6.4.   Type-Definitions

### *6.4.1.   General*

A type-definition shall introduce an identifier to denote a type. Type shall be an attribute that is possessed by every value and every variable. Each occurrence of a new-type shall denote a type that is distinct from any other new-type.

type-definition = identifier "=" type-denoter.
type-denoter = type-identifier | new type.
new-type = new-ordinal-type | new-structured-type | new-pointer-type .

The occurrence of an identifier in a type-definition of a type-definition-part of a block shall constitute its defining-point for the region that is the block. Each applied occurrence of that identifier shall be a type-identifier and shall denote the same type as that which is denoted by its type-denoter. Except for applied occurrences as the domain-type of a new-pointer-type, the type-denoter shall not contain an applied occurrence of the identifier in the type-definition.

Types shall be classified as simple, structured, or pointer types. The required types shall be denoted by predefined type-identifiers (see 6.4.2.2 and 6.4.3.5).

simple-type-identifier = type-identifier .
structured-type-identifier = type-identifier .
pointer-type-identifier = type-identifier .
type-identifier = identifier.

A type-identifier shall be considered as a simple-type-identifier, a structured-type-identifier, or a pointer-type-identifier, according to the type that it denotes.

### 6.4.2.  Simple-Types

*6.4.2.1.  General.*   A simple-type shall determine an ordered set of values. The values of each ordinal-type shall have integer ordinal numbers. An ordinal-type-identifier shall denote an ordinal-type.

simple-type = ordinal-type | real-type.
ordinal-type = new-ordinal-type | integer-type | Boolean-type | char-type |
              ordinal-type-identifier .
new-ordinal-type = enumerated-type | subrange-type .
ordinal-type-identifier = identifier

*6.4.2.2.  Required Simple-Types.*   The following types shall exist:

Integer-type:   The required integer-type-identifier integer shall denote the integer-type. The values shall be a subset of the whole numbers, denoted as specified in 6.1.5 by the signed-integer values (see also 6.7.2.2). The ordinal number of a value of integer-type shall be the value itself.

Real-type:   The required real-type-identifier real shall denote the real-type. The values shall be an implementation-defined subset of the real numbers denoted as specified in 6.1.5 by the signed-real values.

Boolean-type:   The required Boolean-type-identifier Boolean shall denote the Boolean-type. The values shall be the enumeration of truth values denoted by the required constant-identifiers false and true, such that false is the predecessor of true. The ordinal numbers of the truth values denoted by false and true shall be the integer values 0 and 1, respectively.

Char-type: The required char-type-identifier char shall denote the char-type. The values shall be the enumeration of a set of implementation-defined characters, some possibly without graphic representations. The ordinal numbers of the character values shall be values of integer-type, that are implementation-defined, and that are determined by mapping the character values on to consecutive non-negative integer values starting at zero. The mapping shall be order preserving. The following relations shall hold:

(a) The subset of character values representing the digits 0 to 9 shall be numerically ordered and contiguous.

(b) The subset of character values representing the upper-case letters A to Z, if available, shall be alphabetically ordered but not necessarily contiguous.

(c) The subset of character values representing the lower-case letters a to z, if available, shall be alphabetically ordered but not necessarily contiguous.

(d) The ordering relationship between any two character values shall be the same as between their ordinal numbers.

NOTE. Operators applicable to the required simple-types are specified in 6.7.2.

*6.4.2.3. Enumerated-Types.* An enumerated-type shall determine an ordered set of values by enumeration of the identifiers that denote those values. The ordering of these values shall be determined by the sequence in which their identifiers are enumerated, i.e., if x precedes y then x is less than y. The ordinal number of a value that is of an enumerated-type shall be determined by mapping all the values of the type as their identifiers occur in the identifier-list of the enumerated-type on to consecutive non-negative values of integer-type starting from zero.

enumerated-type = "(" identifier-list ")" .
identifier-list = identifier { "," identifier } .

The occurrence of an identifier in the identifer-list of an enumerated-type shall constitute its defining-point as a constant-identifier for the region which is the block closest-containing the enumerated-type.

Examples:

(red,yellow,green,blue,tartan)
(club,diamond,heart,spade)
(married,divorced,widowed,single)

(scanning,found,notpresent)
(Busy,InterruptEnable,ParityError,OutOfPaper,LineBreak)

*6.4.2.4.    Subrange-Types.*    The definition of a type as a subrange of an ordinal-type shall include identification of the smallest and the largest value in the subrange. The first constant of a subrange-type shall specify the smallest value, and this shall be less than or equal to the largest value which shall be specified by the other constant of the subrange-type. Both constants shall be of the same ordinal-type, and that ordinal-type shall be designated the host type of the subrange-type.

> subrange-type  =  constant ".." constant.

Examples:

> 1 . .100
> −10 . . +10
> red . . green
> '0' . . '9'

### 6.4.3.    Structured-Types

*6.4.3.1.    General.*    A new-structured-type shall be classified as an array-type, record-type, set-type, or file-type according to the unpacked-structured-type, closest-contained by the new-structured-type. A component of a value of a structured-type shall be a value.

> structured-type  =  new-structured-type | structured-type-identifier .
> unpacked-structured-type  −  array-type | record-type | set-type | file-type .
> new-structured-type  =  ["packed"] unpacked-structured-type .

The occurrence of the token packed in a new-structured-type shall designate the type denoted thereby as packed. The designation of a structured-type as packed shall indicate to the processor that data-storage of values should be economized, even if this causes operations on, or accesses to components of, variables possessing the type to be less efficient in terms of space or time.

The designation of a structured-type as packed shall affect the representation in data-storage of that structured-type only; that is, if a component is itself structured, the component's representation in data-storage shall be packed only if the type of the component is designated packed.

NOTE. The ways in which the treatment of entities of a type is affected by whether or not the type is designated packed are specified in 6.4.3.2, 6.4.5, 6.6.3.3, 6.6.3.8, 6.6.5.4, and 6.7.1.

*6.4.3.2.    Array-Types.*    An array-type shall be structured as a mapping from each value specified by its index-type onto a distinct component. Each component shall have the type denoted by the type-denoter of the component-type of the array-type.

array-type = "array" "[" index-type { "," index-type } "]" "of" component-type .
index-type = ordinal-type.
component-type = type-denoter .

Examples:

array [1 . . 100] of real
array [Boolean] of color

An array-type that specifies a sequence of two or more index-types shall be an abbreviated notation for an array-type specified to have as its index-type the first index-type in the sequence, and to have a component-type that is an array-type specifying the sequence of index-types without the first and specifying the same component-type as the original specification. The component-type thus constructed shall be designated packed if and only if the original array-type is designated packed. The abbreviated form and the full form shall be equivalent.

NOTE. Each of the following two examples thus contains different ways of expressing its array-type.

Example 1.

array[Boolean] of array[1 . . 10] of array[size] of real
array[Boolean] of array[1 . . 10,size] of real
array[Boolean,1 . . 10[size] of real
array[Boolean,1 . . 10] of array[size] of real

Example 2.

packed array[1 . . 10,1 . .8] of Boolean
packed array[1 . . 10] of packed array [1 . . 8] of Boolean

Let i denote a value of the index-type; let v[i] denote a value of that component of the array-type that corresponds to the value i by the structure of the array-type; let the smallest and largest values specified by the index-type be denoted by m and n; and let k = (ord(n)−ord(m)+1) denote the number of values specified by the index-type. Then the values of the array-type shall be the distinct k-tuples of the form:

$$(v[m], \ldots ,v[n])$$

NOTE. A value of an array-type does not therefore exist unless all of its component values are defined. If the component-type has c values, then it follows that the cardinality of the set of values of the array-type is c raised to the power k.

Any type designated packed and denoted by an array-type having as its index-type a denotation of a subrange-type specifying a smallest value of 1, and having as its component-type a denotation of the char-type, shall be designated a string-type.

The correspondence of character-strings to values of string-types is obtained by relating the individual characters of the character-string, taken in left to right order, to the components of the values of the string-type in order of increasing index.

NOTE. The values of a string-type possess additional properties which allow writing them to textfiles (see 6.9.4.7) and define their use with relational-operators (see 6.7.2.5).

*6.4.3.3.  Record-Types.*   The structure and values of a record-type shall be the structure and values of the field-list of the record-type.

```
record-type = "record" field-list "end" .
field-list = [ (fixed-part [ ";" variant-part ] | variant-part) [";"]] .
fixed-part = record-section { ";" record-section } .
record-section = identifier-list ":" type-denoter .
variant-part = "case" variant-selector "of" variant { ";" variant } .
variant-selector = [tag-field ":"] tag-type .
tag-field = identifier .
variant = case-constant-list ":" "(" field-list ")" .
tag-type = ordinal-type-identifier .
case-constant-list = case-constant { "," case-constant } .
case-constant = constant .
```

A field-list which contains neither a fixed-part nor a variant-part shall have no components, shall define a single null value, and shall be designated empty.

The occurrence of an identifier in the identifier-list of a record-section of a fixed-part of a field-list shall constitute its defining-point as a field-identifier for the region which is the record-type closest-containing the field-list, and shall associate the field-identifier with a distinct component, which shall be designated a field, of the record-type and of the field-list. That component shall have the type denoted by the type-denoter of the record-section.

The field-list closest-containing a variant-part shall have a distinct component which shall have the values and structure defined by the variant-part.

Let Vi denote the value of the i-th component of a non-empty field-list having m components; then the values of the field-list shall be distinct m-tuples of the form

$$(V1, V2, \ldots ; Vm).$$

NOTE. If the type of the i-th component has Fi values, then the cardinality of the set of values of the field-list shall be (F1 $*$ F2 $*$ ... $*$ Fm).

A tag-type shall denote the type denoted by the ordinal-type-identifier of the tag-type. A case-constant shall denote the value denoted by the constant of the case-constant.

The type of each case-constant in the case-constant-list of a variant of a variant-part shall be compatible with the tag-type of the variant-selector of the variant-part. The values denoted by all case-constants of a type that is required to be compatible with a given tag-type shall be distinct and the set thereof shall be equal to the set of values specified by the tag-type. The values denoted by the case-constants of the case-constant-list of a variant shall be designated as corresponding to the variant.

With each variant-part shall be associated a type designated the selector-type possessed by the variant-part. If the variant-selector of the variant-part contains a tag-field, or if the case-constant-list of each variant of the variant-part contains only one case-constant, then the selector-type shall be denoted by the tag-type, and each variant of the variant-part shall be associated with those values specified by the selector-type denoted by the case-constants of the case-constant-list of the variant. Otherwise, the selector-type possessed by the variant-part shall be a new ordinal-type constructed such that there is exactly one value of the type for each variant of the variant-part, and no others, and each variant shall be associated with a distinct value of that type.

Each variant-part shall have a component which shall be designated the selector of the variant-part, and which shall possess the selector-type of the variant-part. If the variant-selector of the variant-part contains a tag-field, then the occurrence of an identifier in the tag-field shall constitute the defining-point of the identifier as a field-identifier for the region which is the record-type closest-containing the variant-part, and shall associate the field-identifier with the selector of the variant-part. The selector shall be designated a field of the record-type if and only if it is associated with a field-identifier.

Each variant of a variant-part shall denote a distinct component of the variant-part; the component shall have the values and structure of the field-list of the variant, and shall be associated with those values specified by the selector-type possessed by the variant-part which are associated with the variant. The value of the selector of the variant-part shall cause the associated variant and component of the variant-part to be in a state that shall be designated active. The values of a variant-part shall be the distinct pairs

$$(k, Xk)$$

where k represents a value of the selector of the variant-part, and Xk is a value of the field-list of the active variant of the variant-part.

NOTES

1. If there are n values specified by the selector-type, and if the field-list of the variant associated with the i-th value has Ti values, then the cardinality of the set of values of the variant-part is $(T1 + T2 + \cdots + Tn)$. There is no component of a value of a variant-part corresponding to any non-active variant of the variant-part.

2. Restrictions placed on the use of fields of a record-variable pertaining to variant-parts are specified in 6.5.3.3, 6.6.3.3, and 6.6.5.3.

Examples:

```
record
    year : 0 . . 2000;
    month : 1 . . 12;
    day : 1 . . 31
end

record
    name, firstname : string;
    age : 0 . . 99;
    case married : Boolean of
    true : (Spousesname : string);
    false : ( )
end

record
    x,y : real;
    area : real;
    case shape of
    triangle :
        (side : real;
        inclination, angle1, angle2 : angle);
    rectangle :
        (side1, side2 : real;
        skew : angle);
    circle :
        (diameter : real);
end
```

**6.4.3.4  Set-Types.**  A set-type shall determine the set of values that is structured as the powerset of its base-type. Thus each value of a set-type shall be a set whose members shall be unique values of the base-type.

set-type = "set" "of" base-type .
base-type = ordinal-type

NOTE. Operators applicable to values of set-types are specified in 6.7.2.4.

Examples:

set of char
set of (club, diamond, heart, spade)

NOTE. If the base-type of a set-type has b values then the cardinality of the set of values is 2 raised to the power b.

For every ordinal-type S, there exists an unpacked set designated the unpacked canonical set-of-T type and there exists a packed set type designated the packed canonical set-of-T type. If S is a subrange-type then T is the host type of S; otherwise T is S. Each value of the type set of S is also a value of the unpacked canonical set-of-T type, and each value of the type packed set of S is also a value of the packed canonical set-of-T type.

### 6.4.3.5.  File-Types.

NOTE. A file-type describes sequences of values of the specified component-type, together with a current position in each sequence and a mode which indicates whether the sequence is being inspected or generated.

file-type  =  "file" "of" component-type.

A type-denoter shall not be permissible as the component-type of a file-type if it denotes either a file-type or a structured-type having any component whose type-denoter is not permissible as the component-type of a file-type.

file of real<br>file of vector

A file-type shall define implicitly a type designated a sequence-type having exactly those values, which shall be designated sequences, defined by the following five rules. NOTE. The notation $x\~y$ represents the concatenation of sequences x and y. The explicit representation of sequences (e.g., S(c)), of concatenation of sequences, of the first, last and rest selectors, and of sequence equality is not part of the Pascal language. These notations are used to define file values, below, and the required file operations in 6.6.5.2 and 6.6.6.5.

(a)  S( ) shall be a value of the sequence-type S, and shall be designated the empty sequence. The empty sequence shall have no components.

(b)  Let c be a value of the specified component-type, and let x be a value of the sequence-type S. Then S(c) shall be a sequence of type S, consisting of the single component value c, and $S(c)\~x$ shall also be a sequence, distinct from S( ), of type S.

(c)  Let c, S, and x be as in (b); let y denote the sequence $S(C)\~x$; and let z denote the sequence $x\~S(c)$; then the notation y.first shall denote x (i.e., the sequence obtained from y by deleting the first component), and z.last shall denote c (i.e., the last component value of z).

(d)  Let x and y each be a non-empty sequence of type S; then x = y shall be true if and only if both (x.first = y.first) and (x.rest = y.rest) are true. If x is the empty sequence, then x = y shall be true if and only if y is also the empty sequence.

(e)  Let x, y, and z be sequences of type S; then $x\~(y\~z) = (x\~y)\~z$, $S( )\~x = x$, and $x\~S( ) = x$ shall be true.

A file-type also shall define implicitly a type designated a mode-type having exactly two values which are designated Inspection and Generation.

NOTE. The explicit denotation of these values is not part of the Pascal language.

A file-type shall be structured as three components. Two of these components, designated f.L and f.R, shall be of the implicit sequence-type. The third component, designated f.M, shall be of the implicit mode-type.

Let f.L and f.R each be a single value of the sequence-type; let f.M be a single value of the mode-type; then each value of the file-type shall be a distinct triple of the form

$$(f.L, f.R, f.M)$$

where f.R shall be the empty sequence if f.M is the value Generation. The value, f, of the file-type shall be designated empty if and only if f.L⁓f.R is the empty sequence.

NOTE. The two components, f.L and f.R, of a value of the file-type may be considered to represent the single sequence f.L⁓f.R together with a current position in that sequence. If f.R is non-empty, then f.R.first may be considered the current component as determined by the current position; otherwise, the current position is designated the end-of-file position.

There shall be a file-type that is denoted by the required structured-type-identifier text. The structure of the type denoted by text shall define an additional sequence-type whose values shall be designated lines. A line shall be a sequence x⁓S(e), where x is a sequence of components having the char-type, and e represents a special component value, which shall be designated an end-of-line, and which shall be indistinguishable from the char value space except by the required function eoln (6.6.6.5) and by the required procedures reset (6.6.5.2) writeln (6.9.5), and page (6.9.6). If x is a line then no component of x other than x.last shall be an end-of-line. This definition shall not be construed to determine the underlying representation, if any, of an end-of-line component used by a processor.

A line-sequence, z, shall be either the empty sequence or the sequence x⁓y where x is a line and y is a line-sequence.

Every value t of the type denoted by text shall satisfy one of the following two rules.

(a)   If t.M = Inspection, then t.L⁓t.R shall be a line-sequence

(b)   If t.M = Generation, then t.L⁓t.R shall be x⁓y where x is a line-sequence and y is a sequence of components having the char-type.

NOTE. In rule (b), y may be considered, especially if it is non-empty, to be a partial line which is being generated. Such a partial line cannot occur during inspection of a file. Also, y does not correspond to t.R since t.R is the empty sequence if t.M = Generation.

A variable that possesses the type denoted by the required structured-type-identifier text shall be designated a textfile.

NOTE. All required procedures and functions applicable to a variable of type file of char are applicable to textfiles. Additional required procedures and functions, applicable only to textfiles, are defined in 6.6.6.5 and 6.9.

### 6.4.4.  Pointer-Types.

The values of a pointer-type shall consist of a single nil-value, and a set of identifying-values each identifying a distinct variable possessing the domain-type of the pointer-type. The set of identifying-values shall be dynamic, in that the variables and the values identifying them, may be created and destroyed during the execution of the program. Identifying-values and the variables identified by them shall be created only by the required procedure new (see 6.6.5.3).

NOTE. Since the nil-value is not an identifying-value it does not identify a variable. The token nil shall denote the nil-value in all pointer-types.

> pointer-type  =  new-pointer-type | pointer-type-identifier .
> new-pointer-type  =  "^" domain-type.
> domain-type  =  type-identifier .

NOTE. The token nil does not have a single type, but assumes a suitable pointer-type to satisfy the assignment-compatibility rules, or the compatibility rules for operators, if possible.

### 6.4.5.  Compatible Types

Types T1 and T2 shall be designated compatible if any of the four statements that follow is true.

(a)  T1 and T2 are the same type.

(b)  T1 is a subrange of T2, or T2 is a subrange of T1, or both T1 and T2 are subranges of the same host type.

(c)  T1 and T2 are designated packed or neither T1 nor T2 is designated packed.

(d)  T1 and T2 are string-types with the same number of components.

### 6.4.6.  Assignment-Compatibility

A value of type T2 shall be designated assignment-compatible with a type T1 if any of the five statements that follow is true.

(a)  T1 and T2 are the same type which is neither a file-type nor a structured-type with a file component (this rule is to be interpreted recursively).

(b)  T1 is the real-type and T2 is the integer-type.

(c)  T1 and T2 are compatible ordinal-types and the value of type T2 is in the closed interval specified by the type T1.

(d)  T1 and T2 are compatible set-types and all the members of the value of type T2 are in the closed interval specified by the base-type of T1.

(e)  T1 and T2 are compatible string-types.

At any place where the rule of assignment-compatibility is used:

(a)  It shall be an error if T1 and T2 are compatible ordinal-types and the value of type T2 is not in the closed interval specified by the type T1.

(b)  It shall be an error if T1 and T2 are compatible set-types and any member of the value of type T2 is not in the closed interval specified by the base-type of the type T1.


**6.4.7.  *Example of a Type-Definition-Part***

```
type
    natural = 0 . . maxint;
    count = integer;
    range = integer;
    color = (red, yellow, green, blue);
    sex = (male, female);
    year = 1900 . . 1999;
    shape = (triangle, rectangle, circle);
    punchedcard = array[1 . . 80] of char;
    charsequence = file of char;
    polar = record
                r : real;
                theta : angle
            end;


    indextype = 1 . . limit;
    vector = array [indextype] of real;
    person = ^persondetails;
            record
                name, firstname : charsequence;
                age : integer;
                married : Boolean;
                father, child, sibling : person;
                case s : sex of
                    male :
                        (enlisted,bearded : Boolean);
                    female :
                        (mother,programmer : Boolean)
            end;
    FileOfInteger = file of integer;
```

NOTES

1. In the above example count, range and integer denote the same type. The types denoted by year and natural are compatible with, but not the same as, the type denoted by range, count and integer.

2. Types occurring in examples in the remainder of this standard should be assumed to have been declared as specified in 6.4.7.

### 6.5. Declarations and Denotations of Variables

*6.5.1. Variable-Declarations*

A variable is an entity to which a (current) value may be a attributed (see 6.8.2.2). Each identifier in the identifier-list of a variable-declaration shall denote a distinct variable possessing the type denoted by the type-denoter of the variable-declaration.

> variable-declaration = identifier-list ":" type-denoter .

The occurrence of an identifier in the identifier-list of a variable-declaration of the variable-declaration-part of a block shall constitute its defining-point as a variable-identifier for the region that is the block. The structure of a variable possessing a structured-type shall be the structure of the structured-type. A use of a variable-access shall be an access, at the time of the use, to the variable thereby denoted. A variable-access, according to whether it is an entire-variable, a component-variable, an identified-variable, or a buffer-variable, shall denote either a declared variable, or a component of a variable, a variable which is identified by a pointer value (see 6.4.4), or a buffer-variable, respectively.

> variable-access = entire-variable : component-variable :
>                   identified-variable : buffer-variable .

An assigning-reference to a variable shall occur if any of the six statements that follow is true.

(a) The variable is denoted by the variable-access of an assignment-statement.

(b) The variable is denoted by an actual variable parameter in a function-designator or procedure-statement.

(c) The variable is denoted by an actual parameter in a procedure-statement that specifies the activation of the required procedure read or the required procedure readln.

(d) The variable occurs as the control-variable of a for-statement.

(e) A procedure-statement or a function-designator contains a procedure-identifier associated with a procedure-block containing an assigning-reference to the variable.

(f)    A procedure-statement or a function-designator contains a function-identifier associated with a function-block containing an assigning-reference to the variable.

Example of a variable-declaration-part:

```
var
    x,y,z,max: real;
    i,j: integer;
    k: 0 . . 9;
    p,q,r: Boolean;
    operator: (plus, minus, times);
    a: array[0 . . 63] of real;
    c: color;
    f: file of char;
    hue1,hue2: set of color;
    p1,p2: person;
    m,m1,m2 : array[1 . . 10,1 . . 10] of real;
    coord : polar;
    pooltape : array[1 . . 4] of FileOfInteger;
    date : record
                        month : 1 . . 12;
                        year : integer
           end;
```

NOTE. Variables occurring in examples in the remainder of this standard should be assumed to have been declared as specified in 6.5.1.

### 6.5.2.    Entire-Variables

entire-variable = variable-identifier .
variable-identifier = identifier .

### 6.5.3.    Component-Variables

*6.5.3.1.    General.*    A component of a variable shall be a variable. A component-variable shall denote a component of a variable. A reference, assigning-reference, or access to a component of a variable shall constitute a reference, assigning-reference, or access, respectively, to the variable. The value, if any, of the component of a variable shall be the same component of the value, if any, of the variable.

component-variable = indexed-variable : field-designator .

*6.5.3.2.    Indexed-Variables.*    A component of a variable possessing an array-type shall be denoted by an indexed-variable.

indexed-variable = array-variable "[" index-expression
                    { "," index-expression } "]" .
array-variable = variable-access .
index-expression = expression .

An array-variable shall be a variable-access that denotes a variable possessing an array-type. For an indexed-variable closest-containing a single index-expression, the value of the index-expression shall be assignment-compatible with the index-type of the array-type. The component denoted by the indexed-variable shall be the component that corresponds to the value of the index-expression by the mapping of the type possessed by the array-variable (see 6.4.3.2).

Examples:

> a[12]
> a[i+j]
> m[k]

If the array-variable is itself an indexed-variable an abbreviation may be used. In the abbreviated form, a single comma shall replace the sequence "]" "[" that occurs in the full form. The abbreviated form and the full form shall be equivalent.

Examples:

> m[k][l]
> m[k,l]

NOTE. The two examples denote the same component variable.

*6.5.3.3.  Field-Designators.*  A field-designator either shall denote that component of the record-variable of the field-designator which is associated with the field-identifier of the field-specifier of the field designator, by the record-type possessed by the record-variable; or shall denote the variable denoted by the field-designator-identifier (see 6.8.3.10) of the field-designator. A record-variable shall be a variable-access that denotes a variable possessing a record-type.

The occurrence of a record-variable in a field-designator shall constitute the defining-point of the field-identifiers associated with components of the record-type possessed by the record-variable, for the region that is the field-specifier of the field-designator.

field-designator = record-variable "." field-specifier |
                    field-designator-identifier .
record-variable = variable-access .
field-specifier = field-identifier .
field-identifier = identifier .

Examples:

$$p2\hat{}. \text{ mother}$$
$$\text{coord.theta}$$

An access to a component of a variant of a variant-part, where the selector of the variant-part is not a field, shall attribute to the selector that value specified by its type which is associated with the variant.

It shall be an error unless a variant is active for the entirety of each reference and access to each component of the variant.

When a variant becomes not active, all of its components shall become totally-undefined.

NOTE. If the selector of a variant-part is undefined, then no variant of the variant-part is active.

### 6.5.4.  Identified-Variables

An identified-variable shall denote the variable (if any) identified by the value of the pointer-variable of the identifier-variable (see 6.4.4 and 6.6.5.3).

identified-variable = pointer-variable "^"
pointer-variable = variable-access .

A variable created by the required procedure new (see 6.6.5.3) shall be accessible until the termination of the activation of the program-block or until the variable is made inaccessible (see the required procedure dispose, 6.6.5.3).

NOTE. The accessibility of the variable also depends on the existence of a pointer-variable which has attributed to it the corresponding identifying value.

A pointer-variable shall be a variable-access that denotes a variable possessing a pointer-type. It shall be an error if the pointer-variable of an identified-variable either denotes a nil-value or is undefined. It shall be an error to remove from its pointer-type the identifying-value of an identified variable (see 6.6.5.3) when a reference to the identified variable exists.

Examples:

p1^
p1^.father^
p1^.sibling^.father^

### 6.5.5.  Buffer-Variables

A file-variable shall be a variable-access that denotes a variable possessing a file-type. A buffer-variable shall denote a variable associated with the variable denoted by the file-variable of the buffer-variable. A buffer-variable associated with a textfile shall possess the char-type: otherwise, a buffer-variable shall possess the component-type of the file-type possessed by the file-variable of the buffer-variable.

> buffer-variable = file-variable "^" .
> file-variable = variable-access .

Examples:

> input^
> pooltape[2]^

It shall be an error to alter the value of a file-variable f when a reference to the buffer-variable f^ exists. A reference or access to a buffer-variable shall constitute a reference or access, respectively, to the associated file-variable.

## 6.6.    Procedure and Function Declarations

### 6.6.1.    Procedure-Declarations

A procedure-declaration shall associate an identifier with a procedure-block so that it can be activated by a procedure-statement. Activation of the procedure shall activate the procedure-block.

> procedure-declaration = procedure-heading ";" directive | procedure-identification
> ";" procedure-block | procedure-heading ";"
> procedure-block .
> procedure-heading = "procedure" identifier [ formal-parameter-list ] .
> procedure-identification = "procedure" procedure-identifier .
> procedure-identifier = identifier .
> procedure-block = block .

The occurrence of a formal-parameter-list in a procedure-heading of a procedure-declaration shall define the formal parameters of the procedure-block, if any, associated with the identifier of the procedure-heading to be those of the formal-parameter-list.

The occurrence of an identifier in the procedure-heading of a procedure-declaration shall constitute its defining-point as a procedure-identifier for the region that is the block closest-containing the the procedure-declaration.

Each identifier having a defining-point as a procedure-identifier in a procedure-heading of a procedure-declaration closest-containing the directive "forward" shall have exactly one of its corresponding occurrences in a procedure-identification of a procedure-declaration, and that shall be in the same procedure-and-function-declaration-part.

The occurrence of a procedure-block in a procedure-declaration associates the procedure-block with the identifier in the procedure-heading, or with the procedure-identifier in the procedure-identification, of the procedure-declaration.

Example of a procedure-and-function-declaration-part:

```
procedure readinteger (var f: text; var x: integer);
var
    i:natural;
begin
    while f^ = " do get(f);
    {The file buffer contains the first non-space char}
    i := 0;
    while f^ in ['0' .. '9'] do begin
        i := (10 * i) + (ord(f^) - ord('0'));
        get(f)
    end;
    {The file buffer contains a non-digit}
    x := i
    {Of course if there are no digits, x is zero}
end;
```

```
procedure AddVectors(var A,B,C: array[low .. high: natural] of real);
var
    i : natural;
begin
    for i := low to high do A[i] := B[i] + C[i]
end { of AddVectors };
```

```
procedure bisect (function f(x : real) : real;
                  a,b: real;
                  var result: real);
{This procedure attempts to find a zero of f(x) in (a,b) by
    the method of bisection. It is assumed that the procedure is
    called with suitable values of a and b such that
        (f(a)<0) and (f(b)>0)
    The estimate is returned in the last parameter.}
const
    Eps = 1e-10;
var
    midpoint: real;
begin
    {The invariant P is true by calling assumption}
    midpoint := a;
    while abs(a−b) > Eps*abs(a) do begin
    midpoint := (a+b)/2;
        if f(midpoint) < 0 then a := midpoint
        else b :=midpoint
        {Which re-establishes the invariant:
            P = (f(a)<0) and (f(b)>0)
```

and reduces the interval (a,b) provided that the value
of midpoint is distinct from both a and b.}
end;
{P together with the loop exit condition assures that a zero
is contained in a small sub-interval. Return the midpoint as
the zero.)
    result := midpoint
end;


    procedure PrepareForAppending (var f: FileOfInteger);
    {This procedure takes a file in an arbitrary state and sets
        it up in a condition for appending data to its end. Simpler
        conditioning is only possible if assumptions are made about the
        initial state of the file.)
    var
        LocalCopy : FileOfInteger;
        procedure CopyFiles(var from,into : FileOfInteger);
        begin
            reset(from); rewrite(into);
            while not eof(from) do begin
                into^ := from^;
                put(into); get(from)
            end;
        end { of CopyFiles };
    begin {of body of PrepareForAppending}
        CopyFiles(f,LocalCopy);
        CopyFiles(LocalCopy,f)
    end { of PrepareForAppending };


## 6.6.2.  Function-Declarations


A function-declaration shall associate an identifier with a function-block so that it
can be activated by a function-designator. Activation of the function shall activate
the function-block.


function-declaration = function-heading ";" directive | function-identification
                    ";" function-block | function-heading ";"
                    function-block .
function-heading = "function" identifier [formal-parameter-list] ":"
                    result-type .
function-identification = "function" function-identifier .
function-identifier = identifier .
result-type = simple-type-identifier | pointer-type-identifier .
function-block = block .

The occurrence of a formal-parameter-list in a function-heading of a function-declaration shall define the formal parameters of the function-block, if any, associated with the identifier of the function-heading to be those of the formal-parameter-list. The function-block shall contain at least one assignment-statement that attributes a value to the function-identifier (see 6.8.2.2). The value of the function shall be the last value attributed to the function-identifier. It shall be an error if the function is undefined upon completion of the algorithm of an activation of the function-block.

The occurrence of an identifier in the function-heading of a function-declaration shall constitute its defining-point as a function-identifier possessing the type denoted by the result-type for the region that is the block closest-containing the the function-declaration.

Each identifier having a defining-point as a function-identifier in the function-heading of a function-declaration closest-containing the directive "forward" shall have exactly one of its corresponding occurrences in a function-identification of a function-declaration, and that shall be in the same procedure-and-function-declaration-part.

The occurrence of a function-block in a function-declaration associates the function-block with the identifier in the function-heading, or with the function-identifier in the function-identification, of the function-declaration.

Example of a procedure-and-function-declaration-part:

```
function Sqrt (x:real): real;
{This function computes the square root of x (x>0)
    using Newton's method.}
var
    old,new: real;
begin
    new := x;
    repeat
        old := new;
        new := (old + x/old) * 0.5;
    until abs(new-old) < Eps * new;
    {Eps being a global constant}
    Sqrt := new
end { of Sqrt };


function max(a: vector): real;
{This function finds the largest component of the value of a.}
var
    largestsofar: real;
    fence: indextype;
begin
    largestsofar := a[1];
    {Establishes largestsofar = max(a[1])}
    for fence := 2 to limit do begin
```

```
        if largestsofar < a[fence] then largestsofar := a[fence]
        (Re-establishing largestsofar = max(a[1], . . . ,a[fence])}
      end;
      {So now largestsofar = max(a[1], . . . ,a[limit])}
      max := largestsofar
    end { of max };
    function GCD(m,n: natural): natural;
    begin
      if n=0 then GCD := m else GCD := GCD(n,m mod n);
    end;
```

This example of the use of forward demonstrates how mutual recursion is helpful in reading a parenthesized expression and converting it to some internal form}

```
function ReadOperand : formula; forward;

function ReadExpression : formula;
        var
          this : formula
        begin
        this := ReadOperand;
        while IsOperator(nextsym) do
          this := MakeFormula(this, ReadOperator, ReadOperand);
        ReadExpression := this
        end;

      function ReadOperand { : formula };
        begin
        if IsOpen(nextsym) then
          begin
          SkipSymbol;
          ReadOperand := ReadExpression;
          {nextsym should be a close}
          SkipSymbol
          end
        else ReadOperand := ReadElement
        end;
```

## 6.6.3. Parameters

*6.6.3.1. General.* The identifier-list in a value-parameter-specification shall be a list of value parameters. The identifier-list in a variable-parameter-specification shall be a list of variable parameters.

```
        formal-parameter-list = "(" formal-parameter-section
                                {";" formal-parameter-section} ")" .
```

formal-parameter-section > value-parameter-specification |
   variable-parameter-specification |
   procedural-parameter-specification |
   functional-parameter-specification .

value-parameter-specification = identifier-list ":",type-identifier .
variable-parameter-specification = "var" identifier-list ":" type-identifier .
procedural-parameter-specification = procedure-heading .
functional-parameter-specification = function-heading .

An identifier that is defined to be a parameter-identifier for the region which is the formal-parameter-list of a procedure-heading shall be designated a formal parameter of the block of the procedure-block, if any, associated with the identifier of the procedure-heading. An identifier that is defined to be a parameter-identifier for the region which is the formal-parameter-list of a function-heading shall be designated a formal parameter of the block of the function-block, if any, associated with the identifier of the function-heading.

The occurrence of an identifier in the identifier-list of a value-parameter-specification or a variable-parameter-specification shall constitute its defining-point as a parameter-identifier for the region that is the formal-parameter-list closest-containing it and its defining-point as the associated variable-identifier for the region that is the block, if any, of which it is a formal parameter.

The occurrence of the identifier of a procedure-heading in a procedural-parameter-specification shall constitute its defining-point as a parameter-identifier for the region that is the formal-parameter-list closest-containing it and its defining-point as the associated procedure-identifier for the region that is the block, if any, of which it is a formal parameter.

The occurrence of the identifier of a function-heading in a functional-parameter-specification shall constitute its defining-point as a parameter-identifier for the region that is the formal-parameter-list closest-containing it and its defining-point as the associated function-identifier for the region that is the block, if any, of which it is a formal parameter.

The occurrence of the identifier of a procedure-heading in a procedural-parameter-specification shall constitute its defining-point as a parameter-identifier for the region that is the formal-parameter-list closest-containing it and its defining-point as the associated procedure-identifier for the region that is the block, if any, of which it is a formal parameter.

The occurrence of the identifier of a function-heading in a functional-parameter-specification shall constitute its defining-point as a parameter-identifier for the region that is the formal-parameter-list closest-containing it and its defining-point as the associated function-identifier for the region that is the block, if any, of which it is a formal parameter.

NOTE. If the formal-parameter-list is contained in a procedural-parameter-specification or a functional-parameter-specification, there is no corresponding procedure-block or function-block.

*6.6.3.2.    Value Parameters.*   The formal parameter and its associated variable-identifier shall denote the same variable. The formal parameter shall possess the type denoted by the type-identifier of the value-parameter-specification. The actual-parameter (see 6.7.3 and 6.8.2.3) shall be an expression whose value is assignment-compatible with the type possessed by the formal parameter. The current value of the expression shall be attributed upon activation of the block to the variable that is denoted by the formal parameter.

*6.6.3.3.    Variable Parameters.*   The actual-parameter shall be a variable-access. The actual-parameters (see 6.7.3 and 6.8.2.3) corresponding to formal parameters that occur in a single variable-parameter-specification shall all possess the same type. The type possessed by the actual-parameters shall be the same as that denoted by the type-identifier, and the formal parameters shall also possess that type. The actual-parameter shall be accessed before the activation of the block, and this access shall establish a reference to the variable thereby accessed during the entire activation of the block; the corresponding formal parameter and its associated variable-identifier shall denote the referenced variable during the activation.

An actual variable parameter shall not denote a field which is the selector of a variant-part. An actual variable parameter shall not denote a component of a variable that possesses a type that is designated packed.

*6.6.3.4.    Procedural Parameters.*   The actual-parameter (see 6.7.3 and 6.8.2.3) shall be a procedure-identifier that has a defining-point contained by the program-block. The procedure denoted by the actual-parameter and the procedure denoted by the formal parameter shall have congruous formal-parameter-lists (see 6.6.3.6) if either has a formal-parameter-list. The formal parameter and its associated procedure-identifier shall denote the actual parameter during the entire activation of the block.

*6.6.3.5.    Functional Parameters.*   The actual-parameter (see 6.7.3 and 6.8.2.3) shall be a function-identifier that has a defining-point contained by the program-block. The function denoted by the actual-parameter and the function denoted by the formal parameter shall have the same result-type and shall have congruous formal-parameter-lists (see 6.6.3.6) if either has a formal-parameter-list. The formal parameter and its associated function-identifier shall denote the actual parameter during the entire activation of the block.

*6.6.3.6.    Parameter List Congruity.*   Two formal-parameter-lists shall be congruous if they contain the same number of formal-parameter-sections and if the formal-parameter-sections in corresponding positions match. Two formal-parameter-sections shall match if any of the statements that follow is true.

(a)    They are both value-parameter-specifications containing the same number of parameters and the type-identifier in each value-parameter-specification denotes the same type.

(b)   They are both variable-parameter-specifications containing the same number of parameters and the type-identifier in each variable-parameter-specification denotes the same type.

(c)   They are both procedural-parameter-specifications and the formal-parameter-lists of the procedure-headings thereof are congruous.

(d)   They are both functional-parameter-specifications, the formal-parameter-lists of the function-headings thereof are congruous, and the type-identifiers of the result-types of the function-headings thereof denote the same type.

(e)   They are both conformant-array-parameter-specifications containing the same number of parameters and equivalent conformant-array-schemas. Two conformant-array-schemas shall be equivalent if all of the four statements which follow are true.

(1)   There is a single index-type-specification in each conformant-array-schema.

(2)   The ordinal-type-identifier in each index-type-specification denotes the same type.

(3)   Either the (component) conformant-array-schemas of the conformant-array-schemas are equivalent or the type-identifiers of the conformant-array-schemas denote the same type.

(4)   Either or both conformant-array-schemas are packed-conformant-array-schemas.

NOTES

**1.**   The abbreviated conformant-array-schema and its corresponding full form are equivalent (see 6.6.3.7)

**2.**   The contents of (e) above do not apply to level 0.

*6.6.3.7.   Conformant Array Parameters.*

NOTE. This clause does not apply to level 0.

The occurrence of an identifier in the identifier-list of a conformant-array-parameter-specification shall constitute its defining-point as a parameter-identifier for the region that is the formal-parameter-list closest-containing it and its defining-point as the associated variable-identifier for the region that is the block, if any, of which it is a formal parameter.

The occurrence of an identifier in an index-type-specification shall constitute its defining-point as a bound-identifier for the region that is the formal-parameter-list closest-containing it and for the region that is the block, if any, whose formal parameters are specified by that formal-parameter-list.

```
formal-parameter-section > conformant-array-parameter-specification .
conformant-array-parameter-specification = "var" identifier-list ":"
                                     conformant-array-schema .
conformant-array-schema = (packed-conformant-array-schema |
                            unpacked-conformant-array-schema) .
```

packed-conformant-array-schema  =  "packed" "array" "["
                                        index-type-specification "]"
                                        "of" type-identifier .
unpacked-conformant-array-schema  =  "array" "[" index-type-specification
                                        { ":" index-type-specification }
                                        "]" "of" ( type-identifier |
                                        conformant-array-schema ) .
index-type-specification  =  identifier ". ." identifier ":"
                                ordinal-type-identifier .
bound-identifier  =  identifier .
factor  >  bound-identifier .

NOTE. There is also a syntax rule for formal-parameter-section in 6.6.3.1. There is also a syntax rule for factor in 6.7.1.

If a conformant-array-schema contains a conformant-array-schema, then an abbreviated form of definition may be used. In the abbreviated form, a single semicolon shall replace the sequence "]" "of" "array" "[" that occurs in the full form. The abbreviated form and the full form shall be equivalent.

Examples:

    array[u . . v: T1] of array[j . . k: T2] of T3
    array[u . . v: T1; j . . k: T2] of T3

During the entire activation of the block, the first bound-identifier of an index-type-specification shall denote the smallest value specified by the corresponding index-type (see 6.6.3.8) possessed by each actual-parameter, and the second bound-identifier of the index-type-specification shall denote the largest value specified by that index-type.

The actual-parameters (see 6.7.3 and 6.8.2.3) corresponding to formal parameters that occur in a single conformant-array-parameter-specification shall all possess the same type. The type possessed by the actual-parameters shall be conformable (see 6.6.3.8) with the conformant-array-schema, and the formal parameters shall possess an array-type which shall be distinct from any other type, and which shall have a component-type that shall be that denoted by the type-identifier contained by the conformant-array-schema in the conformant-array-parameter-specification and which shall have the index-types of the type possessed by the actual-parameters that correspond (see 6.6.3.8) to the index-type-specifications contained by the conformant-array-schema in the conformant-array-parameter-specification.

NOTE. The type of the formal parameter can not be a string-type (see 6.4.3.2) because it is not denoted by an array-type.

The actual-parameter shall be either a variable-access or an expression that is not a factor that is not a variable-access. If the actual-parameter is an expression, the value of the expression shall be attributed before activation of the block to an auxiliary variable which the program does not otherwise contain. The type possessed by this variable shall be the same as that possessed by the expression. This variable, or the actual-parameter if it is denoted by a variable-access, shall be accessed before the activation of the block, and this access shall establish a reference to the variable thereby accessed during the entire activation of the block; the corresponding formal parameter and its associated variable-identifier shall represent the referenced variable during the activation.

NOTE. In using an array variable A as an actual parameter corresponding to a formal parameter that occurs in a conformant-array-parameter-specification the use of an auxiliary variable is ensured by enclosing the variable-access A in parentheses.

An actual-parameter that is a variable-access shall not denote a component of a variable that possesses a type that is designated packed.

If the actual-parameter is an expression whose value is denoted by a variable-access that closest-contains an identifier which has a defining-occurrence in the identifier-list of a conformant-array-parameter-specification, then

(a)   that identifier shall be contained by an indexed-variable contained by the expression, and

(b)   the factor closest-containing the indexed-variable shall closest-contain at least as many index-expressions as the conformant-array-parameter-specification contains index-type-specifications.

NOTE. This ensures that the type of the expression and the anonymous variable will always be known and that, as a consequence, the activation record of a procedure can be of a fixed size.

### 6.6.3.8.   Conformability.

NOTE. This clause does not apply to level 0.

Given a type denoted by an array-type closest-containing a single index-type, and a conformant-array-schema closest-containing a single index-type-specification, then the index-type and the index-type-specification shall be designated as corresponding. Given two conformant-array-schemas closest-containing a single index-type-specification, then the two index-type-specifications shall be designated as corresponding. Let T1 be an array-type with a single index-type and let T2 be the type denoted by the ordinal-type-identifier of the index-type-specification of a conformant-array-schema closest-containing a single index-type-specification, then T1 shall be conformable with the conformant-array-schema if all the following four statements are true.

(a)   The index-type of T1 is compatible with T2.

(b)   The smallest and largest values specified by the index-type of T1 lie within the closed interval specified by T2.

(c)   The component-type of T1 denotes the same type as that which is is denoted by the type-identifier of the conformant-array-schema, or is conformable to the conformant-array-schema in the conformant-array-schema.

(d)   Either T1 is not designated packed and the conformant-array-schema is an unpacked-conformant-array-schema, or T1 is designated packed and the conformant-array-schema is a packed-conformant-array-schema.

NOTE. The abbreviated and full forms of a conformant-array-schema are equivalent (see 6.6.3.7). The abbreviated and full forms of an array-type are equivalent (see 6.4.3.2).

It shall be an error if the smallest or largest value specified by the index-type of T1 lies outside the closed interval specified by T2.

### 6.6.4.  Required Procedures and Functions

*6.6.4.1.  General.*   Required procedures and functions shall be predeclared. The required procedures and functions shall be as specified in 6.6.5 and 6.6.6, respectively.

NOTE. Required procedures and functions do not necessarily follow the rules given elsewhere for procedures and functions.

### 6.6.5.  Required Procedures

*6.6.5.1.  General.*   The required procedures shall be file handling procedures, dynamic allocation procedures, and transfer procedures.

*6.6.5.2.  File Handling Procedures.*   Except for the application of rewrite or reset to the program parameters denoted by input or output, the effects of applying each of the file handling procedures rewrite, put, reset, and get to a file-variable f shall be defined by pre-assertions and post-assertions about f, its components f.L, f.R, and f.M, and about the associated buffer-variable f^. The use of the variable f0 within an assertion shall be considered to represent the state or value, as appropriate, of f prior to the operation, and similarly for f0^ and f^, while f (within an assertion) shall denote the variable after the operation.

It shall be an error if the stated pre-assertion does not hold immediately prior to any use of the defined operation. It shall be an error if any variable explicitly denoted in an assertion of equality is undefined. The post-assertion shall hold prior to the next subsequent access to the file, its components, or its associated buffer-variable. The post-assertions imply corresponding activities on the external entities, if any, to which the file-variables are bound. These activities, and the point at which they are actually performed, shall be implementation-defined.

| rewrite(f) | pre-assertion: | true. |
| | post-assertion: | (f.L = f.R = S( )) and |
| | | (f.M = Generation) and |
| | | (f^ is totally-undefined). |
| put(f) | pre-assertion: | (f0.M = Generation) and |
| | | (f0.L is not undefined) and |
| | | (f0.R = S( )) and |
| | | (f0^ is not undefined). |

|               | post-assertion: | (f.M = Generation) and<br>(f.L = (f0.L⁻S(f0^))) and<br>(f.R = S()) and<br>(f^ is totally-undefined). |
|---------------|-----------------|-------------------------------------------------------------|
| reset(f)      | pre-assertion:  | The components f0.L and<br>f0.R are not undefined. |
|               | post-assertion: | (f.L = S()) and<br>(f.R = (f0.L⁻f0.R⁻X)) and<br>(f.M = Inspection) and<br>(if f.R = S( ) then (f^ is<br>totally-undefined)<br>else (f^ = f.R.first)),<br>where, if f is of the type de-<br>noted by the required struc-<br>tured-type-identifier text and<br>if (f0.L⁻f0.R).last is not des-<br>ignated an end-of-line, then<br>X shall be a sequence having<br>an end-of-line component as<br>its only component; other-<br>wise X = S( ). |
| set(f)        | pre-assertion:  | (f0.M = Inspection) and<br>(neither f0.L nor f0.R are<br>undefined) and (f0.R) < ><br>S( )). |
|               | post-assertion: | (f.M = Inspection) and<br>(f.L = (f0.L⁻S(f0.R.first)))<br>and (f.R = f0.R.rest) and<br>if f.R = S( ) then (f^ is<br>totally-undefined)<br>else (f^ = f.R.first). |

When the file-variable f possesses a type other than that denoted by text, the required procedures read and write shall be defined as follows.

| read | Read(f,vl, . . . ,vn) where vl . . . vn denote variable-accesses shall be equivalent to<br>   begin read(f,vl); . . . ; read(f,vn) end<br>Read(f,v) where v denotes a variable-access shall be equiv-<br>alent to<br>   begin v:= f^; get(f) end |
|------|---------------------------------------------------------------------------------------|

NOTE. The variable-access is not a variable parameter. Consequently it may be a component of a packed structure and the value of the buffer-variable need only be assignment-compatible with it.

Write(f,e1, . . . ,en), where e1 . . . en denote expressions shall be equivalent to

begin write(f,e1); . . . ; write(f,en) end

Write(f,e), where e denotes an expression shall be equivalent to

begin f^ := put(f) end

NOTES

1.  The required procedures read, write, readln, writeln, and page, as applied to textfiles, are described in 6.9.
2.  Since the definitions of read and write include the use of get and put, the implementation-defined aspects of their post-asssertions also apply.

*6.6.5.3.  Dynamic Allocation Procedures*

new(p)                   shall create a new variable that is totally-undefined, shall create a new identifying-value of the pointer-type associated with p, that identifies the new variable, and shall attribute this identifying-value to the variable denoted by the variable-access p. The created variable shall possess the type that is the domain-type of the pointer-type possessed by p.

new(p,c1, . . . ,cn)     shall create a new variable that is totally-undefined, shall create a new identifying-value of the pointer-type associated with p, that identifies the new variable, and shall attribute this identifying-value to the variable denoted by the variable-access p. The created variable shall possess the record-type that is the domain-type of the pointer-type possessed by p and shall have nested variants that correspond to the case-constants c1, . . . cn. The case-constants shall be listed in order of increasing nesting of the variant-parts. Any variant not specified shall be at a deeper level

|  | of nesting than that specified by cn. It shall be an error if a variant of a variant-part within the new variable becomes active and a different variant of the variant-part is one of the specified variants. |
|---|---|
| dispose(q) | shall remove the identifying-value denoted by the expression q from the pointer-type of q. It shall be an error if the identifying-value had been created using the form new(p,c1, . . . ,cn). |
| dispose(q,k1, . . . ,km) | shall remove the identifying-value denoted by the expression q from the pointer-type of q. The case-constants k1, . . . km shall be listed in order of increasing nesting of the variant-parts. It shall be an error if the variable had been created using the form new(p,c1, . . . ,cn) and m is less than n. It shall be an error if the variants in the variable identified by q^ are different from those specified by the case-constants k1, . . . ,km. |

NOTE. The removal of an identifying-value from the pointer-type to which it belongs renders the identified variable inaccessible (see 6.5.4) and makes undefined all variables and functions that have that value attributed (see 6.8.2.2).

It shall be an error if q has a nil-value or is undefined.

It shall be an error if a variable created using the second form of new is accessed by the identified-variable of the variable-access of a factor, of an assignment-statement, or of an actual-parameter.

*6.6.5.4.   Transfer Procedures.*   Let a be a variable possessing a type that can be denoted by array [s2] of T. Let z be a variable possessing a type that can be denoted by packed array [s2] of T, and u and v be the smallest and largest values of the type s2, then the statement pack(a,i,z) shall be equivalent to

```
begin
k := i;
for j := u to v do
```

```
begin
z[j] := a[k];
if j < > v then k := succ(k)
end
end
```

and the statement unpack(z,a,i) shall be equivalent to

```
begin
k := i;
for j := u to v do
  begin
  a[k] := z[j];
  if j < > v then k := succ(k)
  end
end
```

where j and k denote auxiliary variables which the program does not otherwise contain. The type possessed by j shall be s2, the type possessed by k shall be s1, and i shall be an expression whose value shall be assignment-compatible with s1.

### 6.6.6.  Required Functions

*6.6.6.1.  General.*  The required functions shall be arithmetic functions, transfer functions, ordinal functions, and Boolean functions.

*6.6.6.2.  Arithmetic Functions.*  For the following arithmetic functions, the expression x shall be either of real-type or integer-type. For the functions abs and sqr, the type of the result shall be the same as the type of the parameter, x. For the remaining arithmetic functions, the result shall always be of real-type.

| | |
|---|---|
| abs(x) | shall compute the absolute value of x. |
| sqr(x) | shall compute the square of x. It shall be an error if such a value does not exist. |
| sin(x) | shall compute the sine of x, where x is in radians. |
| cos(x) | shall compute the cosine of x, where x is in radians. |
| exp(x) | shall compute the value of the base of natural logairthms raised to the power x. |
| ln(x) | shall compute the natural logarithm of x, if x is greater than zero. It shall be an error if x is not greater than zero. |
| sqrt(x) | shall compute the non-negative square root of x, if x is not negative. It shall be an error if x is negative. |
| arctan(x) | shall compute the principal value, in radians, of the arctangent of x. |

*6.6.6.3. Transfer Functions*

| | |
|---|---|
| trunc(x) | From the expression x that shall be of real-type, this function shall return a result of integer-type. The value of trunc(x) shall be such that if x is positive or zero then 0<=x−trunc(x)<1; otherwise −1<x−trunc(x)<=0. It shall be an error if such a value does not exist. |

Examples:
trunc(3.5) yields 3
trunc(−3.5) yields −3

round(x)      From the expression x that shall be of real-type, this function shall return a result of integer-type. If x is positive or zero, round(x) shall be equivalent to trunc(x+0.5), otherwise round(x) shall be equivalent to trunc(x−0.5). It shall be an error if such a value does not exist.

Examples:
round(3.5) yields 4
round(−3.5) yields −4

*6.6.6.4. Ordinal Functions*

ord(x)      From the expression x that shall be of an ordinal-type, this function shall return a result of integer-type that shall be the ordinal number (see 6.4.2.2 and 6.4.2.3) of the value of the expression x.

chr(x)      From the expression x that shall be of integer-type, this function shall return a result of char-type which shall be the value whose ordinal number is equal to the value of the expression x if such a character value exists. It shall be an error if such a character value does not exist.

For any value, ch, of char-type, the following shall be true:
chr(ord(ch)) = ch

succ(x)      From the expression x that shall be of an ordinal-type, this function shall return a result that shall be of the same type as that of the expression (see 6.7.1). The function shall yield a value whose ordinal number is one greater than that of the expression x, if such a value exists. It shall be an error if such a value does not exist.

pred(x)      From the expression x that shall be of an ordinal-type, this function shall return a result that shall be of the same type as that of the expression (see 6.7.1). The function shall yield a value whose ordinal number is one less than that of the expression x, if such a value exists. It shall be an error if such a value does not exist.

*6.6.6.5.    Boolean Functions*

odd(x) From the expression x that shall be of integer-type, this function shall be equivalent to the expression (abs(x) mod 2 = 1).

eof(f) the parameter f shall be a file-variable; if the actual-parameter-list is omitted, the function shall be applied to the required textfile input (see 6.10). When eof(f) is activated, it shall be an error if f is undefined; otherwise the function shall yield the value true if f.R is the empty sequence (see 6.4.3.5), otherwise false.

eoln(f) the parameter f shall be a textfile; if the actual-parameter-list is omitted, the function shall be applied to the required textfile input (see 6.10). When eoln(f) is activated, it shall be an error if f is undefined or if eof(f) is true; otherwise the function shall yield the value true if f.R.first is an end-of-line component (see 6.4.3.5), otherwise false.

## 6.7. Expressions

### *6.7.1. General*

An expression shall denote a value unless a variable denoted by a variable-access contained by the expression is undefined at the time of its use, in which case that use shall be an error. The use of a variable-access as a factor shall denote the value, if any, attributed to the variable accessed thereby. Operator precedences shall be according to four classes of operators as follows. The operator not shall have the highest precedence, followed by the multiplying-operators, then the adding-operators and signs, and finally, with the lowest precedence, the relational-operators. Sequences of two or more operators of the same precedence shall be left associative.

unsigned-constant = unsigned-number | character-string | constant-identifier | "nil" .

factor > variable-access | unsigned-constant | function-designator | set-constructor | "(" expression ")" | "not" factor .

NOTE. There is also a syntax rule for factor in 6.6.3.7.

set-constructor = "[" [ member-designator { "," member-designator } ] "]" .

term = factor { multiplying-operator factor } .

simple-expression = [ sign ] term { adding-operator term } .

expression = simple-expression [ relational-operator simple-expression ] .

Any factor whose type is S, where S is a subrange of T, shall be treated as of type T. Similarly, any factor whose type is set of S shall be treated as of the unpacked canonical set-of-T type, and any factor whose type is packed set of S shall be treated as of the canonical packed set-of-T type.

NOTE. Consequently an expression that consists of a single factor of type S shall itself be of type T, and an expression that consists of a single factor of type set of S shall itself be of type set of T, and an expression that consists of a single factor of type packed set of S shall itself be of type packed set of T.

A set-constructor shall denote a value of a set-type. The set-constructor [] shall denote that value in every set-type that contains no members. A set-constructor containing one or more member-designators shall denote either a value of the unpacked canonical set-of-T type or, if the context so requires, the packed canonical set-of-T type, where T is the type of every expression of each member-designator of the set-constructor. The type T shall be an ordinal-type. The value denoted by the set-constructor shall contain zero or more members each of which shall be denoted by at least one member-designator of the set-constructor.

The member-designator x, where x is an expression, shall denote the member that shall have the value x. The member-designator x . . y, where x and y are expressions, shall denote zero or more members that shall have the values of the base-type in the closed interval from the value of x to the value of 7.

NOTE. The member-designator x . . y denotes no members if the value of x is greater than the value of y.

Examples are as follows:

| | | |
|---|---|---|
| (a) | Factors: | x |
| | | 15 |
| | | (x+y+z) |
| | | sin(x+y) |
| | | [red,c,green] |
| | | [1,5,10 . . 19,23] |
| | | not p |
| (b) | Terms: | x*y |
| | | i/(1−i) |
| | | (x <= y) and (y < z) |
| (c) | Simple expressions: | p or q |
| | | x+y |
| | | −x |
| | | hue1 + hue2 |
| | | i*j + 1 |
| (d) | Expressions: | x = 1.5 |
| | | p <= q |
| | | p <= q and r |
| | | (i < j) = (j < k) |
| | | c in hue1 |

### 6.7.2. *Operators*

#### 6.7.2.1. *General*

multiplying-operator = "*" | "/" | "div" | "mod" | "and" .
adding-operator = "+" | "−" | "or" .
relational-operator = "=" | "< >" | "<" | ">" | "<=" | ">=" | "in" .

A factor, or a term, or a simple-expression shall be designated an operand. The order of evaluation of the operands of a dyadic operator shall be implementation-dependent.

NOTE. This means, for example, that the operands may be evaluated in textual order, or in reverse order, or in parallel or they may not both be evaluated.

#### 6.7.2.2. *Arithmetic Operators.*  The types of operands and results for dyadic and monadic operations shall be as shown in tables 2 and 3, respectively.

NOTE. The symbols +, −, and * are also used as set operators (see 6.7.2.4).

A term of the form x/y shall be an error if y is zero, otherwise the value of x/y shall be the result of dividing x by y.

A term of the form i div j shall be an error if j is zero, othewise the value of i div j shall be such that

$$abs(i) - abs(j) < abs((i\ div\ j) * j) <= abs(i)$$

where the value shall be zero if abs(i)<abs(j), otherwise the sign of the value shall be positive if i and j have the same sign and negative if i and j have different signs.

**TABLE 2.  Dyadic Arithmetic Operations**

| Operator | Operation | Type of Operands | Type of Result |
|---|---|---|---|
| + | addition | integer-type or real-type | integer-type if both |
| − | subtraction | integer-type or real-type | operands are of integer-type |
| * | multiplication | integer-type or real-type | otherwise real-type |
| / | division | integer-type or real-type | real-type |
| div | division with truncation | integer-type | integer-type |
| mod | modulo | integer-type | integer-type |

TABLE 3.   Monadic Arithmetic Operations

| Operator | Operation | Type of Operands | Type of Result |
|---|---|---|---|
| + | identity | integer-type<br>real-type | integer-type<br>real-type |
| − | sign-inversion | integer-type<br>real-type | integer-type<br>real-type |

A term of the form i and j shall be an error if j is zero or negative, otherwise the value of i mod j shall be that value of (i−(k∗j)) for integral k such that 0 <= i mod j < j.

NOTE. Only for i >= 0 does the relation (i div j) ∗ j + i mod j = i hold.

The required constant-identifier maxint shall denote an implementation-defined value of integer-type. This value shall satisfy the following conditions:

(a)   All integral values in the closed interval from −maxint to +maxint shall be values of the integer-type.

(b)   Any monadic operation performed on an integer value in this interval shall be correctly performed according to the mathematical rules for integer arithmetic.

(c)   Any dyadic integer operation on two integer values in this same interval shall be correctly performed according to the mathematical rules for integer arithmetic, provided that the result is also in this interval.

(d)   Any relational operation on two integer values in this same interval shall be correctly performed according to the mathematical rules for integer arithmetic.

The results of the real arithmetic operators and functions shall be approximations to the corresponding mathematical results. The accuracy of this approximation shall be implementation-defined.

It shall be an error if an integer operation or function is not performed according to the mathematical rules for integer arithmetic.

*6.7.2.3.   Boolean operators.*   Operands and results for Boolean operations shall be of Boolean-type, Boolean operators or, and, and not shall denote respectively the logical operations of disjunction, conjunction, and negation.

Boolean-expression = expression .

A Boolean-expression shall be an expression that denotes a value of Boolean-type.

*6.7.2.4.   Set Operators.*   The types of operands and results for set operations shall be as shown in table 4.

TABLE 4.    Set Operations

| Operator | Operation | Type of Operands | Type of Result |
|---|---|---|---|
| + | set union | ⎫ | ⎫ |
| | | a | same as the |
| − | set difference | canonical | operands |
| | | set-of-T type | |
| * | set intersection | ⎭ | ⎭ |

*6.7.2.5.    Relational Operators.*    The types of operands and results for relational operations shall be as shown in table 5.

The operands of =, < >, <, >, >=, and <= shall be either of compatible types, the same canonical get-of-T type, or one operand shall be of real-type and the other shall be of integer-type.

The operators =, < >, <, > shall stand for "equal to," "not equal to," "less than," and "greater than," respectively.

Except when applied to sets, the operators <= and >= shall stand for "less than or equal to" and "greater than or equal to," respectively.

Where u and v denote simple-expressions of a get-type, u <= v shall denote the inclusion of u in v and u >= v shall denote the inclusion of v in u.

NOTE. Since the Boolean-type is an ordinal-type with false less than true, then if p and q are operands of Boolean-type, p = q denotes their equivalence and p < q means p implies q.

When the relational operators =, < >, <, >, <=, >= are used to compare operands of compatible string-types (see 6.4.3.2), they denote lexicographic relations

TABLE 5.    Relational Operations

| Operator | Type of Operands | Type of Result |
|---|---|---|
| = < > | any simple, pointer or string-type or canonical set-of-T type | Boolean-type |
| < > | any simple or string-type | Boolean-type |
| <= >= | any simple or string-type or canonical set-of-T type | Boolean-type |
| in | left operand:any ordinal type T right operand: a canonical set-of-T type (see 6.7.1) | Boolean-type |

defined below. Lexicographic ordering imposes a total ordering on values of a string-type. If s1 and s2 are two values of compatible string-types then,

s1 = s2 iff for all i in [1 .. n]: s1[i] = s2[i]
s1 < s2 iff there exists a p in [1 .. n]: (for all i in [1 .. p−1]: s1[i] = s2(i])
   and s1[p] < s2[p]

The operator in shall yield the value true if the value of the operand of ordinal-type is a member of the value of the set-type, otherwise it shall yield the value false.

#### 6.7.3.  Function Designators

A function-designator shall yield the value of the function denoted by the function-identifier of the function-designator. The function-designator shall specify the activation of the function. If the function has any formal parameters the function-designator shall contain a list of actual-parameters that shall be bound to their corresponding formal parameters defined in the function-declaration. The correspondence shall be established by the positions of the parameters in the lists of actual and formal parameters, respectively. The number of actual-parameters shall be equal to the number of formal parameters. The types of the actual-parameters shall correspond to the types of the formal parameters as specified by 6.6.3. The order of evaluation, accessing and binding of the actual-parameters shall be implementation-dependent.

function-designator = function-identifier [ actual-parameter-list ] .
actual-parameter-list = "(" actual-parameter { "," actual-parameter } ")" .
actual-parameter = expression | variable-access | procedure-identifier |
         function-identifier .

Examples:

Sum(a,63)
GCD(147,k)
sin(x+y)
eof(f)
ord(f^)

#### 6.8.  Statements

#### 6.8.1.  General

Statements shall denote algorithmic actions, and shall be executable. They may be prefixed by a label.

A label occurring in a statement S shall be designated as prefixing S, and shall be allowed to occur in a goto-statement G (see 6.8.2.4) if and only if any of the following three conditions is satisfied.

(a)  S contains G.

(b)  S is a statement of a statement-sequence containing G.

(c)  S is a statement of the statement-sequence of the compound-statement of the statement-part of a block containing G.

> statement = [ label ":" ] ( simple-statement | structured-statement ) .

NOTE. A goto-statement within a block may refer to a label in an enclosing block, provided that the label prefixes a simple-statement or structured-statement at the outermost level of nesting of the block.

### 6.8.2.  *Simple-Statements*

*6.8.2.1.  General.*  A simple-statement shall be a statement not containing a statement. An empty-statement shall contain no symbol and shall denote no action.

> simple-statement = empty-statement | assignment-statement |
>                    procedure-statement |
>                    goto-statement .
> empty-statement = .

*6.8.2.2.  Assignment-Statements.*  An assignment-statement shall attribute the value of the expression of the assignment-statement either to the variable denoted by the variable-access of the assignment-statement, or to the function-identifier of the assignment-statement; the value shall be assignment-compatible with the type possessed by the variable or function-identifier. The function-block associated (6.6.2) with the function-identifier of an assignment-statement shall contain the assignment-statement.

> assignment-statement = ( variable-access | function-identifier ) ":=" expression .

The decision as to the order of accessing the variable and evaluating the expression shall be implementation-dependent; the access shall establish a reference to the variable during the remaining execution of the assignment-statement.

The state of a variable or function when the variable or function does not have attributed to it a value specified by its type shall be designated undefined. If a variable possesses a structured-type, the state of the variable when every component of the variable is totally-undefined shall be designated totally-undefined. Totally-undefined shall be synonymous with undefined if the variable does not possess a structured-type.

> x := y+z
> p := (1<=i) and (i<100)
> i := sqr(k) − (i∗j)
> hue1 := [blue,succ(c)]
> p1^.mother := true

*6.8.2.3. Procedure-Statements.* A procedure-statement shall specify the activation of the block of the procedure-block associated with the procedure-identifier of the procedure-statement. If the procedure has any formal parameters the procedure-statement shall contain an actual-parameter-list, which is a list of actual-parameters that shall be bound to their corresponding formal parameters defined in the procedure-declaration. The correspondence shall be established by the positions of the parameters in the lists of actual and formal parameters, respectively. The number of actual-parameters shall be equal to the number of formal parameters. The types of the actual-parameters shall correspond to the types of the formal parameters as specified by 6.6.3. The order of evaluation, accessing and binding of the actual-parameters shall be implementation-dependent.

> procedure-statement = procedure-identifier [ actual-parameter-list ] .

Examples:

> printheading
> transpose(a,n,m)
> bisect(fct,−1.0,+1.0,x)
> AddVectors(m[1],(m[2]),(m[k]))

*6.8.2.4. Goto-Statements.* A goto-statement shall indicate that further processing is to continue at the program-point denoted by the label in the goto-statement and shall cause the termination of all activations except

(a)   the activation containing the program-point and

(b)   any activation containing the activation-point of an activation required by these exceptions not to be terminated.

### 6.8.3. Structured-Statements

*6.8.3.1. General*

> structured-statement = compound-statement | conditional-statement |
>                        repetitive-statement | with-statement .
> statement-sequence = statement { ";" statement } .

The execution of a statement-sequence specifies the execution of the statements of the statement-sequence in textual order, except as modified by execution of a goto-statement.

*6.8.3.2. Compound-Statements.* A compound-statement shall specify execution of the statement-sequence of the compound-statement.

> compound-statement = "begin" statement-sequence "end" .

Examples:

> begin z := x ; x := y; y := z end

### 6.8.3.3.   Conditional-Statements

> conditional-statement = if-statement : case-statement .

### 6.8.3.4.   If-Statements

> if-statement = "if" Boolean-expression "then" statement [ else-part ] .
> else-part = "else" statement .

If the Boolean-expression of the if-statement yields the value true, the statement of the if-statement shall be executed. If the Boolean-expression yields the value false, the statement of the if-statement shall not be executed and the statement of the else-part (if any) shall be executed.

An if-statement without an else-part shall not be followed by the token else.

NOTE. An else-part is thus paired with the nearest preceding otherwise unpaired then.

Examples:

> if x < 1.5 then z := x+y else z := 1.5
> if p1 < > nil then p1 := p1^.father
> if j = 0
>    if i = 0 then writeln('indefinite')
>    else writeln('infinite')
> else writeln( i/j )

### 6.8.3.5.   Case-Statements.

The values denoted by the case-constants of the case-constant-lists of the case-list-elements of a case-statement shall be distinct and of the same ordinal-type as the expression of the case-index of the case-statement. On execution of the case-statement the case-index shall be evaluated. That value shall then specify execution of the statement of the case-list-element closest-containing the case-constant denoting that value. One of the case-constants shall be equal to the value of the case-index upon entry to the case-statement.

It shall be an error if none of the case-constants is equal to the value of the case-index upon entry to the case-statement.

NOTE. Case-constants are not the same as statement labels.

> case-statement =
>    "case" case-index "of"
>    case-list-element {";" case-list-element } [";"] "end" .
> case-list-element = case-constant-list ":" statement .
> case-index = expression .

Example:

```
case operator of
   plus:    x := x+y;
   minus:   x := x−y;
   times:   x := x*y
end
```

*6.8.3.6.  Repetitive-Statements.*    Repetitive-statements shall specify that certain statements are to be executed repeatedly.

repetitive-statement = repeat-statement | while-statement | for-statement .

*6.8.3.7.  Repeat-Statements*

repeat-statement = "repeat" statement-sequence "until" Boolean-expression .

The statement-sequence of the repeat-statement shall be repeatedly executed (except as modified by the execution of a goto-statement) until the Boolean-expression of the repeat-statement yields the value true on completion of the statement-sequence. The statement-sequence shall be executed at least once, because the Boolean-expression is evaluated after execution of the statement-sequence.

Example:

```
repeat k := i mod j;
   i := j;
   j := k
until j = 0
```

*6.8.3.8.  While-Statements*

while-statement = "while" Boolean-expression "do" statement .

The while-statement

```
while b do body
```

shall be equivalent to

```
begin
if b then
   repeat
   body
   until not (b)
end
```

Examples:

```
while i>0 do
    begin if odd(i) then z := z*x;
    i := i div 2;
    x := sqr(s)
end
while not eof(f) do
    begin process(f^ ); set(f)
end
```

*6.8.3.9.    For-Statements.*   The for-statement shall specify that the statement of the for-statement is to be repeatedly executed while a progression of values is attributed to a variable that is designated the control-variables of the for-statement.

```
for-statement  =  "for" control-variable ":=" initial-value ( "to" | "downto" )
                  final-value "do" statement .
control-variable  =  entire-variable .
initial-value  =  expression .
final-value  =  expression .
```

The control-variable shall be an entire-variable whose identifier is declared in the variable-declaration-part of the block closest-containing the for-statement. The control-variable shall possess an ordinal-type, and the initial-value and final-value shall be of a type compatible with this type. The statement of a for-statement shall not contain an assigning-reference (see 6.5.1) to the control-variable of the for-statement. The value of the final-value shall be assignment-compatible with the control-variable when the initial-value is assigned to the control-variable. After a for-statement is executed (other than being left by a goto-statement leading out of it) the control-variable shall be undefined. Apart from the restrictions imposed by these requirements, the for-statement

```
                    for v:= e1 to e2 do body
```

shall be equivalent to

```
            begin
            temp1 := e1;
            temp2 := e2;
            if temp2 <= temp2 then
                begin
                v := temp1;
                body;
                while v < > temp2 do
                    begin
                    v := succ(v);
```

```
                    body
                end
            end
        end
```

and the for-statement

```
        for v := e1 downto e2 do body
```

shall be equivalent to

```
            begin
            temp1 := e1;
            temp2 := e2;
            if temp1 >= temp2 then
                begin
                v := temp1;
                body;
                while v < > temp2 do
                    begin
                    v := pred(v);
                    body
                   ` end
                end
            end
```

where temp1 and temp2 denote auxiliary variables that the program does not otherwise contain, and that possess the type possessed by the variable v if that type is not a subrange-type; otherwise the host type of the type possessed by the variable v.

Examples:

```
        for i := 2 to 63 do
            for a[i] > max then max := a[i]
```

Examples:

```
        for i := 1 to 10 do
            for j := 1 to 10 do
                begin
                x := 0;
                for k := 1 to 10 do
                    x := x + m1[i,k]*m2[k,j];
                m[i,j] := x
                end
```

```
for i := 1 to 10 do
  for j := 1 to i-1 do
    m[i][j] := 0.0
for c := blue downto red do q(c)
```

## 6.8.3.10. With-Statements

with-statement = "with" record-variable-list "do" statement .
record-variable-list = record-variable { "," record-variable } .

A with-statement shall specify the execution of the statement of the with-statement. The occurrence of a record-variable as the only record-variable in the record-variable-list of a with-statement shall constitute a defining-point of each of the field-identifiers associated with components of the record-type possessed by the record-variable as a field-designator-identifier for the region which is the statement of the with-statement; each applied occurrence of a field-designator-identifier shall denote that component of the record-variable which is associated with the field-identifier by the record-type. The record-variable shall be accessed before the statement of the with-statement is executed, and that access shall establish a reference to the variable during the entire execution of the statement of the with-statement.

The statement

```
with v1,v2, . . . ,vn do s
```

shall be equivalent to

```
with v1 do
  with v2 do
    . . .
      with vn do s
```

Example:

```
with date do
if month = 12 then
  begin month := 1; year := year + 1
  end
else month := month+1
```

shall be equivalent to

```
if date.month = 12 then
  begin date.month := 1; date.year := date.year+1
  end
else date.month := date.month+1
```

## 6.9.  Input and Output

### 6.9.1.  General

Textfiles (see 6.4.3.5) that are identified in the program-parameters (see 6.10) to a Pascal program shall provide legible input and output.

### 6.9.2.  The Procedure Read

The syntax of the parameter list of read when applied to a textfile shall be:

read-parameter-list  =  "(" [file-variable ","] variable-access
                        {"," variable-access}")" .

If the file-variable is omitted, the procedure shall be applied to the required textfile input.

   The following requirements shall apply for the procedure read (where f denotes a textfile and v1 . . . vn denote variable-accesses possessing the char-type (or a sub-range of char-type), the integer-type (or a subrange of integer-type), or the real-type):

(a)   read(f,v1, . . . ,vn) shall be equivalent to

begin read(f,v1); . . . ; read(f,vn) end

(b)   If v is a variable-access possessing the char-type (or subrange thereof), read(f,v) shall be equivalent to

begin v := f^; set(f) end

NOTE. The variable-access is not a variable parameter. Consequently it may be a component of a packed structure and the value of the buffer-variable need only be assignment-compatible with it.

(c)   If v is a variable-access possessing the integer-type (or subrange thereof), read(f,v) shall cause the reading from f of a sequence of characters. Preceding spaces and end-of-lines shall be skipped. It shall be an error if the rest of the sequence does not form a signed-integer according to the syntax of 6.1.5. The value of the signed-integer thus read shall be assignment-compatible with the type possessed by v, and shall be attributed to v. Reading shall cease as soon as the buffer-variable f^ does not have attributed to it a character contained by the longest sequence available that forms a signed-integer.

(d)   if v is a variable-access possessing the real-type, read(f,v) shall cause the reading from f of a sequence of characters. Preceding spaces and end-of-lines shall be skipped. It shall be an error if the rest of the sequence does not form a signed-number according to the syntax of 6.1.5. The value de-noted by the number thus read shall be attributed to the variable v. Reading shall cease as soon as the buffer-variable f^ does not have attributed to it a character contained by the longest sequence available that forms a signed-number.

(e)    When read is applied to f, it shall be an error if the buffer-variable f̂ is undefined or the pre-assertions for set do not hold (see 6.4.3.5).

### 6.9.3.    The Procedure Readln

The syntax of the parameter list of readln shall be:

> readln-parameter-list  =  ["(" 'file-variable | variable-access)
> {"," variable-access} ")"] .

Readln shall only be applied to textfiles. If the file-variable or the entire readln-parameter-list is omitted, the procedure shall be applied to the required textfile input.

> readln(f,v1, . . . ,vn) shall be equivalent to
> begin read(f,v1, . . . ,vn); readln(f) end
> readln(f) shall be equivalent to
> begin while not eoln(f) do get(f); get(f) end

NOTE. The effect of readln is to place the current file position just past the end of the current line in the textfile. Unless this is the end-of-file position, the current file position is therefore at the start of the next line.

### 6.9.4.    The Procedure Write

The syntax of the parameter list of write when applied to a textfile shall be:

> write-parameter-list  =  "("[file-variable ","] write-parameter
> {"," write-parameter}")" .
> write-parameter  =  expression [":" expression [":" expression ]] .

If the file-variable is omitted, the procedure shall be applied to the required textfile output. When write is applied to a textfile f, it shall be an error if f is undefined or f.M = Inspection (see 6.4.3.5). An application of write to a textfile f shall cause the buffer-variable f̂ to become undefined.

#### 6.9.4.1.    Multiple Parameters.    Write(f,p1, . . . ,pn) shall be equivalent to

> begin write(f,p1); . . . ; write(f,pn) end

where f denotes a textfile, and p1, . . . ,pn denote write-parameters.

*6.9.4.2. Write-Parameters.*    The write-parameters p shall have the following forms:

$$\text{e:TotalWidth:FracDigits} \qquad \text{e:TotalWidth} \qquad \text{e}$$

where e is an expression whose value is to be written on the file f and may be of integer-type, real-type, char-type, Boolean-type, or a string-type, and where Total-Width and FracDigits are expressions of integer-type whose values are the field-width parameters. The values of TotalWidth and FracDigits shall be greater than or equal to one; it shall be an error if either value is less than one.

Write(f,e) shall be equivalent to the form write(f,e:TotalWidth), using a default value for TotalWidth that depends on the type of e; for integer-type, real-type, and Boolean-type the default values shall be implementation-defined.

Write(f,e:TotalWidth:FracDigits) shall be applicable only if e is of real-type (see 6.9.4.5.2)

*6.9.4.3. Char-Type.*    If e is of char-type, the default value of TotalWidth shall be one. The representation written on the file f shall be:

$$(\text{TotalWidth} - 1) \text{ spaces,}$$
$$\text{the character value of e .}$$

*6.9.4.4. Integer-Type.*    If e is of integer-type, the decimal representation of e shall be written on the file f. Assume a function

$$\text{function IntegerSize ( x : integer ) : integer;}$$
$$\text{\{ returns the number of digits, } z \text{, such that}$$
$$10 \text{ to the power } (z-1) <= \text{abs}(x) < 10 \text{ to the power } z \text{ \}}$$

and let IntDigits be the positive integer defined by:

$$\text{if e = 0}$$
$$\text{then IntDigits := 1}$$
$$\text{else IntDigits := IntegerSize(e);}$$

Then the representation shall consist of:

1. If TotalWidth >= IntDigits + 1: (TotalWidth − IntDigits − 1) spaces, the sign character: '−' if e < 0, otherwise a space, IntDigits digit-characters of the decimal representation of abs(e).
2. If TotalWidth < IntDigits + 1: if e < 0 the sign character '−', IntDigits digit-characters of the decimal representation of abs(e).

*6.9.4.5. Real-Type.*    If e is of real-type, a decimal representation of the number e, rounded to the specified number of significant figures or decimal places, shall be written on the file f.

*6.9.4.5.1.   The Floating-Point Representation.*   Write(f,e:TotalWidth) shall cause
a floating-point representation of e to be written. Assume functions

```
function TenPower ( Int : integer ) : real ;
  { Returns 10.0 raised to the power Int }
function RealSize ( y : real ) : integer ;
  { Returns the value, z, such that
  TenPower(z−1) <= abs(y) < TenPower(z) }
    function Truncate ( y : real; DecPlaces : integer )
    : real ;
    { Returns the value of y after truncation
    to DecPlaces decimal places }
```

Let ExpDigits be an implementation-defined value representing the number of digit-
characters written in an exponent; let ActWidth be the positive integer defined by:

```
if TotalWidth >= ExpDigits + 6
  then ActWidth := TotalWidth
  else ActWidth := ExpDigits + 6;
```

and let the non-negative number eWritten and the integer ExpValue be defined by:

```
if e = 0.0
  then begin eWritten := 0.0; ExpValue := 0 end
  else
  begin
  eWritten := abs(e);
  ExpValue := RealSize ( eWritten ) − 1;
  eWritten := eWritten / TenPower ( ExpValue );
  DecPlaces := ActWidth−ExpDigits−5;
  eWritten := eWritten +
    0.5*TenPower( −Decplaces );
  if eWritten >= 10.0
    then
    begin
    eWritten := eWritten / 10.0;
    ExpValue := ExpValue + 1
    end;
  eWritten := Truncate ( eWritten, DecPlaces )
  end;
```

Then the floating-point representation of the value of e shall consist of:

```
the sign character,
  ( '−' if (e < 0) and (eWritten > 0), otherwise a space )
```

> the leading digit-character of the decimal
>     representation of eWritten,
> the character '.' ,
> the next DecPlaces digit-characters
>     of the decimal representation of eWritten,
> an implementation-defined exponent character
>     (either 'e' or 'E'),
> the sign of ExpValue
>     ( '−' if ExpValue < 0, otherwise '+' ),
> the ExpDigits digit-characters of the decimal
>     representation of ExpValue
>     (with leading zeros if the value requires them).

*6.9.4.5.2.    The Fixed-Point Representation.*    Write(f,e:TotalWidth:FracDigits) shall cause a fixed-point representation of e to be written. Assume the function IntegerSize described in clause 6.9.4.4, and the functions TenPower and Truncate described in clause 6.9.4.5.1; let eWritten be the non-negative number defined by:

> if e = 0.0
>     then eWritten := 0.0
>     else
>     begin
>     eWritten := abs(e);
>     eWritten := eWritten + 0.5
>         * TenPower ( − FracDigits );
>     eWritten := Truncate ( eWritten, FracDigits )
>     end;

Let IntDigits be the positive integer defined by:

> if trunc ( eWritten ) = 0
>     then IntDigits := 1
>     else IntDigits:= IntegerSize ( trunc(eWritten) );

and let MinNumChars be the positive integer defined by:

> MinNumChars := IntDigits + FracDigits + 1;
>     if (e < 0.0) and (eWritten > 0)
>         then MinNumChars := MinNumChars + 1;{'−' required}

Then the fixed-point representation of the value of e shall consist of:

> if TotalWidth >= MinNumChars,
>     (TotalWidth − MinNumChars) spaces,
>     the character '−' if (e < 0) and (eWritten > 0),

the first IntDigits digit-characters of the decimal representation
of the value of eWritten,
the character '.',
the next FracDigits digit-characters of the decimal representation
of the value of eWritten.

NOTE. At least MinNumChars characters are written. If TotalWidth is less than this
value, no initial spaces are written.

*6.9.4.6.  Boolean-Type.*  If e is of Boolean-type, a representation of the word true
or the word false (as appropriate to the value of e) shall be written on the file f. This
shall be equivalent to writing the appropriate character-strings 'True' or 'False' (see
6.9.4.7), where the case of each letter is implementation-defined, with a field-width
parameter of TotalWidth.

*6.9.4.7.  String-Types.*  If the type of e is a string-type with n components, the
default value of TotalWidth shall be n. The representation shall consist of:

if TotalWidth > n,
(TotalWidth − n) spaces,
the first through nth characters of the value of e in that order.
if 1 <= TotalWidth <= n,
the first through TotalWidth characters in that order.

**6.9.5.  The Procedure Writeln**

The syntax of the parameter list of writeln shall be:

writeln-parameter-list =
["(" (file-variable | write-parameter)
{"," write-parameter}")"] .

Writeln shall only be applied to textfiles. If the file-variable or the writeln-parameter-
list is omitted, the procedure shall be applied to the required textfile output.

writeln(f,p1, . . . ,pn) shall be equivalent to
begin write(f,p1, . . . ,pn); writeln(f) end

Writeln shall be defined by a pre-assertion and a post-assertion using the notation of
6.6.5.2.

pre-assertion:     (f0 is not undefined) and (f0.M = Generation).
post-assertion:    (f.L = (f0.L⌃S(e))) and
                   (f⌃ is totally-undefined) and
                   (f.R = s()) and (f.M = Generation),

where s(e) is the sequence consisting solely of the
end-of-line component defined in 6.4.3.5.

NOTE. Writeln(f) terminates the partial line, if any, which is being generated. By the
conventions of 6.6.5.2 it is an error if the pre-assertion is not true prior to writeln(f).


*6.9.6. The Procedure Page*

It shall be an error if the pre-assertion required for writeln(f) (see 6.9.5) does not hold
prior to the activation of page(f). If the actual-parameter-list is omitted the procedure
shall be applied to the required textfile output. Page(f) shall cause an implementation-defined effect on the textfile f, such that subsequent text written to f will be on
a new page if the textfile is printed on a suitable device, shall perform an implicit
writeln(f) if f.L is not empty and if f.L.last is not the end-of-line component (see
6.4.3.5), and shall cause the buffer-variable f^ to become totally-undefined. The effect
of inspecting a textfile to which the page procedure was applied during generation
shall be implementation-dependent.


**6.10.  Programs**

program = program-heading ";" program-block "." .
program-heading = "program" identifier [ "(" program-parameters ")" ] .
program-parameters = identifier-list .
program-block = block .

The identifier of the program-heading shall be the program name which shall have
no significance within the program. The identifiers contained by the program-parameters shall be distinct and shall be designated program parameters. Each program
parameter shall be declared in the variable-declaration-part of the block of the program-block. The binding of the variables denoted by the program parameters to
entities external to the program shall be implementation-dependent, except if the
variable possesses a file-type in which case the binding shall be implementation-
defined.

NOTE. The external representation of such external entities is not defined by this
standard, nor is any property of a Pascal program dependent on such representation.
The occurrence of the identifier input or the identifier output as a program parameter
shall constitute its defining-point for the region that is the program-block as a variable-identifier of the required type denoted by text. Such occurrence of the identifier
input shall cause the post-assertions of reset to hold, and of output, the post-assertions of rewrite to hold, prior to the first access to the textfile or its associated
buffer-variable. The effect of the application of the required procedure reset or the
required procedure rewrite to either of these textfiles shall be implementation-defined.

Examples:

```
program copy(f,g);
var f,g: file of real;
begin reset(f); rewrite(g);
    while not eof(f) do
        begin g^ := f^; get(f); put(g)
        end
end.
```

```
program copytext(input,output);
{This program copies the characters and line structure of the
textfile input to the textfile output.}
var ch: char;
begin
    while not eof do
    begin
        while not eoln do
        begin read(ch); write(ch)
        end;
        readln; writeln
    end
end.
```

```
program t6p6p3p3d2revised(output);
var globalone, globaltwo : integer;

procedure dummy;
    begin
    writeln('fail4 . . . 6.6.4.3-2')
    end { of dummy };

procedure p(procedure f(procedure ff; procedure gg);
    procedure g);
    var localtop : integer;
    procedure r;
        begin
        if globalone = 1 then
            begin
            if (globaltwo < > 2) or (localtop < > 1) then
                writeln('fail1 . . . 6.6.3.3-2')
            end
        else if globalone = 2 then
            begin
            if (globaltwo < > 2) or (localtop <> 2) then
                writeln('fail2 . . . 6.6.3.3-2')
```

```
      else
          writeln('pass . . . 6.6.3.3-2')
      end
  else
      writeln('fail3 . . . 6.6.3.3-2');
      globalone := globalone + 1
  end { of r };
  begin { of p }
  globaltwo := globaltwo + 1;
  localtop := globaltwo;
  if globaltwo = 1 then
      p(f,r)
  else
      f(g,r)
  end { of p}:

procedure q(procedure f; procedure g);
  begin
  f;
  end { of q};

begin
globalone := 1;
globaltwo := 0;
p(q,dummy)
end.
```

## 6.11.  Hardware Representation

The representation for lexical tokens and separators given in 6.1 constitutes a reference representation for program interchange. A processor shall accept all the reference symbols and all the alternative symbols except for any symbol whose representation contains a character not available in the character set of the processor. The
reference symbols and the alternative symbols are given in table 6.

TABLE 6.   Alternative Symbols

| Reference Symbol | Alternative Symbol |
|---|---|
| ^ | @ or ↑ |
| { | (* |
| } | *) |
| [ | (. |
| ] | .) |

NOTES

1. The alternative comment delimiters are equivalent to the reference comment delimiters, thus a comment may begin with "{" and close with "*)", or begin with "(*" and close with "}".

2. For any other purpose than program interchange, this representation is not required, and so does not exclude the existence of other alternative symbols.

## COMMENTARY

Some of the notable features of the ISO Draft Standard over the standard Pascal defined by Jensen and Wirth are:

the use of a function or procedure heading

the introduction of a conformant array parameter, which is defined as compliance level 1

The point of the conformant array parameter is to permit the bounds of the index-type of an actual parameter to be restricted to a specified range of values, rather than be fixed. Such parameters would be utilized in library programs containing arrays, so that the bounds on the parameters can be determined at compile time.

In addition to the ISO Draft Standard, there are a number of other standardization efforts that attempt to establish even further extensions. The American National Standards Institute (ANSI), for example, is considering extensions which include such features as:

random access

structured constants

variable length strings

The feature of random access refers to the capability of accessing an individual file element by a number rather than the identifier. The facility used to implement this feature is a "seek" command, which is similar to that currently found in the OMSI Pascal implementation to be discussed in a later chapter.

Structured constants refer to the ability to have a constant identifier be associated with a structured data type.

Variable length strings are another proposal, along with associated string manipulation facilities such as concatenation, insertion, deletion, and substringing.

# 9

# Pascal:
# Sample Programs

Although this book is not intended as a programming text, it would be worthwhile to give a number of examples of Pascal programs in order to give the reader an appreciation of the application and use of the language. The present chapter therefore provides program examples in the following areas:

demonstration program
arithmetic operations
functional calculations
use of arrays
industrial applications

## DEMONSTRATION PROGRAM

The following Pascal program demonstrates the output facility:

```
program demo1 (output)
begin
writeln('the program works');
end.
```

When the above program is executed, the printer or CRT display will produce the following output:

the program works

Some variations of this basic program will illustrate other output facilities.

```
program demo1a (output)
const
  texta = 'Welcome';
  textb = 'to your new computer';
begin
  write (texta);
  write (textb)
end
```

will produce the output

Welcome to your new computer

The statements

```
begin
  writeln (texta)
  writeln (textb)
end
```

will produce the output which includes a carriage return:

Welcome
to your new computer

The following program demonstrates the use of both the input and the output facility:

```
program demo2(input, output)
var
  name : char;
begin
  read (name);
  writeln ('hello', name);
end.
```

This program operates by reading a character string, and then reprinting that same character string together with the word "hello." Thus, if the user inputs

John

the computer will respond with

hello John

## ARITHMETIC OPERATIONS

The following program illustrates a simple arithmetic calculation in Pascal. The program reads three input integers, calculates an arithmetic result, and prints "result is - - - -".

```
program math (input, output) ;
var
    a,b,c, result : integer ;
begin
    read(a,b,c) ;
    result := (a + z) * b * c ;
    writeln ('result is', result)
end.
```

## FUNCTIONAL CALCULATIONS

The following program illustrates the use of Pascal to perform simple functional calculations. A simple function "alpha" is defined, and various values of the function are calculated.

```
program alphatable (output) ;
var
    x : real ;
function alpha(x) : real ;
    begin
    alpha := x / sin(x)
    end ;
begin
    read(x);
    writeln('alpha(' , x,') equals' , alpha(x)) ;
end.
```

## THE USE OF ARRAYS

The use of arrays is illustrated in the following program for calculating prime numbers. The program also illustrates the response of the program when the maximum integer range of the hardware implementation is reached. An examination of the output will reveal that the last real prime computed was 32749. The following numbers are negative, and represent two's complements of the result.

```
program   primes (output)

const     n = 10000; nl = 100; m = 20 ;

var       i,k,x,inc,lim,square,l : integer ;
          prim : boolean ;
          p,v : array[1 . . . nl] of integer ;

begin     l := 0 ;
          x := 1; inc := 4; lim := 1, square := 9 ;
          for i := 3 to n do
          begin
              repeat x := x + inc; inc := 6 − inc
                 if square <= x then
                    begin lim := lim + 1 ;
                        v[lim] := square; square := sqr(p[lim + 1])
                    end

                 k := 2; prim := true ;
                 while prim and (k<lim) do
                 begin k := k+1 ;
                    if v[k] < x then v[k] := v[k] +  2 * p[k] ;
                    prim := x < > v[k]
                 end
              until prim;
              if i< nl then p[i] := x ;
              write (x); l = l − 1 ;
              if l = m then
                    begin writeln; l := 0
                    end
          end;
          writeln
end
```

TABLE 9.1.   Table of Primes (Validity from 5 to 32749)

| 5 | 7 | 11 | 13 | 17 | 19 | 23 | 29 | 31 | 37 | 41 | 43 |
|---|---|----|----|----|----|----|----|----|----|----|----|
| 47 | 53 | 59 | 61 | 67 | 71 | 73 | 79 | 83 | 89 | 97 | 101 |
| 103 | 107 | 109 | 113 | 127 | 131 | 137 | 139 | 149 | 151 | 157 | 163 |
| 167 | 173 | 179 | 181 | 191 | 193 | 197 | 199 | 211 | 223 | 227 | 229 |
| 233 | 239 | 241 | 251 | 257 | 263 | 269 | 271 | 277 | 281 | 283 | 293 |
| 307 | 311 | 313 | 317 | 331 | 337 | 347 | 349 | 353 | 359 | 367 | 373 |
| 379 | 383 | 389 | 397 | 401 | 409 | 419 | 421 | 431 | 433 | 439 | 443 |
| 449 | 457 | 461 | 463 | 467 | 479 | 487 | 491 | 499 | 503 | 509 | 521 |
| 523 | 541 | 547 | 557 | 563 | 569 | 571 | 577 | 587 | 593 | 599 | 601 |
| 607 | 613 | 617 | 619 | 631 | 641 | 643 | 647 | 653 | 659 | 661 | 673 |
| 677 | 683 | 691 | 701 | 709 | 719 | 727 | 733 | 739 | 743 | 751 | 757 |
| 761 | 769 | 773 | 787 | 797 | 809 | 811 | 821 | 823 | 827 | 829 | 839 |
| 853 | 857 | 859 | 863 | 877 | 881 | 883 | 887 | 907 | 911 | 919 | 929 |
| 937 | 941 | 947 | 953 | 967 | 971 | 977 | 983 | 991 | 997 | 1009 | 1013 |
| 1019 | 1021 | 1031 | 1033 | 1039 | 1049 | 1051 | 1061 | 1063 | 1069 | 1087 | 1091 |
| 1093 | 1097 | 1103 | 1109 | 1117 | 1123 | 1129 | 1151 | 1153 | 1163 | 1171 | 1181 |
| 1187 | 1193 | 1201 | 1213 | 1217 | 1223 | 1229 | 1231 | 1237 | 1249 | 1259 | 1277 |
| 1279 | 1283 | 1289 | 1291 | 1297 | 1301 | 1303 | 1307 | 1319 | 1321 | 1327 | 1361 |
| 1367 | 1373 | 1381 | 1399 | 1409 | 1423 | 1427 | 1429 | 1433 | 1439 | 1447 | 1451 |
| 1453 | 1459 | 1471 | 1481 | 1483 | 1487 | 1489 | 1493 | 1499 | 1511 | 1523 | 1531 |
| 1543 | 1549 | 1553 | 1559 | 1567 | 1571 | 1579 | 1583 | 1597 | 1601 | 1607 | 1609 |
| 1613 | 1619 | 1621 | 1627 | 1637 | 1657 | 1663 | 1667 | 1669 | 1693 | 1697 | 1699 |
| 1709 | 1721 | 1723 | 1733 | 1741 | 1747 | 1753 | 1759 | 1777 | 1783 | 1787 | 1789 |
| 1801 | 1811 | 1823 | 1831 | 1847 | 1861 | 1867 | 1871 | 1873 | 1877 | 1879 | 1889 |
| 1901 | 1907 | 1913 | 1931 | 1933 | 1949 | 1951 | 1973 | 1979 | 1987 | 1993 | 1997 |
| 1999 | 2003 | 2011 | 2017 | 2027 | 2029 | 2039 | 2053 | 2063 | 2069 | 2081 | 2083 |
| 2087 | 2089 | 2099 | 2111 | 2113 | 2129 | 2131 | 2137 | 2141 | 2143 | 2153 | 2161 |
| 2179 | 2203 | 2207 | 2213 | 2221 | 2237 | 2239 | 2243 | 2251 | 2267 | 2269 | 2273 |
| 2281 | 2287 | 2293 | 2297 | 2309 | 2311 | 2333 | 2339 | 2341 | 2347 | 2351 | 2357 |
| 2371 | 2377 | 2381 | 2383 | 2389 | 2393 | 2399 | 2411 | 2417 | 2423 | 2437 | 2441 |
| 2447 | 2459 | 2467 | 2473 | 2477 | 2503 | 2521 | 2531 | 2539 | 2543 | 2549 | 2551 |
| 2557 | 2579 | 2591 | 2593 | 2609 | 2617 | 2621 | 2633 | 2647 | 2657 | 2659 | 2663 |
| 2671 | 2677 | 2683 | 2687 | 2689 | 2693 | 2699 | 2707 | 2711 | 2713 | 2719 | 2729 |
| 2731 | 2741 | 2749 | 2753 | 2767 | 2777 | 2789 | 2791 | 2797 | 2801 | 2803 | 2819 |
| 2833 | 2837 | 2843 | 2851 | 2857 | 2861 | 2879 | 2887 | 2897 | 2903 | 2909 | 2917 |
| 2927 | 2939 | 2953 | 2957 | 2963 | 2969 | 2971 | 2999 | 3001 | 3011 | 3019 | 3023 |
| 3037 | 3041 | 3049 | 3061 | 3067 | 3079 | 3083 | 3089 | 3109 | 3119 | 3121 | 3137 |
| 3163 | 3167 | 3169 | 3181 | 3187 | 3191 | 3203 | 3209 | 3217 | 3221 | 3229 | 3251 |
| 3253 | 3257 | 3259 | 3271 | 3299 | 3301 | 3307 | 3313 | 3319 | 3323 | 3329 | 3331 |
| 3343 | 3347 | 3359 | 3361 | 3371 | 3373 | 3389 | 3391 | 3407 | 3413 | 3433 | 3449 |
| 3457 | 3461 | 3463 | 3467 | 3469 | 3491 | 3499 | 3511 | 3517 | 3527 | 3529 | 3533 |
| 3539 | 3541 | 3547 | 3557 | 3559 | 3571 | 3581 | 3583 | 3593 | 3607 | 3613 | 3617 |
| 3623 | 3631 | 3637 | 3643 | 3659 | 3671 | 3673 | 3677 | 3691 | 3697 | 3701 | 3709 |
| 3719 | 3727 | 3733 | 3739 | 3761 | 3767 | 3769 | 3779 | 3793 | 3797 | 3803 | 3821 |
| 3823 | 3833 | 3847 | 3851 | 3853 | 3863 | 3877 | 3881 | 3889 | 3907 | 3911 | 3917 |

TABLE 9.1. (*continued*)

| | | | | | | | | | | | |
|---|---|---|---|---|---|---|---|---|---|---|---|
| 3919 | 3923 | 3929 | 3931 | 3943 | 3947 | 3967 | 3989 | 4001 | 4003 | 4007 | 4013 |
| 4019 | 4021 | 4027 | 4049 | 4051 | 4057 | 4073 | 4079 | 4091 | 4093 | 4099 | 4111 |
| 4127 | 4129 | 4133 | 4139 | 4153 | 4157 | 4159 | 4177 | 4201 | 4211 | 4217 | 4219 |
| 4229 | 4231 | 4241 | 4243 | 4253 | 4259 | 4261 | 4271 | 4273 | 4283 | 4289 | 4297 |
| 4327 | 4337 | 4339 | 4349 | 4357 | 4363 | 4373 | 4391 | 4397 | 4409 | 4421 | 4423 |
| 4441 | 4447 | 4451 | 4457 | 4463 | 4481 | 4483 | 4493 | 4507 | 4513 | 4517 | 4519 |
| 4523 | 4547 | 4549 | 4561 | 4567 | 4583 | 4591 | 4597 | 4603 | 4621 | 4637 | 4639 |
| 4643 | 4649 | 4651 | 4657 | 4663 | 4673 | 4679 | 4691 | 4703 | 4721 | 4723 | 4729 |
| 4733 | 4751 | 4759 | 4783 | 4787 | 4789 | 4793 | 4799 | 4801 | 4813 | 4817 | 4831 |
| 4861 | 4871 | 4877 | 4889 | 4903 | 4909 | 4919 | 4931 | 4933 | 4937 | 4943 | 4951 |
| 4957 | 4967 | 4969 | 4973 | 4987 | 4993 | 4999 | 5003 | 5009 | 5011 | 5021 | 5023 |
| 5039 | 5051 | 5059 | 5077 | 5081 | 5087 | 5099 | 5101 | 5107 | 5113 | 5119 | 5147 |
| 5153 | 5167 | 5171 | 5179 | 5189 | 5197 | 5209 | 5227 | 5231 | 5233 | 5237 | 5261 |
| 5273 | 5279 | 5281 | 5297 | 5303 | 5309 | 5323 | 5333 | 5347 | 5351 | 5381 | 5387 |
| 5393 | 5399 | 5407 | 5413 | 5417 | 5419 | 5431 | 5437 | 5441 | 5443 | 5449 | 5471 |
| 5477 | 5479 | 5483 | 5501 | 5503 | 5507 | 5519 | 5521 | 5527 | 5531 | 5557 | 5563 |
| 5569 | 5573 | 5581 | 5591 | 5623 | 5639 | 5641 | 5647 | 5651 | 5653 | 5657 | 5659 |
| 5669 | 5683 | 5689 | 5693 | 5701 | 5711 | 5717 | 5737 | 5741 | 5743 | 5749 | 5779 |
| 5783 | 5791 | 5801 | 5807 | 5813 | 5821 | 5827 | 5839 | 5843 | 5849 | 5851 | 5857 |
| 5861 | 5867 | 5869 | 5879 | 5881 | 5897 | 5903 | 5923 | 5927 | 5939 | 5953 | 5981 |
| 5987 | 6007 | 6011 | 6029 | 6037 | 6043 | 6047 | 6053 | 6067 | 6073 | 6079 | 6089 |
| 6091 | 6101 | 6113 | 6121 | 6131 | 6133 | 6143 | 6151 | 6163 | 6173 | 6197 | 6199 |
| 6203 | 6211 | 6217 | 6221 | 6229 | 6247 | 6257 | 6263 | 6269 | 6271 | 6277 | 6287 |
| 6299 | 6301 | 6311 | 6317 | 6323 | 6329 | 6337 | 6343 | 6353 | 6359 | 6361 | 6367 |
| 6373 | 6379 | 6389 | 6397 | 6421 | 6427 | 6449 | 6451 | 6469 | 6473 | 6481 | 6491 |
| 6521 | 6529 | 6547 | 6551 | 6553 | 6563 | 6569 | 6571 | 6577 | 6581 | 6599 | 6607 |
| 6619 | 6637 | 6653 | 6659 | 6661 | 6673 | 6679 | 6689 | 6691 | 6701 | 6703 | 6709 |
| 6719 | 6733 | 6737 | 6761 | 6763 | 6779 | 6781 | 6791 | 6793 | 6803 | 6823 | 6827 |
| 6829 | 6833 | 6841 | 6857 | 6863 | 6869 | 6871 | 6883 | 6899 | 6907 | 6911 | 6917 |
| 6947 | 6949 | 6959 | 6961 | 6967 | 6971 | 6977 | 6983 | 6991 | 6997 | 7001 | 7013 |
| 7019 | 7027 | 7039 | 7043 | 7057 | 7069 | 7079 | 7103 | 7109 | 7121 | 7127 | 7129 |
| 7151 | 7159 | 7177 | 7187 | 7193 | 7207 | 7211 | 7213 | 7219 | 7229 | 7237 | 7243 |
| 7247 | 7253 | 7283 | 7297 | 7307 | 7309 | 7321 | 7331 | 7333 | 7349 | 7351 | 7369 |
| 7393 | 7411 | 7417 | 7433 | 7451 | 7457 | 7459 | 7477 | 7481 | 7487 | 7489 | 7499 |
| 7507 | 7517 | 7523 | 7529 | 7537 | 7541 | 7547 | 7549 | 7559 | 7561 | 7573 | 7577 |
| 7583 | 7589 | 7591 | 7603 | 7607 | 7621 | 7639 | 7643 | 7649 | 7669 | 7673 | 7681 |
| 7687 | 7691 | 7699 | 7703 | 7717 | 7723 | 7727 | 7741 | 7753 | 7757 | 7759 | 7789 |
| 7793 | 7817 | 7823 | 7829 | 7841 | 7853 | 7867 | 7873 | 7877 | 7879 | 7883 | 7901 |
| 7907 | 7919 | 7927 | 7933 | 7937 | 7949 | 7951 | 7963 | 7993 | 8009 | 8011 | 8017 |
| 8039 | 8053 | 8059 | 8069 | 8081 | 8087 | 8089 | 8093 | 8101 | 8111 | 8117 | 8123 |
| 8147 | 8161 | 8167 | 8171 | 8179 | 8191 | 8209 | 8219 | 8221 | 8231 | 8233 | 8237 |
| 8243 | 8263 | 8269 | 8273 | 8287 | 8291 | 8293 | 8297 | 8311 | 8317 | 8329 | 8353 |
| 8363 | 8369 | 8377 | 8387 | 8389 | 8419 | 8423 | 8429 | 8431 | 8443 | 8447 | 8461 |
| 8467 | 8501 | 8513 | 8521 | 8527 | 8537 | 8539 | 8543 | 8563 | 8573 | 8581 | 8597 |
| 8599 | 8609 | 8623 | 8627 | 8629 | 8641 | 8647 | 8663 | 8669 | 8677 | 8681 | 8689 |

TABLE 9.1. (*continued*)

| | | | | | | | | | | | |
|---|---|---|---|---|---|---|---|---|---|---|---|
| 8693 | 8699 | 8707 | 8713 | 8719 | 8731 | 8737 | 8741 | 8747 | 8753 | 8761 | 8779 |
| 8783 | 8803 | 8807 | 8819 | 8821 | 8831 | 8837 | 8839 | 8849 | 8861 | 8863 | 8867 |
| 8887 | 8893 | 8923 | 8929 | 8933 | 8941 | 8951 | 8963 | 8969 | 8971 | 8999 | 9001 |
| 9007 | 9011 | 9013 | 9029 | 9041 | 9043 | 9049 | 9059 | 9067 | 9091 | 9103 | 9109 |
| 9127 | 9133 | 9137 | 9151 | 9157 | 9161 | 9173 | 9181 | 9187 | 9199 | 9203 | 9209 |
| 9221 | 9227 | 9239 | 9241 | 9257 | 9277 | 9281 | 9283 | 9293 | 9311 | 9319 | 9323 |
| 9337 | 9341 | 9343 | 9349 | 9371 | 9377 | 9391 | 9397 | 9403 | 9413 | 9419 | 9421 |
| 9431 | 9433 | 9437 | 9439 | 9461 | 9463 | 9467 | 9473 | 9479 | 9491 | 9497 | 9511 |
| 9521 | 9533 | 9539 | 9547 | 9551 | 9587 | 9601 | 9613 | 9619 | 9623 | 9629 | 9631 |
| 9643 | 9649 | 9661 | 9677 | 9679 | 9689 | 9697 | 9719 | 9721 | 9733 | 9739 | 9743 |
| 9749 | 9767 | 9769 | 9781 | 9787 | 9791 | 9803 | 9811 | 9817 | 9829 | 9833 | 9839 |
| 9851 | 9857 | 9859 | 9871 | 9883 | 9887 | 9901 | 9907 | 9923 | 9929 | 9931 | 9941 |
| 9949 | 9967 | 9973 | 10007 | 10009 | 10037 | 10039 | 10061 | 10067 | 10069 | 10079 | 10091 |
| 10093 | 10099 | 10103 | 10111 | 10133 | 10139 | 10141 | 10151 | 10159 | 10163 | 10169 | 10177 |
| 10181 | 10193 | 10211 | 10223 | 10243 | 10247 | 10253 | 10259 | 10267 | 10271 | 10273 | 10289 |
| 10301 | 10303 | 10313 | 10321 | 10331 | 10333 | 10337 | 10343 | 10357 | 10369 | 10391 | 10399 |
| 10427 | 10429 | 10433 | 10453 | 10457 | 10459 | 10463 | 10477 | 10487 | 10499 | 10501 | 10513 |
| 10529 | 10531 | 10559 | 10567 | 10589 | 10597 | 10601 | 10607 | 10613 | 10627 | 10631 | 10639 |
| 10651 | 10657 | 10663 | 10667 | 10687 | 10691 | 10709 | 10711 | 10723 | 10729 | 10733 | 10739 |
| 10753 | 10771 | 10781 | 10789 | 10799 | 10831 | 10837 | 10847 | 10853 | 10859 | 10861 | 10867 |
| 10883 | 10889 | 10891 | 10903 | 10909 | 10937 | 10939 | 10949 | 10957 | 10973 | 10979 | 10987 |
| 10993 | 11003 | 11027 | 11047 | 11057 | 11059 | 11069 | 11071 | 11083 | 11087 | 11093 | 11113 |
| 11117 | 11119 | 11131 | 11149 | 11159 | 11161 | 11171 | 11173 | 11177 | 11197 | 11213 | 11239 |
| 11243 | 11251 | 11257 | 11261 | 11273 | 11279 | 11287 | 11299 | 11311 | 11317 | 11321 | 11329 |
| 11351 | 11353 | 11369 | 11383 | 11393 | 11399 | 11411 | 11423 | 11437 | 11443 | 11447 | 11467 |
| 11471 | 11483 | 11489 | 11491 | 11497 | 11503 | 11519 | 11527 | 11549 | 11551 | 11579 | 11587 |
| 11593 | 11597 | 11617 | 11621 | 11633 | 11657 | 11677 | 11681 | 11689 | 11699 | 11701 | 11717 |
| 11719 | 11731 | 11743 | 11777 | 11779 | 11783 | 11789 | 11801 | 11807 | 11813 | 11821 | 11827 |
| 11831 | 11833 | 11839 | 11863 | 11867 | 11887 | 11897 | 11903 | 11909 | 11923 | 11927 | 11933 |
| 11939 | 11941 | 11953 | 11959 | 11969 | 11971 | 11981 | 11987 | 12007 | 12011 | 12037 | 12041 |
| 12043 | 12049 | 12071 | 12073 | 12097 | 12101 | 12107 | 12109 | 12113 | 12119 | 12143 | 12149 |
| 12157 | 12161 | 12163 | 12197 | 12203 | 12211 | 12227 | 12239 | 12241 | 12251 | 12253 | 12263 |
| 12269 | 12277 | 12281 | 12289 | 12301 | 12323 | 12329 | 12343 | 12347 | 12373 | 12377 | 12379 |
| 12391 | 12401 | 12409 | 12413 | 12421 | 12433 | 12437 | 12451 | 12457 | 12473 | 12479 | 12487 |
| 12491 | 12497 | 12503 | 12511 | 12517 | 12527 | 12539 | 12541 | 12547 | 12553 | 12569 | 12577 |
| 12583 | 12589 | 12601 | 12611 | 12613 | 12619 | 12637 | 12641 | 12647 | 12653 | 12659 | 12671 |
| 12689 | 12697 | 12703 | 12713 | 12721 | 12739 | 12743 | 12757 | 12763 | 12781 | 12791 | 12799 |
| 12809 | 12821 | 12823 | 12829 | 12841 | 12853 | 12889 | 12893 | 12899 | 12907 | 12911 | 12917 |
| 12919 | 12923 | 12941 | 12953 | 12959 | 12967 | 12973 | 12979 | 12983 | 13001 | 13003 | 13007 |
| 13009 | 13033 | 13037 | 13043 | 13049 | 13063 | 13093 | 13099 | 13103 | 13109 | 13121 | 13127 |
| 13147 | 13151 | 13159 | 13163 | 13171 | 13177 | 13183 | 13187 | 13217 | 13219 | 13229 | 13241 |
| 13249 | 13259 | 13267 | 13291 | 13297 | 13309 | 13313 | 13327 | 13331 | 13337 | 13339 | 13367 |
| 13381 | 13397 | 13399 | 13411 | 13417 | 13421 | 13441 | 13451 | 13457 | 13463 | 13469 | 13477 |
| 13487 | 13499 | 13513 | 13523 | 13537 | 13553 | 13567 | 13577 | 13591 | 13597 | 13613 | 13619 |
| 13627 | 13633 | 13649 | 13669 | 13679 | 13681 | 13687 | 13691 | 13693 | 13697 | 13709 | 13711 |

TABLE 9.1. (*continued*)

| | | | | | | | | | | | |
|---|---|---|---|---|---|---|---|---|---|---|---|
| 13721 | 13723 | 13729 | 13751 | 13757 | 13759 | 13763 | 13781 | 13789 | 13799 | 13807 | 13829 |
| 13831 | 13841 | 13859 | 13873 | 13877 | 13879 | 13883 | 13901 | 13903 | 13907 | 13913 | 13921 |
| 13931 | 13933 | 13963 | 13967 | 13997 | 13999 | 14009 | 14011 | 14029 | 14033 | 14051 | 14057 |
| 14071 | 14081 | 14083 | 14087 | 14107 | 14143 | 14149 | 14153 | 14159 | 14173 | 14177 | 14197 |
| 14207 | 14221 | 14243 | 14249 | 14251 | 14281 | 14293 | 14303 | 14321 | 14323 | 14327 | 14341 |
| 14347 | 14369 | 14387 | 14389 | 14401 | 14407 | 14411 | 14419 | 14423 | 14431 | 14437 | 14447 |
| 14449 | 14461 | 14479 | 14489 | 14503 | 14519 | 14533 | 14537 | 14543 | 14549 | 14551 | 14557 |
| 14561 | 14563 | 14591 | 14593 | 14621 | 14627 | 14629 | 14633 | 14639 | 14653 | 14657 | 14669 |
| 14683 | 14699 | 14713 | 14717 | 14723 | 14731 | 14737 | 14741 | 14747 | 14753 | 14759 | 14767 |
| 14771 | 14779 | 14783 | 14797 | 14813 | 14821 | 14827 | 14831 | 14843 | 14851 | 14867 | 14869 |
| 14879 | 14887 | 14891 | 14897 | 14923 | 14929 | 14939 | 14947 | 14951 | 14957 | 14969 | 14983 |
| 15013 | 15017 | 15031 | 15053 | 15061 | 15073 | 15077 | 15083 | 15091 | 15101 | 15107 | 15121 |
| 15131 | 15137 | 15139 | 15149 | 15161 | 15173 | 15187 | 15193 | 15199 | 15217 | 15227 | 15233 |
| 15241 | 15259 | 15263 | 15269 | 15271 | 15277 | 15287 | 15289 | 15299 | 15307 | 15313 | 15319 |
| 15329 | 15331 | 15349 | 15359 | 15361 | 15373 | 15377 | 15383 | 15391 | 15401 | 15413 | 15427 |
| 15439 | 15443 | 15451 | 15461 | 15467 | 15473 | 15493 | 15497 | 15511 | 15527 | 15541 | 15551 |
| 15559 | 15569 | 15581 | 15583 | 15601 | 15607 | 15619 | 15629 | 15641 | 15643 | 15647 | 15649 |
| 15661 | 15667 | 15671 | 15679 | 15683 | 15727 | 15731 | 15733 | 15737 | 15739 | 15749 | 15761 |
| 15767 | 15773 | 15787 | 15791 | 15797 | 15803 | 15809 | 15817 | 15823 | 15859 | 15877 | 15881 |
| 15887 | 15889 | 15901 | 15907 | 15913 | 15919 | 15923 | 15937 | 15959 | 15971 | 15973 | 15991 |
| 16001 | 16007 | 16033 | 16057 | 16061 | 16063 | 16067 | 16069 | 16073 | 16087 | 16091 | 16097 |
| 16103 | 16111 | 16127 | 16139 | 16141 | 16183 | 16187 | 16189 | 16193 | 16217 | 16223 | 16229 |
| 16231 | 16249 | 16253 | 16267 | 16273 | 16301 | 16319 | 16333 | 16339 | 16349 | 16361 | 16363 |
| 16369 | 16381 | 16411 | 16417 | 16421 | 16427 | 16433 | 16447 | 16451 | 16453 | 16477 | 16481 |
| 16487 | 16493 | 16519 | 16529 | 16547 | 16553 | 16561 | 16567 | 16573 | 16603 | 16607 | 16619 |
| 16631 | 16633 | 16649 | 16651 | 16657 | 16661 | 16673 | 16691 | 16693 | 16699 | 16703 | 16729 |
| 16741 | 16747 | 16759 | 16763 | 16787 | 16811 | 16823 | 16829 | 16831 | 16843 | 16871 | 16879 |
| 16883 | 16889 | 16901 | 16903 | 16921 | 16927 | 16931 | 16937 | 16943 | 16963 | 16979 | 16981 |
| 16987 | 16993 | 17011 | 17021 | 17027 | 17029 | 17033 | 17041 | 17047 | 17053 | 17077 | 17093 |
| 17099 | 17107 | 17117 | 17123 | 17137 | 17159 | 17167 | 17183 | 17189 | 17191 | 17203 | 17207 |
| 17209 | 17231 | 17239 | 17257 | 17291 | 17293 | 17299 | 17317 | 17321 | 17327 | 17333 | 17341 |
| 17351 | 17359 | 17377 | 17383 | 17387 | 17389 | 17393 | 17401 | 17417 | 17419 | 17431 | 17443 |
| 17449 | 17467 | 17471 | 17477 | 17483 | 17489 | 17491 | 17497 | 17509 | 17519 | 17539 | 17551 |
| 17569 | 17573 | 17579 | 17581 | 17597 | 17599 | 17609 | 17623 | 17627 | 17657 | 17659 | 17669 |
| 17681 | 17683 | 17707 | 17713 | 17729 | 17737 | 17747 | 17749 | 17761 | 17783 | 17789 | 17791 |
| 17807 | 17827 | 17837 | 17839 | 17851 | 17863 | 17881 | 17891 | 17903 | 17909 | 17911 | 17921 |
| 17923 | 17929 | 17939 | 17957 | 17959 | 17971 | 17977 | 17981 | 17987 | 17989 | 18013 | 18041 |
| 18043 | 18047 | 18049 | 18059 | 18061 | 18077 | 18089 | 18097 | 18119 | 18121 | 18127 | 18131 |
| 18133 | 18143 | 18149 | 18169 | 18181 | 18191 | 18199 | 18211 | 18217 | 18223 | 18229 | 18233 |
| 18251 | 18253 | 18257 | 18269 | 18287 | 18289 | 18301 | 18307 | 18311 | 18313 | 18329 | 18341 |
| 18353 | 18367 | 18371 | 18379 | 18397 | 18401 | 18413 | 18427 | 18433 | 18439 | 18443 | 18451 |
| 18457 | 18461 | 18481 | 18493 | 18503 | 18517 | 18521 | 18523 | 18539 | 18541 | 18553 | 18583 |
| 18587 | 18593 | 18617 | 18637 | 18661 | 18671 | 18679 | 18691 | 18701 | 18713 | 18719 | 18731 |
| 18743 | 18749 | 18757 | 18773 | 18787 | 18793 | 18797 | 18803 | 18839 | 18859 | 18869 | 18899 |
| 18911 | 18913 | 18917 | 18919 | 18947 | 18959 | 18973 | 18979 | 19001 | 19009 | 19013 | 19031 |

TABLE 9.1. (*continued*)

| | | | | | | | | | | | |
|---|---|---|---|---|---|---|---|---|---|---|---|
| 19037 | 19051 | 19069 | 19073 | 19079 | 19081 | 19087 | 19121 | 19139 | 19141 | 19157 | 19163 |
| 19181 | 19183 | 19207 | 19211 | 19213 | 19219 | 19231 | 19237 | 19249 | 19259 | 19267 | 19273 |
| 19289 | 19301 | 19309 | 19319 | 19333 | 19373 | 19379 | 19381 | 19387 | 19391 | 19403 | 19417 |
| 19421 | 19423 | 19427 | 19429 | 19433 | 19441 | 19447 | 19457 | 19463 | 19469 | 19471 | 19477 |
| 19483 | 19489 | 19501 | 19507 | 19531 | 19541 | 19543 | 19553 | 19559 | 19571 | 19577 | 19583 |
| 19597 | 19603 | 19609 | 19661 | 19681 | 19687 | 19697 | 19699 | 19709 | 19717 | 19727 | 19739 |
| 19751 | 19753 | 19759 | 19763 | 19777 | 19793 | 19801 | 19813 | 19819 | 19841 | 19843 | 19853 |
| 19861 | 19867 | 19889 | 19891 | 19913 | 19919 | 19927 | 19937 | 19949 | 19961 | 19963 | 19973 |
| 19979 | 19991 | 19993 | 19997 | 20011 | 20021 | 20023 | 20029 | 20047 | 20051 | 20063 | 20071 |
| 20089 | 20101 | 20107 | 20113 | 20117 | 20123 | 20129 | 20143 | 20147 | 20149 | 20161 | 20173 |
| 20177 | 20183 | 20201 | 20219 | 20231 | 20233 | 20249 | 20261 | 20269 | 20287 | 20297 | 20323 |
| 20327 | 20333 | 20341 | 20347 | 20353 | 20357 | 20359 | 20369 | 20389 | 20393 | 20399 | 20407 |
| 20411 | 20431 | 20441 | 20443 | 20477 | 20479 | 20483 | 20507 | 20509 | 20521 | 20533 | 20543 |
| 20549 | 20551 | 20563 | 20593 | 20599 | 20611 | 20627 | 20639 | 20641 | 20663 | 20681 | 20693 |
| 20707 | 20717 | 20719 | 20731 | 20743 | 20747 | 20749 | 20753 | 20759 | 20771 | 20773 | 20789 |
| 20807 | 20809 | 20849 | 20857 | 20873 | 20879 | 20887 | 20897 | 20899 | 20903 | 20921 | 20929 |
| 20939 | 20947 | 20959 | 20963 | 20981 | 20983 | 21001 | 21011 | 21013 | 21017 | 21019 | 21023 |
| 21031 | 21059 | 21061 | 21067 | 21089 | 21101 | 21107 | 21121 | 21139 | 21143 | 21149 | 21157 |
| 21163 | 21169 | 21179 | 21187 | 21191 | 21193 | 21211 | 21221 | 21227 | 21247 | 21269 | 21277 |
| 21283 | 21313 | 21317 | 21319 | 21323 | 21341 | 21347 | 21377 | 21379 | 21383 | 21391 | 21397 |
| 21401 | 21407 | 21419 | 21433 | 21467 | 21481 | 21487 | 21491 | 21493 | 21499 | 21503 | 21517 |
| 21521 | 21523 | 21529 | 21557 | 21559 | 21563 | 21569 | 21577 | 21587 | 21589 | 21599 | 21601 |
| 21611 | 21613 | 21617 | 21647 | 21649 | 21661 | 21673 | 21683 | 21701 | 21713 | 21727 | 21737 |
| 21739 | 21751 | 21757 | 21767 | 21773 | 21787 | 21799 | 21803 | 21817 | 21821 | 21839 | 21841 |
| 21851 | 21859 | 21863 | 21871 | 21881 | 21893 | 21911 | 21929 | 21937 | 21943 | 21961 | 21977 |
| 21991 | 21997 | 22003 | 22013 | 22027 | 22031 | 22037 | 22039 | 22051 | 22063 | 22067 | 22073 |
| 22079 | 22091 | 22093 | 22109 | 22111 | 22123 | 22129 | 22133 | 22147 | 22153 | 22157 | 22159 |
| 22171 | 22189 | 22193 | 22229 | 22247 | 22259 | 22271 | 22273 | 22277 | 22279 | 22283 | 22291 |
| 22303 | 22307 | 22343 | 22349 | 22367 | 22369 | 22381 | 22391 | 22397 | 22409 | 22433 | 22441 |
| 22447 | 22453 | 22469 | 22481 | 22483 | 22501 | 22511 | 22531 | 22541 | 22543 | 22549 | 22567 |
| 22571 | 22573 | 22613 | 22619 | 22621 | 22637 | 22639 | 22643 | 22651 | 22669 | 22679 | 22691 |
| 22697 | 22699 | 22709 | 22717 | 22721 | 22727 | 22739 | 22741 | 22751 | 22769 | 22777 | 22783 |
| 22787 | 22807 | 22811 | 22817 | 22853 | 22859 | 22861 | 22871 | 22877 | 22901 | 22907 | 22921 |
| 22937 | 22943 | 22961 | 22963 | 22973 | 22993 | 23003 | 23011 | 23017 | 23021 | 23027 | 23029 |
| 23039 | 23041 | 23053 | 23057 | 23059 | 23063 | 23071 | 23081 | 23087 | 23099 | 23117 | 23131 |
| 23143 | 23159 | 23167 | 23173 | 23189 | 23197 | 23201 | 23203 | 23209 | 23227 | 23251 | 23269 |
| 23279 | 23291 | 23293 | 23297 | 23311 | 23321 | 23327 | 23333 | 23339 | 23357 | 23369 | 23371 |
| 23399 | 23417 | 23431 | 23447 | 23459 | 23473 | 23497 | 23509 | 23531 | 23537 | 23539 | 23549 |
| 23557 | 23561 | 23563 | 23567 | 23581 | 23593 | 23599 | 23603 | 23609 | 23623 | 23627 | 23629 |
| 23633 | 23663 | 23669 | 23671 | 23677 | 23687 | 23689 | 23719 | 23741 | 23743 | 23747 | 23753 |
| 23761 | 23767 | 23773 | 23789 | 23801 | 23813 | 23819 | 23827 | 23831 | 23833 | 23857 | 23869 |
| 23873 | 23879 | 23887 | 23893 | 23899 | 23909 | 23911 | 23917 | 23929 | 23957 | 23971 | 23977 |
| 23981 | 23993 | 24001 | 24007 | 24019 | 24023 | 24029 | 24043 | 24049 | 24061 | 24071 | 24077 |
| 24083 | 24091 | 24097 | 24103 | 24107 | 24109 | 24113 | 24121 | 24133 | 24137 | 24151 | 24169 |
| 24179 | 24181 | 24197 | 24203 | 24223 | 24229 | 24239 | 24247 | 24251 | 24281 | 24317 | 24329 |

TABLE 9.1. (continued)

| | | | | | | | | | | |
|---|---|---|---|---|---|---|---|---|---|---|
| 24337 | 24359 | 24371 | 24373 | 24379 | 24391 | 24407 | 24413 | 24419 | 24421 | 24439 | 24443 |
| 24469 | 24473 | 24481 | 24499 | 24509 | 24517 | 24527 | 24533 | 24547 | 24551 | 24571 | 24593 |
| 24611 | 24623 | 24631 | 24659 | 24671 | 24677 | 24683 | 24691 | 24697 | 24709 | 24733 | 24749 |
| 24763 | 24767 | 24781 | 24793 | 24799 | 24809 | 24821 | 24841 | 24847 | 24851 | 24859 | 24877 |
| 24889 | 24907 | 24917 | 24919 | 24923 | 24943 | 24953 | 24967 | 24971 | 24977 | 24979 | 24989 |
| 25013 | 25031 | 25033 | 25037 | 25057 | 25073 | 25087 | 25097 | 25111 | 25117 | 25121 | 25127 |
| 25147 | 25153 | 25163 | 25169 | 25171 | 25183 | 25189 | 25219 | 25229 | 25237 | 25243 | 25247 |
| 25253 | 25261 | 25301 | 25303 | 25307 | 25309 | 25321 | 25339 | 25343 | 25349 | 25357 | 25367 |
| 25373 | 25391 | 25409 | 25411 | 25423 | 25439 | 25447 | 25453 | 25457 | 25463 | 25469 | 25471 |
| 25523 | 25537 | 25541 | 25561 | 25577 | 25579 | 25583 | 25589 | 25601 | 25603 | 25609 | 25621 |
| 25633 | 25639 | 25643 | 25657 | 25667 | 25673 | 25679 | 25693 | 25703 | 25717 | 25733 | 25741 |
| 25747 | 25759 | 25763 | 25771 | 25793 | 25799 | 25801 | 25819 | 25841 | 25847 | 25849 | 25867 |
| 25873 | 25889 | 25903 | 25913 | 25919 | 25931 | 25933 | 25939 | 25943 | 25951 | 25969 | 25981 |
| 25997 | 25999 | 26003 | 26017 | 26021 | 26029 | 26041 | 26053 | 26083 | 26099 | 26107 | 26111 |
| 26113 | 26119 | 26141 | 26153 | 26161 | 26171 | 26177 | 26183 | 26189 | 26203 | 26209 | 26227 |
| 26237 | 26249 | 26251 | 26261 | 26263 | 26267 | 26293 | 26297 | 26309 | 26317 | 26321 | 26339 |
| 26347 | 26357 | 26371 | 26387 | 26393 | 26399 | 26407 | 26417 | 26423 | 26431 | 26437 | 26449 |
| 26459 | 26479 | 26489 | 26497 | 26501 | 26513 | 26539 | 26557 | 26561 | 26573 | 26591 | 26597 |
| 26627 | 26633 | 26641 | 26647 | 26669 | 26681 | 26683 | 26687 | 26693 | 26699 | 26701 | 26711 |
| 26713 | 26717 | 26723 | 26729 | 26731 | 26737 | 26759 | 26777 | 26783 | 26801 | 26813 | 26821 |
| 26833 | 26839 | 26849 | 26861 | 26863 | 26879 | 26881 | 26891 | 26893 | 26903 | 26921 | 26927 |
| 26947 | 26951 | 26953 | 26959 | 26981 | 26987 | 26993 | 27011 | 27017 | 27031 | 27043 | 27059 |
| 27061 | 27067 | 27073 | 27077 | 27091 | 27103 | 27107 | 27109 | 27127 | 27143 | 27179 | 27191 |
| 27197 | 27211 | 27239 | 27241 | 27253 | 27259 | 27271 | 27277 | 27281 | 27283 | 27299 | 27329 |
| 27337 | 27361 | 27367 | 27397 | 27407 | 27409 | 27427 | 27431 | 27437 | 27449 | 27457 | 27479 |
| 27481 | 27487 | 27509 | 27527 | 27529 | 27539 | 27541 | 27551 | 27581 | 27583 | 27611 | 27617 |
| 27631 | 27647 | 27653 | 27673 | 27689 | 27691 | 27697 | 27701 | 27733 | 27737 | 27739 | 27743 |
| 27749 | 27751 | 27763 | 27767 | 27773 | 27779 | 27791 | 27793 | 27799 | 27803 | 27809 | 27817 |
| 27823 | 27827 | 27847 | 27851 | 27883 | 27893 | 27901 | 27917 | 27919 | 27941 | 27943 | 27947 |
| 27953 | 27961 | 27967 | 27983 | 27997 | 28001 | 28019 | 28027 | 28031 | 28051 | 28057 | 28069 |
| 28081 | 28087 | 28097 | 28099 | 28109 | 28111 | 28123 | 28151 | 28163 | 28181 | 28183 | 28201 |
| 28211 | 28219 | 28229 | 28277 | 28279 | 28283 | 28289 | 28297 | 28307 | 28309 | 28319 | 28349 |
| 28351 | 28387 | 28393 | 28403 | 28409 | 28411 | 28429 | 28433 | 28439 | 28447 | 28463 | 28477 |
| 28493 | 28499 | 28513 | 28517 | 28537 | 28541 | 28547 | 28549 | 28559 | 28571 | 28573 | 28579 |
| 28591 | 28597 | 28603 | 28607 | 28619 | 28621 | 28627 | 28631 | 28643 | 28649 | 28657 | 28661 |
| 28663 | 28669 | 28687 | 28697 | 28703 | 28711 | 28723 | 28729 | 28751 | 28753 | 28759 | 28771 |
| 28789 | 28793 | 28807 | 28813 | 28817 | 28837 | 28843 | 28859 | 28867 | 28871 | 28879 | 28901 |
| 28909 | 28921 | 28927 | 28933 | 28949 | 28961 | 28979 | 29009 | 29017 | 29021 | 29023 | 29027 |
| 29033 | 29059 | 29063 | 29077 | 29101 | 29123 | 29129 | 29131 | 29137 | 29147 | 29153 | 29167 |
| 29173 | 29179 | 29191 | 29201 | 29207 | 29209 | 29221 | 29231 | 29243 | 29251 | 29269 | 29287 |
| 29297 | 29303 | 29311 | 29327 | 29333 | 29339 | 29347 | 29363 | 29383 | 29387 | 29389 | 29399 |
| 29401 | 29411 | 29423 | 29429 | 29437 | 29443 | 29453 | 29473 | 29483 | 29501 | 29527 | 29531 |
| 29537 | 29567 | 29569 | 29573 | 29581 | 29587 | 29599 | 29611 | 29629 | 29633 | 29641 | 29663 |
| 29669 | 29671 | 29683 | 29717 | 29723 | 29741 | 29753 | 29759 | 29761 | 29789 | 29803 | 29819 |
| 29833 | 29837 | 29851 | 29863 | 29867 | 29873 | 29879 | 29881 | 29917 | 29921 | 29927 | 29947 |

**TABLE 9.1.** (*continued*)

```
29959 29983 29989 30011 30013 30029 30047 30059 30071 30089 30091 30097
30103 30109 30113 30119 30133 30137 30139 30161 30169 30181 30187 30197
30203 30211 30223 30241 30253 30259 30269 30271 30293 30307 30313 30319
30323 30341 30347 30367 30389 30391 30403 30427 30431 30449 30467 30469
30491 30493 30497 30509 30517 30529 30539 30553 30557 30559 30577 30593
30631 30637 30643 30649 30661 30671 30677 30689 30697 30703 30707 30713
30727 30757 30763 30773 30781 30803 30809 30817 30829 30839 30841 30851
30853 30859 30869 30871 30881 30893 30911 30931 30937 30941 30949 30971
30977 30983 31013 31019 31033 31039 31051 31063 31069 31079 31081 31091
31121 31123 31139 31147 31151 31153 31159 31177 31181 31183 31189 31193
31219 31223 31231 31237 31247 31249 31253 31259 31267 31271 31277 31307
31319 31321 31327 31333 31337 31357 31379 31387 31391 31393 31397 31469
31477 31481 31489 31511 31513 31517 31531 31541 31543 31547 31567 31573
31583 31601 31607 31627 31643 31649 31657 31663 31667 31687 31699 31721
31723 31727 31729 31741 31751 31769 31771 31793 31799 31817 31847 31849
31859 31873 31883 31891 31907 31957 31963 31973 31981 31991 32003 32009
32027 32029 32051 32057 32059 32063 32069 32077 32083 32089 32099 32117
32119 32141 32143 32159 32173 32183 32189 32191 32203 32213 32233 32237
32251 32257 32261 32297 32299 32303 32309 32321 32323 32327 32341 32353
32359 32363 32369 32371 32377 32381 32401 32411 32413 32423 32429 32441
32443 32467 32479 32491 32497 32503 32507 32531 32533 32537 32561 32563
32569 32573 32579 32587 32603 32609 32611 32621 32633 32647 32653 32687
32693 32707 32713 32717 32719 32749-32765-32763-32759-32757-32753-32747
-32745-32739-32735-32733-32729-32727-32717-32715-32705-32703-32699-32697
-32693-32687-32673-32669-32667-32663-32655-32649-32645-32639-32637-32627
-32625-32619-32613-32603-32597-32595-32585-32583-32579-32567-32565-32559
-32553-32549-32543-32537-32523-32519-32517-32513-32507-32499-32493-32489
-32487-32483-32475-32465-32463-32453-32445-32435-32433-32429-32427-32423
-32417-32409-32405-32397-32387-32385-32375-32363-32357-32355-32345-32339
-32337-32333-32325-32315-32313-32309-32303-32289-32279-32277-32265-32259
-32253-32249-32247-32235-32225-32223-32219-32207-32205-32193-32189-32187
-32183-32177-32175-32159-32147-32145-32135-32133-32127-32123-32109-32105
-32103-32093-32079-32075-32073-32069-32067-32057-32055-32049-32045-32043
-32037-32033-32027-32015-32013-32007-32003-31989-31985-31973-31967-31959
-31955-31949-31947-31943-31937-31935-31929-31923-31919-31917-31913-31907
-31899-31895-31889-31883-31877-31869-31863-31857-31845-31839-31835-31833
-31823-31817-31815-31805-31797-31787-31785-31779-31769-31767-31763-31745
-31739-31737-31727-31725-31719-31715-31713-31709-31707-31685-31683-31679
-31677-31673-31665-31653-31647-31643-31637-31625-31617-31613-31605-31595
-31595-31589-31575-31569-31539-31529-31517-31509-31505-31503-31499-31497
-31487-31479-31475-31467-31455-31449-31445-31443-31439-31433-31419-31415
-31413-31409-31407-31397-31395-31389-31379-31377-31373-31365-31353-31343
-31329-31325-31323-31319-31313-31305-31299-31283-31277-31275-31269-31263
-31259-31253-31239-31235-31233-31223-31217-31215-31209-31199-31187-31185
-31175-31173-31169-31167-31157-31155-31143-31133-31119-31115-31109-31107
```

## INDUSTRIAL APPLICATIONS

The following program, written in Hewlett-Packard Pascal/1000, and reproduced courtesy of Hewlett-Packard Company, illustrates the use of Pascal for a simple industrial application.

The program monitors a pressure transducer which provides a single variable pressure. The variable pressure is of the subrange data type, which varies between the limits 0 and 100. The program also defines various constants within the pressure range which the application programmer considers to be "low," "normal," or "high" pressure. The use of the CONST declaration to define such values should be noted here, since if the values of low, normal, and high pressure are to be redefined at a later time, the programmer need only change the declaration of the constants, and not the procedures or other executable statements of the program.

The next portion of the program defines two procedures—reading the pressure, and sounding an alarm. Note that the parameter pressure is presented in the parameter list immediately following the procedure identifier.

The executable portion of the program itself is marked by the first BEGIN statement, which is followed by the first procedure "read_pressure." An iterative operation is defined next by use of a WHILE . . . DO statement. The action to be taken during the period when the condition is true (i.e., when the value of the pressure is less than or equal to the constant defined as the maximum safe pressure) is defined in the indented BEGIN . . . END block. The indented BEGIN . . . END block defines an operation of printing the pressure value that has been read, and defining the Range as being either Low, Normal, or High, depending upon whether the value corresponds to one of three ranges defined within the CASE statement. If the WHILE . . . DO is not true, then the sound_alarm procedure is entered and executed.

```
PROGRAM pressure (INPUT,OUTPUT);

TYPE    pressure_range = 0 . . 100;

TYPE    low  = 0;    low_max  = 19;
        norm = 20;   norm_max = 59;
        high = 60;   max_safe = 79;

VAR     pressure: pressure_range;

PROCEDURE read_pressure $ALIAS 'RDPRS'$
          (VAR pressure: pressure_range); EXTERNAL;

PROCEDURE sound_alarm $ALIAS 'ALARM'$; EXTERNAL;
```

```
BEGIN
read_pressure(pressure);
WHILE pressure <= max_safe DO
  BEGIN
  write ('Pressure =' ,pressure);
  write ('Range = ');
  CASE pressure OF
    low . . low_max:
       writeln('Low ');
    norm . . norm_max:
       writeln('Normal ');
    high . . max_safe:
       writeln('High ');
    END;
  read_pressure(pressure);
  END
sound_alarm;
END.
```

# 10

# Pascal Implementations: Mini- and Microcomputers

There are a large number of different implementations of Pascal, and it would be impractical to discuss them all here. However, it would be worth-while to list the more widely known implementations, and to discuss in detail a few of the more significant ones to indicate the various types of extensions to standard Pascal which are done by various vendors.

Table 10.1 lists the more popular implementations of Pascal on mini- and microcomputers, and identifies their vendors. Appendix C gives the addresses and telephone numbers of the vendors for those readers desiring further information.

As examples of Pascal implementations, the present chapter considers the following:

Hewlett-Packard Pascal 1000

Texas Instruments Pascal

OMSI Pascal

TABLE 10.1  Pascal Implementations

| Vendor | Name | CPU or Computer |
|---|---|---|
| Advanced Computer | ACT Pascal | any CPU |
| Apple Computer | Apple Pascal | Apple II |
| Boston Systems Office | BSO/Pascal | DEC PDP-11 |
| California Computer Systems | Pascal | Calif Computer Systems 200, 300, 400 |
| Chapin Associates | P-code Translator | 8080, Z80 |
|  | Z8000 P-code Interpreter | Z8000 |
| Cogitronics Corp. | Pascal Compiler | 8080, Z80 |
| Commodore International | Pascal | Commodore PET, CBM |
| Data General | AOS Pascal | DG Eclipse |
|  | MP/Pascal | DG microNOVA, NOVA 4 |
| Digicomp Research | UCSD Pascal Version III | Digicomp Pascal-100 |
| Digital Equipment | Pascal | DEC VAX-11 |
| Enertec, Inc. | MAC (Micro Concurrent Pascal) | 8080, Z80 |
| Harris | Pascal P4 | Harris |
| Hewlett-Packard | Pascal 1000 | HP 1000 |
| Intellimac | RSI Pascal | 68000 code |
| International Electronic Machinery | Pascal-35, -45 | HP9835, 9845 |
| Ithaca Intersystems | Pascal/Z | Z80 |
| Language Resources | LRPS-80,86 | 8080, 8086 |
| Ontel | Pascal | 8085 |
| Oregon Software | OMSI Pascal | DEC PDP-11 |
| PCD Systems | UCSD Pascal | DEC LSI-11 Radio Shack TRS-80 II |
| Rational Data Systems | Pascal | DG ECLIPSE DG NOVA |
| Softech Microsystems | UCSD Pascal | LSI-11, 8080, etc. |
|  | UCSD p-System | 8086, 68000 |
| Sorcim | Pascal/M | 8080, Z80, 8086 |
| Supersoft Associates | Tiny Pascal | 8080, Z80, 8085 |
| Texas Instruments | Pascal | TI 990, 9900 |
| Xycom | Industrial Pascal | Xycom |

## HEWLETT-PACKARD PASCAL 1000

The HP Pascal/1000 compiler is an implementation of Pascal for the HP 1000 computer system operating under the HP RTE-IVB real-time operating system. As a compiler, the system translates the Pascal source code to RTE assembly language source code, which is then assembled to produce object code, which may then be executed.

Pascal/1000 is a superset of standard Pascal and includes a number of extensions which take advantage of the capabilities of the HP 1000. Some of the most important extensions are:

1. 32-bit integer and double-precision floating point data types.

2. Predefined procedures for directed access I/O.

3. Subroutine compilation with load-time linking of modules (in "standard" Pascal, the entire program must be compiled at the same time). Segmentation can be accomplished in a straightforward manner.

4. The CASE statement can have subrange labels and an OTHERWISE clause.

5. Constant-valued expressions are allowed in most places that a constant is allowed in "standard" Pascal.

6. Structured constants allow arrays, records, and sets to be easily initialized.

7. Declarations may be in any order, except that LABEL must be first if it is used at all. More than one of each declaration section is allowed (such as two or more sections of TYPE, CONST, and/or VAR declarations).

8. Identifiers may be up to a source line in length with all characters significant, versus only the first eight characters in "standard" Pascal.

9. A function may return any type of data including arrays, records, or sets, but excluding files or data types containing files.

10. MARK and RELEASE procedures supplement the "standard" Pascal facilities for dynamic memory management.

11. EXEC, FMP, Pascal, FORTRAN, or Assembly language routines external to the Pascal program may be called by it.

12. The Heap can reside in logical address space, or in the Extended Memory Area (EMA) for Pascal programs running under RTE-IVB.

The following sections summarize the character set, data types, and program vocabulary of Pascal 1000.

## Character Set

**Alphabetic characters.** All upper- and lower-case characters (A through Z and a through z).

**Numeric characters.** The ten digits 0 through 9.

**Special characters.** Blank; currency symbol ($); apostrophe ('); left and right parentheses; comma (,); plus, minus, equals, less than, and greater than symbols (+, −, =, <, >); decimal point(.); slash; colon and semicolon; left and right brackets; left and right braces; caret (^); @ symbol; # sign; asterisk(*); and underscore (_).

## Data Types

**Integer.** A 32-bit quantity, including sign, that ranges from −2,147,483,648 to +2,147,483,647.

**Real.** A 32-bit quantity with sign, exponent, and mantissa that ranges from $\pm 2^{-127}$ to $+2^{+127}$, providing 6 to 7 decimal digit accuracy.

**Longreal.** A 64-bit quantity with sign, exponent, and mantissa that ranges from $\pm 2^{-127}$ to $+2^{+127}$, providing 16 to 17 decimal digit accuracy.

**Boolean.** A 16-bit variable in which only the low order bit is used to determine the Boolean value true (1) or false (0).

**Char.** Values are the set of characters defined by the 8-bit ASCII character set.

**Subrange type.** A data type can be identified as a subrange of another ordinal type (Integer, Boolean, Char, or enumeration type) in which the least and largest values of the subrange are identified.

**Array type.** A structure consisting of a fixed number of components which are all of the same type, called the component type in which the elements of the array are designated by indices. The array type definition specifies the component type and the index type. Component type may be any type, including another standard type.

**Record type.** A structure consisting of a fixed number of components that can be of different types. For each component, called a field, the record definition specifies its type and an identifier.

**Set type.** Defines a range of values which is the powerset of a base type, which can be Integer, Boolean, char, or subrange or any enumeration type.

**File type.** Defines a structure consisting of a sequence of components that are all of the same type. The number of components (length) of the file is not fixed by the file definition.

## Program Vocabulary

In the following program vocabulary tabulation, all reserved words, predefined data types, and key words are given in capital letters, even though that
would not be necessary in an actual program. The described vocabulary item
is in bolder type. Vocabulary items that are extensions to Wirth Pascal are
flagged with a →

| Program Vocabulary Items | Uses |
|---|---|
| **PROGRAM, PROCEDURE AND FUNCTION IDENTIFICATION STATEMENTS** | |
| **PROGRAM** name (INPUT, OUTPUT, otherfile1, otherfile2); | Identifies program by name and specifies the names of the standard files and/or any user-defined files with which it does I/O. |
| **PROCEDURE** name (VAR num, den: INTEGER); | Identifies procedure by name, which may be followed by a list of reference and/or value parameters. |
| **FUNCTION** name (value: Real): REAL. | Identifies function by name, along with parameter(s) used, followed by the type of function. |
| **DECLARATIONS** | |
| **LABEL** 2 | Declares an integer to be used in the program as the destination point of a GOTO |
| **CONST** pi = 3.1415926; multiplier = 0.8598; i = −10; j = 20; k = i+j; | Declares the names and values of constants used in the program. |
| **TYPE** MATRIX = ARRAY [SUB1, SUB2] OF | Declares structured data types, such as arrays, records, sets, |

Program Vocabulary Items      Uses
(*continued*)

| | |
|---|---|
| REAL;<br>SUB1 = 1 . . 5;<br>SUB2 = 10 . . 20; | files, scalars, and subranges. |
| **VAR**<br>rpm : INTEGER;<br>oiltemp, watertemp :<br>REAL;<br>charging : BOOLEAN;<br>P : PACKED ARRAY<br>[i . . j] of SUB1;<br>**GENERAL PROGRAM<br>STATEMENTS** | Declares the names of integer,<br>real, Boolean, or other<br>types of variables used in the<br>program. |
| **BEGIN**<br>*<br>*<br><br><br>**END** | Delimits a series of program<br>statements, such as the execut-<br>able part of a program, pro-<br>cedure, function or the state-<br>ments following FOR-DO,<br>WHILE-DO, or IF-THEN-<br>ELSE statements. |
| **REPEAT**<br>*<br>*<br>**UNTIL** m> n; | Delimits a series of program<br>statements that are executed<br>repeatedly until the condi-<br>tion specified in the UNTIL<br>statement becomes true. |
| **FOR** n := 1 TO m **DO**<br>or<br>**FOR** n := 50 DOWNTO m<br>**DO** | Sets up repeated execution of<br>one or more statements until<br>the specified condition (n =<br>m in this example) is satisfied. |
| **WHILE** m < n **DO** | Sets up repeated execution of<br>one or more statements while<br>the specified condition (m <n<br>in this example) continues to<br>be true. |
| **IF** condition<br>  **THEN** action<br>**ELSE IF** condition<br>  **THEN** other action<br>**ELSE** other action | Sets up execution of alternate<br>actions contingent upon result<br>of one or a series of IF con-<br>dition tests. |

Program Vocabulary Items    Uses
(*continued*)

| | |
|---|---|
| **CASE** expression **OF**<br>list of values;<br>action;<br>list of values;<br>action;<br>*<br>*<br>list of values;<br>action;<br>→ **OTHERWISE**<br>default action;<br>**END**; | Sets up execution of one of<br>several actions according to<br>the value of a scalar or sub-<br>range expression. |
| variable := expression | Assigns the value of the expres-<br>sion to the variable. |
| **GOTO** i | Causes a direct transfer to the<br>statement labeled with the in-<br>ger constant i. |
| **WITH** recordident DO | Identifies a series of records<br>whose fields can be accessed<br>without having to respecify the<br>record names. |
| program statement<br>{**comment**}<br>or<br>program statement<br>(* **comment** *) | Braces or (* and *) provide<br>delimiters for comments. |

## ARITHMETIC OPERATORS

NOTE. In general, if both operands are of type integer, type real,
or type longreal, the result is of that type. If one of the operands is
real or longreal, the result is of that type.

| | |
|---|---|
| result := value 1 + value 2 | Addition of real, longreal, or<br>integer values. |
| result := value 1 − value 2 | Subtraction of real, longreal,<br>or integer values. |
| result := multiplicand *<br>multiplier | Multiplication of real, longreal,<br>or integer values. |

| Program Vocabulary Items (*continued*) | Uses |
|---|---|
| result := dividend/divisor | Division of real, longreal, or integer values. The result is always real or longreal. |
| result := dividend **DIV** divisor | Gives remainder of an integer number after division by an integer divisor. |
| result := number **MOD** divisor | |
| **BOOLEAN OPERATORS** | |
| **NOT** empty | Negation of Boolean operand. |
| finished **AND** empty | Logical AND. |
| coffee **OR** tea | Logical OR. |
| **SET OPERATORS** | |
| [ . . . ] | Brackets function as set delimiters. |
| [apples] + [sugar] = [apples, sugar] | Set union operator (+) and set equality (=). |
| [paper,pen] − [pen] = [paper] | Set difference operator (−) and set equality (=). |
| [h2,0] * [h2,cl] = [h2] | Set intersection operator (*) and set equality (=) |
| [apples] <= [apples, apricots, oranges, peaches] | First set is contained in (<=) the second set. |
| [apples, apricots, peaches] >= [apricots] | First set contains (>=) the second set. |
| pen **IN** [pen,paper,ink] | Tests whether an element is included in a set. |
| [icecream] <> [ice,cream] | First set is not equal to the second set. |
| [] | Empty set. |
| **RELATIONAL OPERATORS** (produce Boolean results) | |
| IF dividend <0 | Less than (<). |
| IF result <= mininumber | Less than or equal to (<=). |
| IF number = result − 0.456 | Equal to (=). |
| IF press1 < > press2 | Unequal to (< >). |
| IF oiltemp >= 220 | Greater than or equal to (>=). |
| IF watertemp > 220 | Greater than (>). |

Program Vocabulary Items
(*continued*)

Uses

---

**STANDARD ARITHMETIC
FUNCTIONS**

**abs** (x)               Computes absolute value of
                          real, longreal, or integer x with
                          result of same type as x.

**sqr** (x)               Computes square of real,
                          longreal, or integer x with re-
                          sult of the same type as x.

**sin** (x)               Computes sine of x radians for
                          real, longreal, or integer x with
                          real or longreal result.

**cos** (x)               Computes cosine of x radians
                          for real, longreal, or integer x
                          with real or longreal result.

**exp** (x)               Computes base e exponential
                          value of real, longreal, or inte-
                          ger x with real or longreal result.

**ln** (x)                Gives base e logarithm of real,
                          longreal, or integer x with real
                          or longreal result.

**sqrt** (x)              Calculates square root of real,
                          longreal, or integer x with real
                          or longreal result.

**arctan** (x)            Calculates Arc Tangent of
                          real, longreal, or integer x with
                          real or longreal result in
                          radians.

**STANDARD PREDICATE
FUNCTIONS**

**odd** (x)               Tests integer x with result true
                          if x is odd and false otherwise.

**eof** (f)               Indicates whether file f is in
                          End-Of-File status.

**eoln** (f)              Indicates whether text file f is
                          at the end of a line.

**STANDARD TRANSFER
FUNCTIONS**

**trunc** (x)             Converts real or longreal x to
                          an integer result which is the

Program Vocabulary Items   Uses
(*continued*)

|  |  |
|---|---|
|  | integral part of x (deletes fractional part of x). |
| **round** (x) | Converts real or longreal x to an integer result that is the value of x rounded to the nearest integer. |
| **STANDARD ORDINAL FUNCTIONS** | |
| **ord** (x) | Returns an integer result that is the ordinal number of x in its defined list of values. |
| **chr** (x) | Returns the character value whose ordinal number is equal to the value of the integer expression x. |
| **succ** (x) | Returns a value whose ordinal number is one greater than that of ordinal expression x, if there is such a value. |
| **pred** (x) | Returns a value whose ordinal number is one less than that of ordinal expression x, if there is such a value. |
| → **linepos** (f) | Returns an integer number of characters read from, or written to, textfile f, since the last eoln. |
| → **position** (f) | Returns an integer representing the current position of the file buffer in direct access file f, starting from 1. This is the index of the next component which will be read or written by a call to read or write. |
| → **maxpos** (f) | Returns an integer representing the position of the last element of direct access file f which may ever be accessed. |

Program Vocabulary Items          Uses
(*continued*)

## INPUT AND OUTPUT PROCEDURES

**read** (fn,p1,p2, . . . ,pn)     Reads input data or text from a named file (fn).

**readln** (fn,p1,p2, . . . pn)    Similar to read, but for text files only with skipping to the start of the next line after the last-specified parameter has been read in the current line.

→ **readdir** (f,k,v1, . . . ,vn)    Reads values v1 through vn from direct access file f, starting at component k.

**write** (fn,p1,p2, . . . pn)     Writes output data or text to a named file.

**writeln** (fn,p1,p2, . . . pn)    Similar to write, but for text file only with addition of an end-of-line marker after the last parameter.

→ **writedir** (f,k,v1, . . . ,vn)    Writes values v1 through vn to direct access file f, starting at component k.

## FILE HANDLING PROCEDURES

**rewrite** (f)     Opens file for writing, with index positioned to the first component; any previously existing information in the file is discarded.

→ **append** (f)     Opens file f for writing, with index positioned just beyond the last-written component for addition of components to f.

**reset** (f)     Opens file f for reading, with index positioned at the first component.

**put** (f^)     Writes the value of buffer variable f^ to file f and advances to the next component.

Program Vocabulary Items          Uses
(*continued*)

| | |
|---|---|
| **get(f^)** | Advances, then assigns the value of the current file f component to buffer variable f^ if the component exists, and advances to the next component; if the component does not exist, the eof condition is set for f. |
| → **close** (f) | Closes file f. A second parameter can be used to cause the closed file to be either saved or purged. |
| → **open** (f) | Opens nontext file for direct access, positioned at the first component. |
| → **seek** (f,k) | Positions direct access file f at component k. If k > component bound of f, eof is set. |
| **DYNAMIC ALLOCATION PROCEDURES** | |
| **new** (p) | Allocates new variable v and assigns a pointer to v to the pointer variable p. |
| **new** (p,t1, . . . ,tn) | Allocates a variable of record type with tag fields t1, . . . tn. |
| **dispose** (p) | Releases storage such that it is available for re-use by a subsequent call to new. |
| **dispose** (p,t1, . . . ,tn) | Releases storage for variable previously allocated using the new (p,t1, . . . ,tn) procedure. |
| → **mark** (p) | Marks the state of the heap in the variable p, which may be of any pointer type. |
| → **release** (p) | restores the state of the heap to the value in the variable p. This has the effect of disposing of all heap objects created by the new procedure since p was marked. |

Program Vocabulary Items    Uses
(*continued*)

| DATA TRANSFER AND MISCELLANEOUS PROCEDURES | |
|---|---|
| pack (a,i,z) | Packs array a into array z, using index factor i. |
| unpack (z,a,i) | Unpacks array z into array a, using index factor i. |
| → halt (i) | Causes abnormal termination of program with display of optional integer i, if provided. |
| → page (f) | Causes skipping to the top of a new page when textfile f is printed. |
| → prompt (f) | Similar to writeln, but no line marker is written. |
| → overprint (f) | Similar to writeln, but the next line prints over the current line. |

**Compiler Options**

**ANSI.** ON causes an error message to be issued for any feature of Pascal/1000 which is not part of "standard" Pascal. Default is OFF.

**Partial_Eval.** ON suppresses evaluation of the right operand of the AND operator when the left operand is false or of the right operand of the OR operator when the left operand is true. OFF causes all operands of Boolean operators to be evaluated. Default is ON.

**List.** ON causes the source to be listed. OFF suppresses the listing except for lines that contain errors. Default is ON.

**PAGE.** Causes the listing to resume on top of the next page if LIST is ON.

**Include.** The string parameter names a file which contains text to be included at the current position in the program. Included code may not contain additional INCLUDE options.

**Width.** Number of significant characters in source lines. Additional characters in the line are ignored. Default is 72.

**Asmb.** Specifies the option string to be passed to the Assembler for control of the nature of assembler OUTPUT, such as whether a listing of the assembled code is provided. Default is R (no listing).

→ Identifies extension to Wirth Pascal.

**Autopage.**    ON specifies that each procedure or function is to be listed on a new page. Page eject is performed after each routine has been compiled, so that a nested routine and the the body of its enclosing routine are listed on separate pages. Default is OFF.

**Ema.**    Specifies parameters of the EMA instruction emitted for HEAP 2 programs. The string is of the form 'emasize,msegsize' (such as '65,2') where emasize and msegsize are integer literals. Default is '0,0'.

**Buffers = n.**    Specifies compile time file options, such as buffer size. Default is 'BUFFERS = 1'.

**Heap.**    0 specifies that no heap is used. 1 specifies that the heap/stack area resides in the area between the end of the program and the end of the partition in which the program is currently executing. Pointers are one-word addresses. 2 specifies that the heap/stack resides in EMA. Pointers are two-word double integer offsets from the start of EMA. 3 is similar to 2, but memory mapping and paging is done by user-written routines. Default is 1.

**List_Code.**    ON specifies that the program listing is to contain emitted code in symbolic (assembly language) form. Default is OFF.

**Code.**    ON specifies that executable code is to be emitted. Default is ON.

**Range.**    ON specifies that run-time checks of array indexing and subrange assignments and pointer values are to be emitted. Default is ON.

**Recursive.**    OFF specifies that subsequent procedures cannot be called recursively. Default is ON.

**Title.**    The first 25 characters of the string parameter will be printed on the top of the next and subsequent pages of the source listing.

**Pascal.**    The string parameter follows the name on the NAM record of the program, subprogram, or segment, and is used to specify program type, priority, etc., and a comment. In addition, the system utilities COMPL and CLOAD look for '$PASCAL' as the first characters of a source file in order to schedule the Pascal compiler.

**Segment.**    ON specifies that the current compilation unit is a segment, rather than a subprogram or main program. A segment is similar to a subprogram, except that it can be loaded dynamically. Default is OFF.

**Static.**    The number specifies the amount of contiguous space from the dynamic memory area that is not to be used by the heap and stack. Default is 0.

**Subprogram.**    ON specifies that the current compilation unit is a subprogram. A subprogram is similar to a main program, except that there is no body for the main. Each outer level routine in a subprogram unit is an entry point.

**Subtitle.** The first 25 characters of the string parameter will be printed under the title string, if any, at the top of the next and subsequent pages of the listing.

**Tables.** ON specifies that symbol table information is to be dumped following each procedure and the main program. Default is OFF.

**Trace.** ON specifies that calls are to be placed in the emitted code that invoke runtime trace procedures to keep a history of procedure entry and exit. Default is OFF.

**Alias.** Followed by a character string provides alternate identification of a procedure or function within the procedure or function heading.

**Direct.** ON bypasses normal .ENTR parameter handling to speed up program execution in nonrecursive routines. Default is OFF.

**Errorexit.** Specifies that an external routine's calling sequence includes an error return.

**Heapparm.** ON changes Heap 2 parameter handling to be the same as Heap 1 parameter handling to realize savings in memory and execution time where VAR parameters are assumed not to be in the Heap. Default is OFF.

**XREF.** ON generates Pascal cross-reference. Default is OFF.


## TEXAS INSTRUMENTS PASCAL

Texas Instruments (TI) Pascal is an implementation of Pascal for the TI 990 minicomputer and the TI 9900 microprocessor family. The following are extensions to Pascal which are implemented in TI Pascal:

Random access files

Common variables having global extent and scope as specified by ACCESS declarations

Dynamic bounds for arrays and sets

Multiprecision integer variables

Multiprecision real variables

FIXED data type

DECIMAL data type

ESCAPE statement for exit from structured statements

Explicit type override operator

ASSERT statement

External procedures and functions using FORTRAN linkage

Standard Model 990 Computer dependent procedures and functions

Additional type-checking for procedure and function parameters

Underscore (_) and dollar sign ($) in identifiers

Constant expressions

FOR statement with IN generator

Function LOCATION

Dynamic array and set parameters

Empty parameter lists for procedures and functions

CLOSE procedure

SIZE function

HALT procedure

MESSAGE procedure

Hexadecimal constants

ENCODE and DECODE procedures

More reliable form of WITH statement

OTHERWISE clause and subrange case labels with CASE statement

Formatted READ operation

DATE procedure

TIME procedure

The relational operators $<$ and $>$ may be applied to sets


The modifications to Pascal are:


Restriction of side effects of user defined functions

Restricted use of GOTO statement

Local scope of FOR statement control variable

Altered precedence for Boolean operators

More flexible I/O functions and procedures

Predefined symbol MAXINT is not supported

RESET procedure required for textfile INPUT

REWRITE procedure permitted for textfile OUTPUT

WRITE procedure replaces PUT

READ procedure replaces GET

Types of parameters of routines that are passed as parameters must be declared

**OMSI PASCAL**

OMSI Pascal is a Pascal compiler for the DEC PDP-11 family of computers, including the LSI-11 microcomputer. Some of the important features of OMSI Pascal are:

NONPASCAL call interface (for FORTRAN and MACRO)
EXTERNAL Pascal call interface
in-line macrocode is supported
extensions for process control applications
supports the use of overlays

The features of OMSI Pascal make it particularly useful in the real-time process control environment, since the language is capable of handling interrupts very rapidly. The language is therefore particularly suited for real-time graphics.

OMSI Pascal requires a minimum of 40K bytes of user memory, and includes a number of utilities such as

source code formatter
cross-reference generator
dynamic string package

In addition, OMSI Pascal includes an interactive symbolic debugger which provides stored breakpoints and a program execution history retrace.

OMSI Pascal is a proprietary product of Oregon Software, of Portland, Oregon.

Some of the important extensions to Pascal found in OMSI Pascal are as follows:

functions:
  **bitsize**
  **loophole**
  **ref**
  **size**
  **time**
reserved words
  **external**
  **forward**

nonpascal
origin
otherwise
procedures
**break**
**close**
**seek**

An explanation of a few of these extensions would be in order.

The **bitsize** and **size** functions are used by the programmer to determine the storage space allocated to a particular type identifier. The function **size** specifies the number of bytes used under normal storage allocation procedure, while the function **bitsize** indicates the number of bits allocated when the argument is a component of a packed record.

The **loophole** function enables the programmer to deviate from the type restrictions of Pascal. For example,

$$L := \text{\textbf{loophole} } (integer, S)$$

is a **loophole** function in which the first argument represents the result type of the function, while the second argument is the expression which is operated upon by the function. The result of the **loophole** function is to convert the bit pattern of the argument expression into a value of the type indicated in the first argument.

The **ref** function takes an argument of data type T and produces a pointer to that variable as a result.

# 11

# Pascal: UCSD Pascal Microcomputer Implementations

One of the most popular implementations of Pascal for microcomputers has been the UCSD Pascal version. In the present chapter we consider UCSD Pascal in general, using UCSD Pascal on specific microcomputer systems, and the Western Digital Pascal Microengine implementation of UCSD Pascal.

## UCSD PASCAL

UCSD Pascal is an implementation of Pascal done at the University of California, San Diego (UCSD) intended for a wide variety of mini- and microcomputers. Because of the widespread availability of microcomputers, and the interest in implementing high level languages with extensive capabilities on such systems, considerable attention has been focused on UCSD Pascal, and it would therefore be appropriate to describe the implementation in detail.

In order to present UCSD in an organized manner, this section is broken into the following topics:

UCSD Pascal overview
screen editor
file handler
compiler
comparison of UCSD Pascal with Standard Pascal

## UCSD Pascal Overview

UCSD Pascal is an implementation of Pascal with various extensions from Standard Pascal that was originally implemented at UCSD on the Digital Equipment LSI-11 and later on other microprocessor-based systems in the mid-1970s. Although the software was originally licensed by UCSD directly to users, its distribution has now been taken over by a commercial firm, SofTech Microsystems, Inc., of San Diego, which supports the system and licenses new users. The name itself, UCSD Pascal, is registered as a trademark by the Regents of the University of California.

The UCSD implementation was originally intended for single-user student use in an interactive environment. The Pascal software was therefore based upon an interpreter, and support programs for editing and file management were also included. Thus a single user at a microcomputer could write and edit programs, execute them on the computer, and save them on a floppy disk for later use.

The presently available version of UCSD Pascal, available on floppy disk, includes the same editing and file support programs as in the original implementation. Moreover, various bootstrapping routines are available to interface UCSD Pascal with many of the microcomputer operating systems currently used.

The UCSD Pascal System basically includes three parts: the screen editor, the file handler, and the compiler. These are three system programs which enable the user to more efficiently and effectively use the computer facilities to execute a Pascal program. It must be pointed out that these system programs are optional; in fact other microcomputer implementations of Pascal based upon the UCSD Pascal interpreter exist which do not include them at all, or include their own system support programs.

### Outermost Level Commands

There are eight general commands which are presented in the form of a prompt line and form the outermost level of the system software, that is, the most general commands that are at the top of the hierarchy of system programs. After specifying one of the eight general commands, the prompt line changes and the user descends onto a branch of the system software, such as suggested in Figure 11.1, and must return to that level before entering another branch.

The eight commands are:

E(dit

F(iler

C(omp

R(un

X(ecute

A(ssem

D(ebug

L(ink

These commands may be invoked by merely typing the first character at the keyboard in response to the prompt line, for example, "E" will evoke the edit command, as will "Eabcd" or "Edit." The left-hand parenthesis after the first letter in the above list is used merely to remind the user that the subsequent list of letters is merely for mnemonic purposes, and is not necessary to invoke the command.

The Edit command results in the editor system program being called from the disk. The purpose of the editor is to permit the user to "edit" or change the contents of the displayed portion of a working file (called a workfile) through the use of the keyboard.

The Filer command results in the filer system program being called from the disk. The Filer program is concerned with maintaining files on the disks.

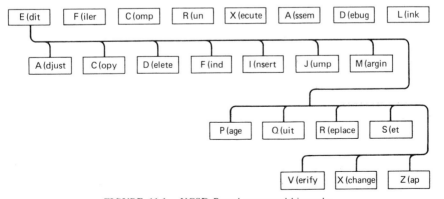

FIGURE 11.1.   UCSD Pascal command hierarchy.

The Comp command results in the compiler system program being called from the disk. The user's current workfile is then compiled, that is, translated into an object program for running on the computer. Another function of the compiler is error detection. If the compiler detects a programming error, an error message is printed out on the CRT display unit identifying the nature of the error. Once the user has identified and understood the error, it may be corrected by calling the Editor program and making a suitable change in the text of the program.

The Run command results in execution of the object program associated with the current workfile.

The Xecute command is similar to the Run command in that it executes an object program. However the file execute is *not* necessarily the workfile but any specifically named previously compiled code file.

The Assem command results in the assembler program being called from the disk. The assembler program functions to convert the source program in Pascal to an assembly language program for a specific processor. Many programmers find it useful to have assembly language programs that can perform operations which might not have been possible using Pascal, or to obtain assembly language object code versions of their Pascal programs for running on a host processor independent of the operating system.

The Debug command results in execution of the object program associated with the current workfile. If an error is detected, a system debugger program is called to analyze the error. In the UCSD Pascal Version II.0 available at the time this was written, the debug command was not yet implemented.

The Link command calls the system linker, which permits the programmer to link together sections of compiled or assembled routines from various files.

**Screen Editors**

The Screen Editor is a system program designed to handle user interaction with the keyboard and CRT display. The program is an interactive one using a series of prompting questions to which the user responds by pressing specified keys on the keyboard, such as

specific upper-case letters
the "return" key
the "escape" key

The overall purpose of the Screen Editor is to permit the user to create a text file that can be stored in the computer with user comments or other documentation, and later modified or executed as a program. The principal operations of the Screen editor, as the name implies, is to allow the user to "edit" the text or program that appears on the screen of the CRT.

In summarizing the Screen Editor in this section, it would be useful to first list all of the Screen Editor commands, and then turn to a description of the specific operation of each of them.

1. Cursor movement commands
   ↑
   ↓
   →
   ←

2. Repeat command: implemented by typing an integer before a command.

3. Commands:
   A(djust
   C(opy
   D(elete
   F(ind
   I(nsert
   J(ump
   M(argin
   P(age
   Q(uit
   R(eplace
   S(et
   V(erify
   eX(change
   Z(ap

*Cursor Movement Commands.*   The cursor is a visual indicator placed by the user at a specific position in a text. The various Screen Editor commands are operative at the text specified by the cursor, so the user's first task is to move the cursor to the desired position.

The basic cursor movement commands consist of four arrow keys on most keyboards. The up arrow ↑ key moves the cursor up one line. The down arrow ↓ key moves the cursor down one line. The right arrow → key moves the cursor to the right by one space, and the left arrow ← key moves the cursor to the left by one space.

On keyboards that do not have the four arrow keys, it is possible to evoke the cursor movement commands by the use of certain letters on the keyboard in combination with the control key on the keyboard.

**P(age**. The P(age command moves the cursor up or down by several lines, or a "page" depending upon the repeat factor. Using the P(age command, the cursor jumps from page to page, always retaining the same position in each line.

**J(ump**. The J(ump command permits the cursor to be moved automatically from one predetermined start location to another. There are three possibilities for the destination location:

beginning of the workfile

end of the workfile

a marker location

The marker location is one placed at a specific point in the workfile by the S(et commnd.

**S(et**. The S(et command is used for setting markers in the workfile which are used by the J(ump instruction. The position of the marker that is set corresponds to the position of the cursor at the time the S(et command is entered.

*Repeat Command.*   On some intelligent keyboards, the repetition of a typed key is implemented by simultaneously pressing another key which is called "repeat." Thus if one wanted to move the cursor position at the beginning of a line to a point in the middle of the line, it would not be necessary to press the cursor key 10, 20, or 30 times; one would merely press the right arrow → key together with the repeat key and simultaneously hold both keys down until the desired point on the line for positioning the cursor was reached.

The Screen Editor provides another method for implementation of the Repeat Function. Using the Screen Editor, one merely types a specific integer before typing the command. Thus, if one wanted to move the cursor 18 places to the right, one would type 18 followed by the right arrow → key. The cursor will then jump 18 positions to the right. Such a facility is particularly useful if one knows the exact number of positions the cursor should be moved. The other technique of using the repeat key requires considerable eye-finger coordination to make the cursor stop exactly on the position desired.

*Commands: Text Editing.*   Since the objective of the Screen Editor is to permit the user to "edit" the text that appears on the screen, it is not surprising that many of the Screen Editor commands are directed to text editing functions.

**I(nsert.**   The I(nsert command permits the user to enter text into the file under consideration, which is called the workfile. The cursor is positioned at the point in the text of the existing workfile where new text is desired to be entered. The user then types the I key, which lets the Editor enter the Insert mode, and types the new text. When the user is finished entering the text, the ETX (End of Text) key is pressed, and the Insert mode is terminated. The new text is then incorporated into the workfile in the position specified.

**D(elete.**   The D(elete command permits the user to delete a specific portion of text stored in the workfile. The cursor is first positioned at the first character where the deletion is to begin, called the anchor or entry point, and the D(elete command entered. The cursor is then moved to another position specifying where the deleted text ends. The ETX key is then pressed to terminate the delete operation, and the text between the anchor position and the current position of the cursor is deleted.

**eX(change.**   The eX(change command combines the Delete and Insert commands by simply permitting the user to type over characters in the workfile with new characters to be inserted.

*Commands: Text Processing.*   The Screen Editor includes a number of commands that can be said to "process" the text in the workfile.

**A(djust.** The A(djust command is used to shift a line of text on which the cursor is located to the left or right of the page to left justify, indent, or right justify.

**F(ind.** F(ind is used for jumping to a position in the workfile defined by a particular string of characters. For example, if one is looking for a previously entered procedure by the name of "beta," one would type

/beta/

and the Screen editor would search thorugh the workfile for the string of characters "beta."

**C(opy**. C(opy is used to insert text into the workfile at the current position of the cursor. The text may be derived from either a buffer or a particularly named file.

**R(eplace**. The R(eplace command is similar to the find command in that it but goes beyond just finding the target, finds a target string, and replaces it with a substitute string.

The replace command, like the find command, operates in either the token or literal mode.

**V(erify**. The V(erify command is used to redisplay the contents of the current workfile on the screen. During the use of the Editor, certain characters or text that have been changed due to subsequent operations on the workfile may still appear on the screen (i.e., although the text may have been replaced in the workfile in main memory, the old text may still appear in the screen buffer memory, and may therefore still appear on the screen). The verify command is used to update the screen with the current contents of the workfile.

**Z(ap**. The Z(ap command is used to correct an error while using the find, replace, or insert commands after the ETX key is pressed.

**Q(uit**. The quit command leaves the Editor. The user has a menu presented:

U(pdate
E(xit
W(rite
R(eturn

## File Handler

The File Handler is a system program that permits the user to store, maintain, and access files on the disk. The File Handler operates in basically the same manner as the Screen Editor: a prompt is provided, together with a list of common commands:

Filter: G(et, S(ave, W(hat, N(ew, L(dir, R(em, C(hng, T(rans, D(ate, Q(uit

The user responds by pressing a specific key on the keyboard, for example, "G," and the corresponding File Handler mode, in this case "Get," is entered.

As with the Screen Editor, we begin by summarizing the list of commands, and then turn to a description of the operation associated with each of them.

### File Handler Commands

B(ad blocks
C(hange
D(ate
E(xtended list
G(et
K(runch
L(dir
M(ake

N(ew
P(refix
Q(uit
R(emove
S(ave
T(ransfer
W(hat
V(olumes
eX(amine
Z(ero

The File Handler refers to files that are stored on the disks. Specific files are identified by the disk they are on, and the name of the file. Each disk is given a volume identifier, which names the disk. Each disk also contains a list of all the files on that disk, called a directory. Each file has a name, which is placed in the directory and is referred to as the "directory name."

Files store information which may be classified as either "text," "code," or "data." The type of information is made part of the file name by appending it to the file name, separated by a period. For example, a text file named alpha is identified as:

alpha.text

A code file named beta may be identified as:

beta.code

The full file name includes the volume identifier, followed by the directory name. The volume identifier and the directory name are separated by a colon (:). Using the examples above, if the volume identifier was DISKB, the full name would be:

diskb:alpha.text

and

diskb:beta.code

### Commands: Workfile Processing

**G(et**. The G(et command is used to load an existing file as the present workfile.

**S(ave.** S(ave is used after the creation of a workfile to give the file a name, and then to "save" the file on the disk for later use.

**N(ew.** N(ew is used to clear the current workfile from memory so that the user can begin creating a new workfile.

**W(hat.** W(hat displays the name of the currently active workfile.

*Commands: Directory Management Commands*

**R(emove.** R(emove functions to completely remove a specified file from the directory. The information stored in the file remains in the file.

**C(hange.** C(hange enables the user to change the title of a file which is listed in the directory.

**M(ake.** M(ake creates a new directory entry for later use by a file yet to be saved. The user may specify a certain number of blocks to reserve a file of a given size on the disk.

**K(runch.** K(runch moves existing files on the disk to the beginning of the disk, so that all unused areas are shifted to the end.

**Z(ero.** Z(ero destroys the directory on a specified disk and creates an empty directory on that disk.

*Commands: File Management*

**T(ransfer.** T(ransfer is used to copy one or more files from a first device to a second device. Typically, both devices will be disks and the command operates as an instruction to transfer a file on one disk to the other disk.

**L(ist.** L(ist functions to list the directory of a selected device volume.

**V(olumes.** V(olumes functions to list the identifiers of volumes that are currently available.

**E(xtended directory list.** The E(xtended directory list instruction is similar to the list command but provides more information, such as the starting address on the disk, the date the file was entered, the blocksize, and the type file information (code, text, data).

**P(refix.** The P(refix command is used to change the default volume name of the system, or to display the current default volume name. The default volume name is the volume designated by the system when the user refers to a diskfile while using the File Handler but does not make explicit reference to any volume name.

**Date.** The D(ate command is used to change the date information associated with a disk, or merely to display the date information that is already contained therein. The date information is represented as day-month-year, as for example 26-Jul-1980.

*Commands: Error Management*

eX(amine. The eX(amine command is used to "examine" a specific group of blocks on a given disk. The File Handler reads the information from the designated blocks, performing a cyclic redundancy check. It then rewrites the same information found in the blocks back onto the disk, and rereads the block, making a comparison between the two reads. If the two reads are the same, the tentative conclusion is that, as far as the eX(amine command is concerned, the blocks are without recording errors.

B(ad blocks. The B(ad blocks command is another error checking command that reads all the blocks of a given disk checking for errors. If a bad block is detected, that is, a block that contains an error that cannot be eliminated after repeated reading, then the command will display the block number of that block.

### Compiler

The compiler system program is evoked by the C(omp command. The compiler operates on the current workfile, provided a workfile exists. If no workfile exists, the system will prompt the user for the name of the source code file to be compiled. The function of the compiler is two-fold:

error detection
generation of the object code file

The compiler checks the syntax of the Pascal statements according to the correct syntax of Pascal as defined, for example, in the syntax diagrams. If a syntax error is found, the text containing the error will be displayed, together with a marker pointing to the source of the error, and an error number indicating the type of error.

If there are no errors, the compiler proceeds to compile the source code, and writes the object code as a codefile on the disk with the name *SYSTEM.WRK.CODE.

### UCSD p-SYSTEM

The UCSD p-System is a proprietary software product of SofTech Microsystems, Inc., for the Intel 8086/8087 microprocessors, and the Motorola 68000 microprocessor. Like UCSD Pascal for 8-bit microprocessors, the software enables programs to be developed using UCSD Pascal, but goes beyond UCSD Pascal in that the user may also develop applications programs in BASIC, FORTRAN, or assembly language, and use the languages together in the same program. The UCSD p-System is also expected to be made available on the IBM Personal Computer, which uses the Intel 8088 microprocessor. (The Intel 8088 is an 8-bit microprocessor using the 16-bit internal architecture of the Intel 8086.)

In addition, several important new features have been added to the UCSD p-System. These innovations include the native code generator for the 8086, increased memory utilization of up to 128K bytes, 64-bit real number support, and system enhancements to support printer spooling and graphics. Support for 8087 numeric processor and larger memory utilization will be available in a second release.

The 8086 Native Code Generator enables designers to exploit the full CPU speed of the 86/87 by translating directly into the microprocessor's native code, which results in faster execution speed than with systems using an interpreter. Thus, in applications requiring high performance, code segments which will be executed many times or are otherwise critical to execution efficiency can be translated into native code. The less critical portions of the application may be left to the somewhat slower, but more memory-efficient interpretive object code.

Because of the portability of the UCSD system, programs developed for most popular 8-bit microprocessors can also be run on the 8086 and 68000. This makes available to 8086 and 68000 users a wide range of UCSD application programs written on other microprocessors. UCSD Version IV presently can be used on personal computers or microcomputer development systems based on Z80, 8080/8085, 6502, 9900, PDP-11$^{TM}$, and LSI-11$^{TM}$ microprocessors. The UCSD p-System not only allows the program portability associated with language standards and language compatibility, but permits the migration of entire software applications among all these processors in an operation no more complicated than moving object-code from one computer system to another. Such object-code portability allows the application developer to design systems across the entire range of microprocessors running under UCSD p-System.

## WESTERN DIGITAL WD/9000 PASCAL MICROENGINE

The Pascal Microengine is a set of five MOS integrated circuits for the direct execution of the UCSD Pascal P-code. The five chips are:

an ALU, containing the arithmetic/logic unit, microinstruction decode, and register file

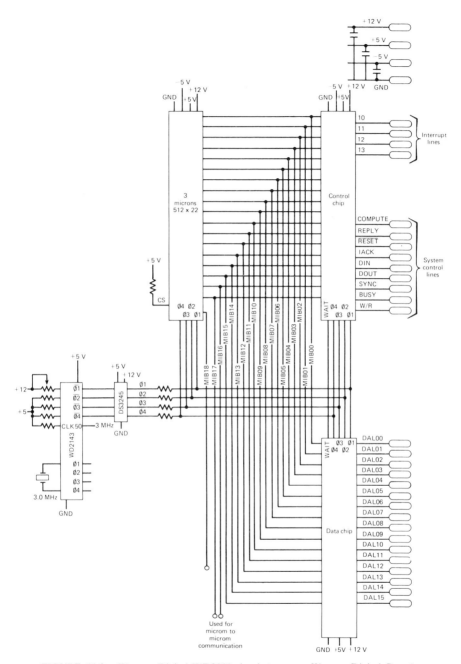

**FIGURE 11.2.** Western Digital WD9000 circuit (courtesy Western Digital Corp.).

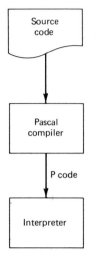

FIGURE 11,3.   Interpretive Pascal.

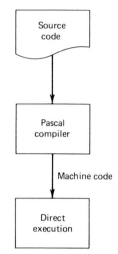

FIGURE 11.4.   Compiler based Pascal system.

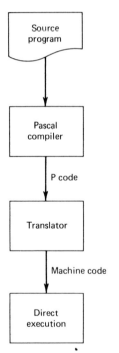

FIGURE 11.5.   P-code translator Pascal system.

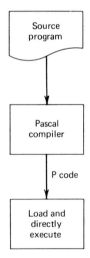

FIGURE 11.6.   Direct execution P-code system.

a control processor, containing the control ciruitry, instruction decoder, microinstruction counters, and I/O logic.

three Microms, a microprogram store containing 512 words × 22 bits

The interconnections of the chip set are shown in Figure 11.2.

It is important to understand the significance of the direct execution of P-code. Most microprocessor compilers are interpretive: the Pascal compiler produces P-code, as is shown in Figure 11.3, which is then decoded and executed by an interpreter. Some of the older Pascal compilers directly convert Pascal source code into the machine language of the target machine, typically a mainframe computer, as is suggested in Figure 11.4. Yet another approach is the translator system, shown in Figure 11.5, in which previously compiled P-code is translated into the machine language of the target processor.

The direct execution approach of the Pascal Microengine is represented in Figure 11.6. The Pascal compiler converts programs into P-code, which is executed directly on the Pascal Microengine. The previous P-code implementations resulted in the conversion of each P-code instruction into one or more machine instructions, and thus had less throughput than a system that executes P-code directly as its native instruction set.

The format of the instruction set of the Pascal Microengine is shown in Table 11.1.

**TABLE 11.1.   Pascal MICROENGINE™ Instruction Set Format**

Instructions are one byte long, followed by zero to four parameters. Most parameters specify one word of information, and are one of five basic types.

UB   Unsigned byte: high order byte of parameter is implicitly zero.

SB   Signed byte: high order byte is sign extension of bit 7.

DB   Don't care byte: can be treated as SB or UB, as value is always in the range 0 . . . 127.

B   Big: this parameter is one byte long when used to represent values in the range 0 . . . 127, and is two bytes long when representing values in the range 128 . . . 32767. If the first byte is in 0 . . . 127, the high byte of the parameter is implicitly zero. Otherwise, bit 7 of the first byte is cleared and it is used as the high order byte of the parameter. The second byte is used as the low order byte.

W   Word: the next two bytes, low byte first, are the parameter value.

More detailed information on the Pascal MICROENGINE™ instructions (P-Code) is contained in the Pascal Operations Manual.

(*continued*)

**TABLE 11.1.** (*continued*)

These mnemonics are intended only for further understanding of P-code. Neither the Microengine Company nor the University of California at San Diego provide P-code assembler software.

| Mnemonic | Instruction Code | Parameters | Description |
|---|---|---|---|
| | *Constant One-Word Loads* | | |
| SLDC | 0 . . . 31 | | Short load word constant (value 0-31) |
| LDCN | 152 | | Load constant nil |
| LDCB | 128 | UB | Load constant byte |
| LDCI | 129 | W | Load constant word |
| LCA | 130 | B | Load constant address |
| | *Local One-Word Loads and Store* | | |
| SLDL1 . . .16 | 32 . . . 47 . | | Short load local word |
| LDL | 135 | B | Load local word |
| LLA | 132 | B | Load local address |
| STL | 164 | B | Store local |
| | *Global One-Word Loads and Store* | | |
| SLDO1 . . . 16 | 48 . . . 63 | | Short load global word |
| LDO | 133 | B | Load global word |
| LAO | 134 | B | Load global address |
| SRO | 165 | B | Store global word |
| | *Intermediate One-Word Loads and Store* | | |
| LOD | 137 | DB, B | Load intermediate word |
| LDA | 136 | DB, B | Load Intermediate address |
| STR | 166 | DB, B | Store intermediate word |
| | *Indirect One-Word Loads and Store* | | |
| STO | 196 | | Store indirect |
| | *Extended One-Word Loads and Store* | | |
| LDE | 154 | UB, B | Load word extended |
| LAE | 155 | UB, B | Load address extended |
| STE | 217 | UB, B | Store word extended |
| | *Multiple Word Loads and Stores (Sets and Reals)* | | |
| LDC | 131 | B, UB | Load multiple word constant |
| LDM | 208 | UB | Load multiple words |
| STM | 142 | UB | Store multiple words |

**256**

**TABLE 11.1.** (*continued*)

| Mnemonic | Instruction Code | Parameters | Description |
|---|---|---|---|
| | *Byte Arrays* | | |
| LDB | 167 | | Load byte |
| STB | 200 | | Store byte |
| | *Record and Array Indexing and Assignment* | | |
| MOV | 197 | B | Move words |
| SIND0 . . . 7 | 120 . . . 127 | | Short index and load word |
| IND | 230 | B | Static index and load word |
| INC | 231 | B | Increment field pointer |
| IXA | 215 | B | Index array |
| IXP | 216 | $UB_1$, $UB_2$ | Index packed array |
| LDP | 201 | | Load a packed field |
| STP | 202 | | Store into a packed field |
| | *Logicals* | | |
| LAND | 161 | | Logical and |
| LOR | 160 | | Logical or |
| LNOT | 229 | | Logical not |
| LEUSW | 180 | | Compare unsigned word $<=$ |
| GEUSW | 181 | | Compare unsigned word $>=$ |
| | *Integers* | | |
| ABI | 224 | | Absolute value of integer |
| NGI | 225 | | Negate integer |
| ADI | 162 | | Add integers |
| SBI | 163 | | Subtract integers |
| MPI | 140 | | Multiply integers |
| DUPI | 226 | | Copy integer |
| DVI | 141 | | Divide integers |
| MODI | 143 | | Modulo integers |
| CHK | 203 | | Check against sub-range bounds |
| EQUI | 176 | | Compare integer $=$ |
| NEQI | 177 | | Compare integer $<>$ |
| LEQI | 179 | | Compare integer $<=$ |
| GEQI | 179 | | Compare integer $>=$ |

**TABLE 11.1.** (*continued*)

| Mnemonic | Instruction Code | Parameters | Description |
|---|---|---|---|
| *Reals (All Over/Underflows Cause a Run-Time Error)* | | | |
| FLT | 204 | | Float top-of-stack |
| TNC | 190 | | Truncate real |
| RND | 191 | | Round real |
| ABR | 227 | | Absolute value of real |
| ADR | 192 | | Add reals |
| NGR | 228 | | Negate real |
| SBR | 193 | | Subtract reals |
| MPR | 194 | | Multiply reals |
| DUP2 | 198 | | Copy real |
| DVR | 195 | | Divide reals |
| EQUREAL | 205 | | Compare Real = |
| LEQREAL | 206 | | Compare Real <= |
| GEQREAL | 207 | | Compare Real >= |
| *Sets* | | | |
| ADJ | 199 | UB | Adjust set |
| SRS | 188 | | Build subrange set |
| INN | 218 | | Set membership |
| UNI | 219 | | Set union |
| INT | 220 | | Set intersection |
| DIF | 221 | | Set difference |
| EQUPWR | 182 | | Set compare = |
| LEQPWR | 183 | | Set compare <= (subset of) |
| GEOPWR | 184 | | Set compare >= (superset of) |
| *Byte Arrays* | | | |
| EQUBYT | 185 | B | Byte array compare = |
| LEQBYT | 186 | B | Byte array compare <= |
| GEQBYT | 187 | B | Byte array compare >= |
| *Jumps* | | | |
| UJP | 138 | SB | Unconditional jump |
| FJP | 212 | SB | False jump |
| EFJ | 210 | SB | Equal false jump |
| NFJ | 211 | SB | Not equal false jump |
| UJPL | 139 | W | Unconditional long jump |
| FJPL | 213 | W | False long jump |
| XJP | 214 | B | Case jump |

**258**

**TABLE 11.1.** *(continued)*

| Mnemonic | Instruction Code | Parameters | Description |
|---|---|---|---|
| | | *Procedure and function calls and returns* | |
| CPL | 144 | UB | Call local procedure |
| CPG | 145 | UB | Call global procedure |
| CPI | 146 | DB, UB | Call intermediate procedure |
| CXL | 147 | $UB_1$, $UB_2$ | Call local external procedure |
| CXG | 148 | $UB_1$, $UB_2$ | Call global external procedure |
| CXI | 149 | $UB_1$, DB, $UB_2$ | Call intermediate external procedure |
| CPF | 151 | | Call formal procedure |
| RPU | 150 | B | Return from user procedure |
| | | *Processor Control* | |
| LSL | 153 | DB | Load static link onto stack |
| SIGNAL | 222 | | Signal |
| WAIT | 223 | | Wait on semaphore |
| LPR | 157 | | Load processor register |
| SPR | 209 | | Store processor register |
| | | *Debugger* | |
| BPT | 158 | | Breakpoint |
| RBP | 159 | | Return from breakpoint |
| | | *Miscellaneous* | |
| NOP | 156 | | No operation |
| SWAP | 189 | | Swap top-of-stack with next to top-of-stack |

# 12

# Modula-2 and Ada

*The [Babbage Analytical] Engine can arrange and combine its numerical quantities exactly as if they were letters or any other general symbols; and in fact it might bring out its results in algebraical notation were provisions made accordingly.*

*Ada Augusta, Countess of Lovelace (1844)*

In addition to Pascal, it is also important to make note of two other structured high level languages—Modula-2 and Ada. These languages incorporate many of the features of Pascal, and may in fact be considered as evolutionary descendants of Pascal. Although implementations of these languages are not as extensive as those for Pascal, there is expected to be greater interest in such languages, particularly Ada, in the future.

## MODULA-2

Modula-2 is a high level programming language developed by Professor Niklaus Wirth of ETH in the late 1970s. It was principally intended as a systems programming language, and extended many of the concepts found in the earlier languages Pascal and Modula.

As the name of the language implies, one of the key features of Modula-2 is the *module*. A module is a building block of a Modula-2 program, much like begin and end pairs form building blocks of a Pascal program. A module is simply a group of declarations and a sequence of statements enclosed by the brackets MODULE and END. (The keywords in Modula-2 are writ-

260

ten in upper case. A comparison of the keywords in Pascal, Modula-2, and Ada are presented in Appendix B.)

Modules are used in Modula-2 to implement concurrent processing. Individual modules are separately compilable and may include machine dependent code. In one of the early implementations of Modula-2, on the PDP-11 each module may be assigned a priority level, with execution of a particular module's priority being suspended if an interrupting module has higher priority.

An important feature of the concurrent processing modules in Modula-2 is that the particular synchronization between modules is not included in the language itself, so that the programmer may select a process scheduling algorithm that is customized to the particular requirements of the application.

Many of the other features of Modula-2, such as data types, statements, and procedures, are similar to Pascal. One extension of the data types in Pascal is the procedure type. Variables of a procedure type in Modula-2 may assume as their value a procedure P.

## ADA

The programming language Ada was developed under the auspices of the United States Department of Defense (DOD) as a common high level language for future computer systems. The language is a structured language similar to Pascal, but goes beyond Pascal in including new software components which are called subprograms, packages, and tasks, as well as a number of real-time facilities. The DOD standardization, as well as the inherent reliability and maintainability of the language itself, is expected to ensure that Ada will become one of the most important programming languages of the 1980s. Ada, incidentally, was named after Ada Augusta, Countess of Lovelace (1816–1852), who worked on Charles Babbage's Analytic Engine, a mechanical calculating machine that is considered a forerunner of today's computers. She was also the daughter of the poet Lord Byron.

Ada was developed in response to a series of language requirement documents issued by DOD and noted in the references. Alternative language proposals were developed by competing teams, and the language originally dubbed "Green" proposed by a CII-Honeywell group was finally selected and renamed Ada in June 1979.

In the present section we review the following features of Ada:

basic elements

multitasking

packages and subprograms

## Basic Elements

The basic elements of Ada are similar to those of Pascal, but generally more extensive. There are 62 reserved words in Ada, listed in Table 12.1, compared to 34 in Pascal. The operators in Ada, shown in Table 12.2, and the symbols used in Ada, shown in Table 12.3, are slightly more extensive.

## Multitasking

Multitasking is concerned with the concurrent execution of distinct programs or "tasks." Multitasking capability is intended to be implemented on either a multiprocessor configuration (many processors sharing a single memory), or a distributed processor configuration (many processors with separate memories, all interconnected).

Two of the key requirements for implementing a multitasking capability are synchronization of execution of the tasks, and communication between tasks. A task consists of an interface portion or specification, and an implementation portion or body. The body may contain local variables and executable statements. A task is entered much like a procedural call. The task

**TABLE 12.1.   Reserved Words**

| | | | | |
|---|---|---|---|---|
| abort | declare | generic | of | select |
| accept | delay | goto | or | separate |
| access | delta | | others | subtype |
| all | digits | | out | |
| and | do | if | | |
| array | | in | package | task |
| at | | is | pragma | terminate |
| | | | | then |
| | | | | type |
| | else | | private | |
| | elsif | limited | procedure | |
| | end | loop | | use |
| begin | entry | | raise | |
| body | exception | mod | range | |
| | exit | | record | when |
| | | | rem | |
| | | | renames | while |
| | | new | | with |
| case | for | not | return | |
| constant | function | null | reverse | xor |

**TABLE 12.2. Ada Operators**

| Operator | Operation | Left Operand | Right Operand | Result |
|---|---|---|---|---|
| *Arithmetic* | | | | |
| + <br> − <br> * <br> / | Addition <br> Subtraction <br> Multiplication <br> Division | Both integer type <br> Both floating type <br> (One integer, one fixed type)[a] | | Same integer type <br> Same floating type <br> (same fixed type)[a] |
| mod | Remainder | Integer type | | Same integer type |
| ** | Exponentiation | Integer <br> Floating | Positive <br> Integer | Same integer type <br> Same floating type |
| *Logical* | | | | |
| and | Conjunction | Boolean | | Same Boolean type |
| or | Inclusive disjunction | Boolean | | |
| xor | Exclusive disjunction | Boolean array | | |
| *Relational* | | | | |
| = | Equality | Both the same type | | Boolean |
| /= | Inequality | | | |
| < | Less than | | | |
| <= | Less than or equal | Both the same scalar type | | Boolean |
| > | Greater than | | | |
| >= | Greater than or equal | | | |

[a] Only for multiplication.

263

TABLE 12.3.  Symbols

| | | |
|---|---|---|
| := | Assignment | Right-side value assigned to left side of symbol |
| & | Concatenation | Right-side string suffixed to left-side string |
| \| | Alternate | Separates members of a list of values |
| ' | Object delimiter | Separates members of a list of objects |
| ` | Attribute delimiter | Separates object from attribute |
| . | Record delimiter | Separates record component from object |
| ; | STATEMENT delimiter | Functions as right-hand statement bracket |
| . . | Range | From value at left to value at right |
| : | Replacement character | Used for initialization and declaration |
| << >> | Label brackets | Used as statement labels for **goto** reference |

must contain an accept statement, and the activation of a task takes place when there is a "rendezvous" between the entry call and the accept statement.

**Packages and Subprograms**

In addition to tasks, there are two other major subunits of an Ada program—packages and subprograms, data types, and data objects which are all logically related in some manner. Packages are distinguished from tasks in that packages are units for sequential processing, whereas tasks are units for concurrent processing. Examples of packages include routines for text processing, or routines for arithmetic calculation. Packages and tasks are sometimes referred to as "modules."

In addition to modules, the other type of separately compilable unit in Ada is known as a *subprogram*. A subprogram is a group of executable statements that perform a specific application, like calculating a specific function. Subprograms fall into two categories—procedures and functions. The difference between a procedure and a function is that a procedure executes an algorithm, whereas a function performs a calculation and returns a value.

Both packages and subprograms consist of a specification portion and an implementation or body portion. The specification portion of a subprogram specifies the name of the subprogram, as well as formal parameters and other declarations that are local to the subprogram. The specification portion of a function also specifies the data type of the result of the computation.

# REFERENCES

## Modula-2

N. Wirth, Modula: A Language for Modula Multiprogramming, *Software Practice and Experience* **7**, 3-35 (1977).

N. Wirth, *MODULA-2*, ETH, Zürich, Switzerland, 1980.

## Ada

D. Fisher, *Woodenman—Set of Criteria and Needed Characteristics for a Common DoD Higher Order Programming Language*, Institute for Defense Analyses, Washington, DC, August 1975.

Department of Defense Requirements for High Order Computer Programming Languages "TINMAN," High Order Language Working Group, U.S. Dept. of Defense, June 1976.

Department of Defense Requirements for High Order Computer Programming Langue "Revised IRONMAN," High Order Language Working Group, U.S. Dept. of Defense, July 1977.

Department of Defense Requirements for High Order Computer Programming Languages "STEELMAN," U.S. Dept. of Defense, June 1978.

"Preliminary Ada Reference Manual," *ACM SIGPLAN Notices* **14**, No. 6 (June 1979).

J. D. Ichbiah et al., "Rationale for the Design of the Ada Programming Language," *ACM SIGPLAN Notices* **14**, No. 6 (June 1979).

Reference Manual for the Ada Programming Language Proposed Standard Document, U.S. Dept. of Defense, July 1980.

Department of Defense Requirements for Ada Programming Support Environments "STONEMAN," U.S. Dept. of Defense, Feb. 1980.

Ada Language System, Contract No. DAAK80-80-C-0507, U.S. Army Communications Research and Development Command (CORADCOM), Fort Monmouth, NJ, June 1980.

# Pascal
# Syntax Diagrams

IDENTIFIER

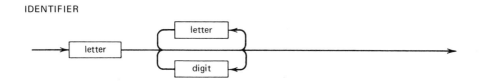

LETTER

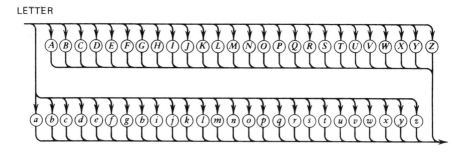

DIGIT

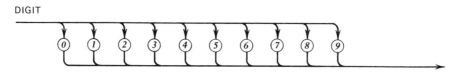

EXPRESSION

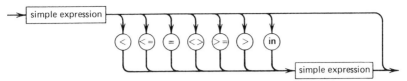

SIMPLE EXPRESSION

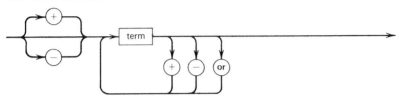

TERM

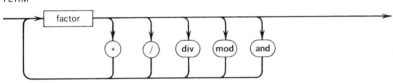

FACTOR

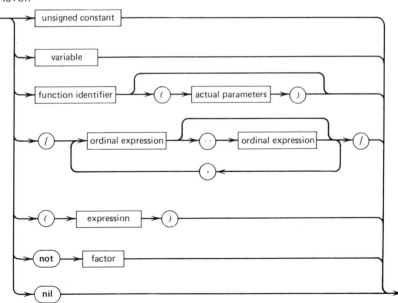

267

TYPE

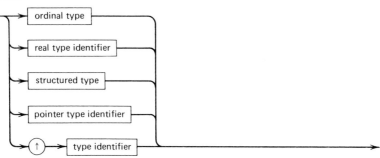

ORDINAL TYPE

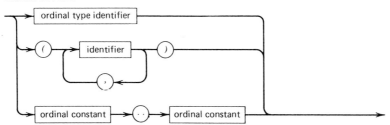

STRUCTURED TYPE

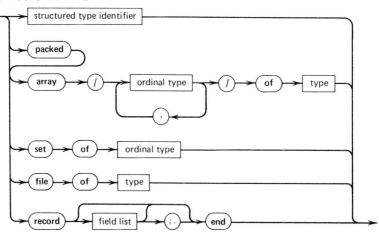

268

FIELD LIST

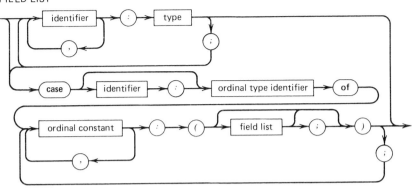

CONSTANT

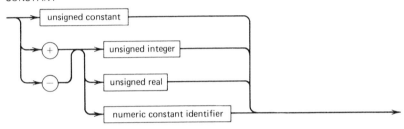

UNSIGNED CONSTANT

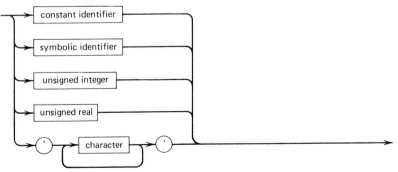

ORDINAL CONSTANT

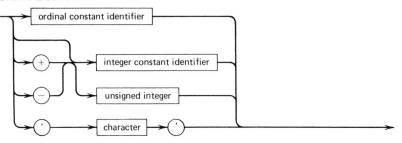

UNSIGNED INTEGER

UNSIGNED REAL

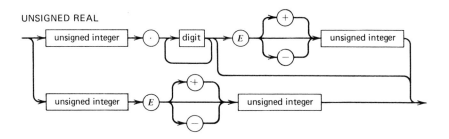

VARIABLE

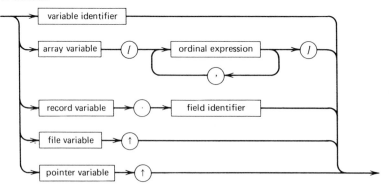

270

STATEMENT

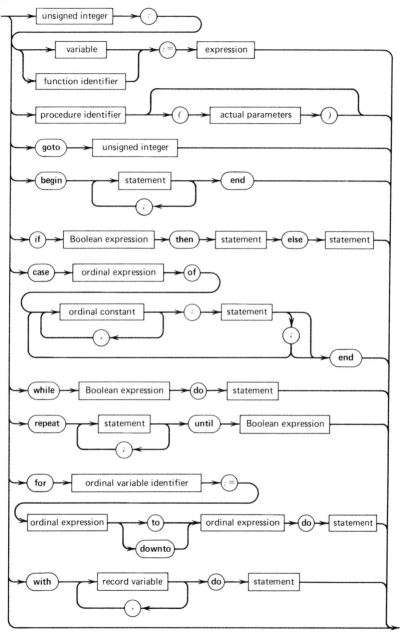

271

ACTUAL PARAMETERS

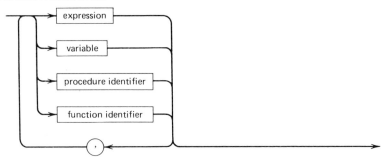

PROCEDURE HEADING

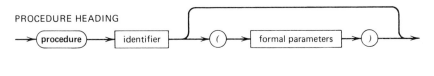

FUNCTION HEADING

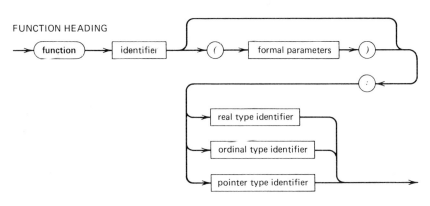

FORMAL PARAMETERS

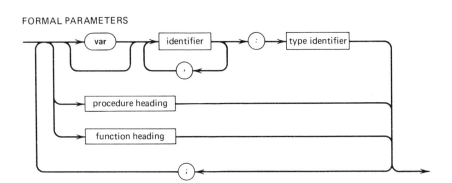

272

PROGRAM

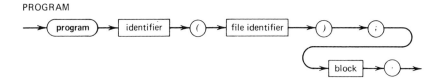

BLOCK

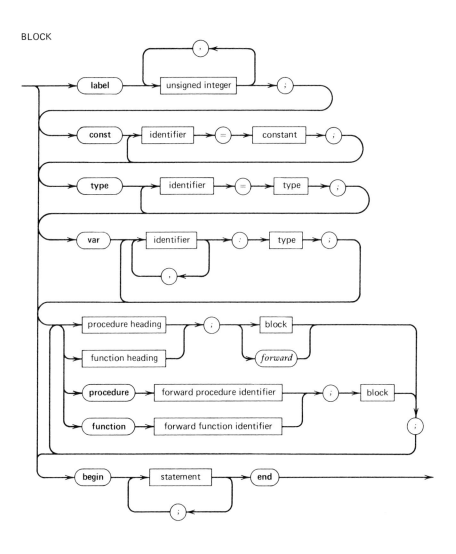

273

APPENDIX B

# Reserved Words

## PASCAL RESERVED WORDS

| and | downto | if | or | then |
|-----|--------|------|----------|-------|
| array | else | in | packed | to |
| begin | end | label | procedure | type |
| case | file | mod | program | until |
| const | for | nil | record | var |
| div | function | not | repeat | while |
| do | goto | of | set | with |

## ADA RESERVED WORDS

| | | |
|---------|-----------|---------|
| abort | delay | generic |
| accept | delta | goto |
| access | digits | if |
| all | do | in |
| and | else | is |
| array | else if | limited |
| at | end | loop |
| begin | entry | mod |
| body | exception | new |
| case | exit | not |
| constant | for | null |
| declare | function | of |

274

| or        | record   | terminate |
|-----------|----------|-----------|
| others    | rem      | then      |
| out       | renames  | type      |
| package   | return   | use       |
| pragma    | reverse  | when      |
| private   | select   | while     |
| procedure | separate | with      |
| raise     | subtype  | xor       |
| range     | task     |           |

## MODULA II RESERVED WORDS

| AND        | FOR            | PROCEDURE |
|------------|----------------|-----------|
| ARRAY      | FROM           | QUALIFIED |
| BEGIN      | IF             | RECORD    |
| BY         | IMPLEMENTATION | REPEAT    |
| CASE       | IMPORT         | RETURN    |
| CONST      | IN             | SET       |
| DEFINITION | LOOP           | THEN      |
| DIV        | MOD            | TO        |
| DO         | MODULE         | TYPE      |
| ELSE       | NOT            | UNTIL     |
| ELSEIF     | OF             | VAR       |
| END        | OR             | WHILE     |
| EXIT       | POINTER        | WITH      |
| EXPORT     |                |           |

# Pascal
# Software Vendors

Advanced Computer Techniques Corp.
437 Madison Ave.
New York, NY 10022
(212) 421-4688

Apple Computer
10260 Bandley Dr.
Cupertino, CA 95014
(408) 996-1010

Boston Systems Office
469 Moody St.
Waltham, MA 02154
(617) 894-7800

California Computer Systems
250 Caribbean Dr.
Sunnyvale, CA 94086
(408) 734-5811

Chapin Associates
11568 Sorrento Valley Rd.
San Diego, CA 92121
(714) 452-9340

Cogitronics Corp.
5470 N.W. Innisbrook Pl.
Portland, OR 97229
(503) 645-5043

Commodore International
681 Moore Rd.
King of Prussia, PA 19406
(215) 337-7100

Data General (DG)
440 Computer Dr.
Westboro, MA 01581
(617) 366-8911

Digicomp Research Corp.
Terrace Hill
Ithaca, NY 14850
(607) 273-5900

Digital Equipment Corp. (DEC)
146 Main St.
Maynard, MA 01754
(617) 897-5111

Enertec, Inc.
19 Jenkins Ave.
Lansdale, PA 19446
(215) 362-0966

Harris Computer Systems
2101 Cypress Creek Rd.
Ft. Lauderdale, FL 33309
(305) 974-1700

Hewlett-Packard Co.
1501 Page Mill Rd.
Palo Alto, CA 94304
(415) 857-1501

Intellimac, Inc.
51 Monroe St.
Rockville, MD 20850
(301) 840-0700

International Electronic Machinery
P. O. Box 1818
Fort Collins, CO 80522
(303) 226-6672

Ithaca Intersystems
1650 Hanshaw Rd.
Ithaca, NY 14850
(607) 257-0190

Language Resources Inc.
4885 Riverbend Rd.
Boulder, CO 80301
(303) 449-8087

Ontel Corporation
250 Crossway Park Dr.
Woodbury, NY 11797
(516) 364-2121

PCD Systems Inc.
323 Keuka St.
Penn Yan, NY 14527

Rational Data Systems
245 W. 55th St.
New York, NY 10019
(212) 757-0011

Softech Microsystems
San Diego, CA
(714) 589-3906

Sorcim Corporation
1333 Lawrence Expressway
Santa Clara, CA 95051
(408) 248-5543

Supersoft Associates
40 E. Main St.
Champaign, IL 61820

Xycom, Inc.
P. O. Box 984
Ann Arbor, MI 48106
(313) 429-4970

APPENDIX **D**

# Steelman*

## PREFACE

The Department of Defense Common High Order Language program was
established in 1975 with the goal of establishing a single high order computer
programming language appropriate for DoD embedded computer systems.
A High Order Language Working Group (HOLWG) was established to
formulate the DoD requirements for high order languages, to evaluate existing languages against those requirements, and to implement the minimal set
of languages required for DoD use. As an administrative initiative toward
the eventual goal, DoD Directive 5000.29 provides that any new defense
systems should be programmed in a DoD approved and centrally controlled
high order language. DoD Instruction 5000.31 gives an interim list of approved languages: COBOL, FORTRAN, TACPOL, CMS-2, SPL/1, and
JOVIAL J3 and J73. Economic analyses that were used to quantify the
benefits from increased use of high order languages, also showed that the
rapid introduction of a single modern language would increase the benefits
considerably. The requirements have been widely distributed for comment
throughout the military and civil communities, producing successively more
refined versions from STRAWMAN through WOODENMAN, TINMAN,
IRONMAN, and the present STEELMAN. During the requirement development process, it was determined that the single set of requirements generated was both necessary and sufficient for all major DoD applications. Formal evaluation was performed on dozens of existing languages concluding
that no existing language could be adopted as a single common HOL for the

* (Department of Defense Requirements for High Order Computer Programming Languages,
Defense Advanced Research Projects Agency, Arlington, VA, June 1978).

DoD but that a single language meeting essentially all the requirements was both feasible and desirable. Four contractors were funded to produce competing prototype designs. After analysis of these preliminary designs the number of design teams was reduced to two. Their designs will be completed and a single language will emerge. Further steps in the program will include test and evaluation of the language, production of compilers and other tools for software development and maintenance, control of the language, and validation of compilers. Government-funded compilers and software tools, as well as the compiler validation facility, will be widely and inexpensively available and well maintained.

## THE TECHNICAL REQUIREMENTS

The technical requirements for a common DoD high order programming language given here are a synthesis of the requirements submitted by the Military Departments. They specify a set of constraints on the design of languages that are appropriate for embedded computer applications (i.e., command and control, communications, avionics, shipboard, test equipment, software development and maintenance, and support applications). We would especially like to thank the phase one analysis teams, the language design teams, and the many other individuals and organizations that have commented on the Revised Ironman and have identified weaknesses and trouble spots in the technical requirements. A primary goal in this revision has been to reduce the complexity of the resulting language.

This revision incorporates the following changes. Care has been taken to ensure that the paragraph numbers remain the same as in the Revised Ironman. There have been several changes in terminology and many changes in wording to improve the understandability and preciseness of the requirements. Several requirements have been restated to remove constraints that were unintended but were implied because the requirement suggested a particular mechanism rather than giving the underlying requirement. The requirements for embedded comments (2I), unordered enumeration types (3-2B), associative operator specifications (7D), dynamic aliasing of array components (10B), and multiple representations of data (11B) have been deleted because they have been found unnnecessary or are not adequately justified. The minimal source language character set has been reduced to 55 characters to make it compatible with the majority of existing input devices (2A). The do together model for parallel processing has been found inadequate for embedded computer applications and has been replaced by a requirement for parallel processes (section 9). The preliminary designs have demonstrated the need for additional requirements for explicit conversion between types (3B), subtype constraints (3D), renaming (3-5B), a language distinction between open and closed scopes (5G), and the ability, but preferably not special mechanisms, to pass data between parallel processes (9H), to write nonverifiable assertions (10F), to wait for several signals simultaneously (9J), and to mark shared variables (9C).

The Steelman is organized with an outline similar to that expected in a language defining document. Section 1 gives the general design criteria. These provide the major goals that influenced the selection of more specific requirements in later sections and provide a basis for language design decisions that are not otherwise addressed in this document. Sections 2 through 12 give more specific constraints on the language and its translators. The Steelman calls for the inclusion of features to satisfy specific needs in the design, implementation, and maintenance of military software, specifies both general and specific characteristics desired for the language, and calls for the exclusion of certain undesirable characteristics. Section 13 gives some of the intentions and expectations for development, control, and use of the language. The intended use and environment for the language has strongly influenced the requirements, and should influence the language design.

A precise and consistent use of terms has been attempted throughout the document. Many potentially ambiguous terms have been defined in the text. Care has been taken to distinguish between requirements, given as text, and comments, given as bracketed notes.

The following terms have been used throughout the text to indicate where and to what degree individual constraints apply:

| | |
|---|---|
| shall | indicates a requirement placed on the language or translator |
| should | indicates a desired goal but one for which there is no objective test |
| shall attempt | indicates a desired goal but one that may not be achievable given the current state-of-the-art, or may be in conflict with other more important requirements |
| shall require | indicates a requirement placed on the user by the language and its translators (language is subject) |
| shall permit | indicates a requirement placed on the language to provide an option to the user (language is subject) |
| must | indicates a requirement placed on the user by the language and its translators (user is subject) |
| may | indicates a requirement placed on the language to provide an option to the user (user is subject) |

---

| will | indicates a consequence that is expected to follow or indicates an intention of the DoD; it does not in any case by itself constrain the design of the language |
|---|---|
| translation | refers to any processing applied to a program by the host or object machine before execution; it includes lexical analysis, syntactic error checking, program analysis, syntactic error checking, program analyses, optimization, code generation, assembly, and loading |
| execution | refers to the processing by the object machine to carry out the actions prescribed by the program. |

## General Design Criteria

*1A. Generality.* The language shall provide generality only to the extent necessary to satisfy the needs of embedded computer applications. Such applications involve real time control, self diagnostics, input-output to nonstandard peripheral devices, parallel processing, numeric computation, and file processing.

*1B. Reliability.* The language should aid the design and development of reliable programs. The language shall be designed to avoid error prone features and to maximize automatic detection of programming errors. The language shall require some redundant, but not duplicative, specifications in programs. Translators shall produce explanatory diagnostic and warning messages, but shall not attempt to correct programming errors.

*1C. Maintainability.* The language should promote ease of program maintenance. It should emphasize program readability (i.e., clarity, understandability, and modifiability of programs). The language should encourage user documentation of programs. It shall require explicit specification of programmer decisions and shall provide defaults only for instances where the default is stated in the language definition, is always meaningful, reflects the most frequent usage in programs, and may be explicitly overridden.

*1D. Efficiency.* The language design should aid the production of efficient object programs. Constructs that have unexpectedly expensive implementations should be easily recognizable by translators and by users. Features should be chosen to have a simple and efficient implementation in many object machines, to avoid execution costs for available generality where it is not needed, to maximize the number of safe optimizations available to translators, and to ensure that unused and constant portions of programs will not add to execution costs. Execution time support packages of the language shall not be included in object code unless they are called.

*1E. Simplicity.* The language should not contain unnecessary complexity. It should have a consistent semantic structure that minimizes the number of underlying concepts. It should be as small as possible consistent with the needs of the intended applications. It should have few special cases and should be composed from features that are individually simple in their semantics. The language should have uniform syntactic conventions and should not provide several notations for the same concept. No arbitrary restriction should be imposed on a language feature.

*1F. Implementability.* The language shall be composed from features that are understood and can be implemented. The semantics of each feature should be sufficiently well specified and understandable that it will be possible to predict its interaction with other features. To the extent that it does not interfere with other requirements, the language shall facilitate the production of translators that are easy to implement and are efficient during translation. There shall be no language restrictions that are not enforceable by translators.

*1G. Machine Independence.* The design of the language should strive for machine independence. It shall not dictate the characteristics of object machines or operating systems except to the extent that such characteristics are implied by the semantics of control structures and built-in operations. It shall attempt to avoid features whose semantics depend on characteristics of the object machine or of the object machine operating system. Nevertheless, there shall be a facility for defining those portions of programs that are dependent on the object machine configuration and for conditionally compiling programs depending on the actual configuration.

*1H. Complete Definition.* The language shall be completely and unambiguously defined. To the extent that a formal definition assists in achieving the above goals (i.e., all of section 1), the language shall be formally defined.

## 2. General Syntax

*2A. Character Set.* The full set of character graphics that may be used in source programs shall be given in the language definition. Every source program shall also have a representation that uses only the following 55-character subset of the ASCII graphics:

%&'( )*+,−./:;<=>?
0123456789
ABCDEFGHIJKLMNOPQRSTUVWXYZ

Each additional graphic (i.e., one in the full set but not in the 55-character set) may be replaced by a sequence of (one or more) characters from the 55-character set without altering the semantics of the program. The replacement sequence shall be specified in the language definition.

*2B.   Grammar.*   The language should have a simple, uniform, and easily parsed grammar and lexical structure. The language shall have free form syntax and should use familiar notations where such use does not conflict with other goals.

*2C.   Syntactic Extensions.*   The user shall not be able to modify the source language syntax. In particular the user shall not be able to introduce new precedence rules or to define new syntactic forms.

*2D.   Other Syntactic Issues.*   Multiple occurrences of a language defined symbol appearing in the same context shall not have essentially different meanings. Lexical units (i.e., identifiers, reserved words, single and multi-character symbols, numeric and string literals, and comments) may not cross line boundaries of a source program. All key word forms that contain declarations or statements shall be bracketed (i.e., shall have a closing as well as an opening key word). Programs may not contain unmatched brackets of any kind.

*2E.   Mnemonic Identifiers.*   Mnemonically significant identifiers shall be allowed. There shall be a break character for use within identifiers. The language and its translators shall not permit identifiers or reserved words to be abbreviated. [Note that this does not preclude reserved words that are abbreviations of natural language words.]

*2F.   Reserved Words.*   The only reserved words shall be those that introduce special syntactic forms (such as control structures and declarations) or that are otherwise used as delimiters. Words that may be replaced by identifiers shall not be reserved (e.g., names of functions, types, constants, and variables shall not be reserved). All reserved words shall be listed in the language definition.

*2G. Numeric Literals.* There shall be built-in decimal literals. There shall be no implicit truncation or rounding of integer and fixed point literals.

*2H. String Literals.* There shall be a built-in facility for fixed length string literals. String literals shall be interpreted as one-dimensional character arrays.

*2I. Comments.* The language shall permit comments that are introduced by a special (one or two character) symbol and terminated by the next line boundary of the source program.

# Types

*3A. Strong Typing.* The language shall be strongly typed. The type of each variable, array and record component, expression, function, and parameter shall be determinable during translation.

*3B. Type Converisons:* The language shall distinguish the concepts of type (specifying data elements with common properties, including operations), subtype (i.e., a subset of the elements of a type that is characterized by further constraints), and representations (i.e., implementation characteristics). There shall be no implicit conversions between types. Explicit conversion operations shall be automatically defined between types that are characterized by the same logical properties.

*3C. Type Definitions.* It shall be possible to define new data types in programs. A type may be defined as an enumeration, an array or record type, an indirect type, an existing type, or a subtype of an existing type. It shall be possible to process type definitions entirely during translation. An identifier may be associated with each type. No restriction shall be imposed on user defined types unless it is imposed on all types.

*3D. Subtype Constraints.* The constraints that characterize subtypes shall include range, precision, scale, index ranges, and user defined constraints. The value of a subtype constraint for a variable may be specified when the variable is declared. The language should encourage such specifications. [Note that such specifications can aid the clarity, efficiency, maintainability, and provability of programs.]

## 3.1.   Numeric Types

*3-1A.   Numeric Values.*   The language shall provide distinct numeric types for exact and for approximate computation. Numeric operations and assignment that would cause the most significant digits of numeric values to be truncated (e.g., when overflow occurs) shall constitute an exception situation.

*3-1B.   Numeric Operations.*   There shall be built-in operations (i.e., functions) for conversion between the numeric types. There shall be operations for addition, subtraction, multiplication, division, negation, absolute value, and exponentiation to integer powers for each numeric type. There shall be built-in equality (i.e., equal and unequal) and ordering operations (i.e., less than, greater than, less than or equal, and greater than or equal) between elements of each numeric type. Numeric values shall be equal if and only if they have exactly the same abstract value.

*3-1C.   Numeric Variables.*   The range of each numeric variable must be specified in programs and shall be determined by the time of its allocation. Such specifications shall be interpreted as the minimum range to be implemented and as the maximum range needed by the application. Explicit conversion operations shall not be required between numeric ranges.

### Approximate Arithmetic

*3-1D.   Precision.*   The precision (of the mantissa) of each expression result and variable in approximate computations must be specified in programs, and shall be determinable during translation. Precision specifications shall be required for each such variable. Such specifications shall be interpreted as the minimum accuracy (not significance) to be implemented. Approximate results shall be implicitly rounded to the implemented precision. Explicit conversions shall not be required between precisions.

*3-1E.   Approximate Arithmetic Implementation.*   Approximate arithmetic will be implemented using the actual precisions, radix, and exponent range available in the object machine. There shall be built-in operations to access the actual precision, radix, and exponent range of the implementation.

### Exact Arithmetic

*3-1F.   Integer and Fixed Point Numbers.*   Integer and fixed point numbers shall be treated as exact numeric values. There shall be no implicit truncation or rounding in integer and fixed point computations.

*3-1G. Fixed Point Scale.* The scale or step size (i.e., the minimal representable difference between values) of each fixed point variable must be specified in programs and be determinable during translation. Scales shall not be restricted to powers of two.

*3-1H. Integer and Fixed Point Operations.* There shall be integer and fixed point operations for modulo and integer division and for conversion between values with different scales. All built-in and predefined operations for exact arithmetic shall apply between arbitrary scales. Additional operations between arbitrary scales shall be definable within programs.

## 3.2. Enumeration Types

*3-2A. Enumeration Type Definitions.* There shall be types that are definable in programs by enumeration of their elements. The elements of an enumeration type may be identifiers or character literals. Each variable of an enumeration type may be restricted to a contiguous subsequence of the enumeration.

*3-2B. Operations on Enumeration Types.* Equality, inequality, and the ordering operations shall be automatically defined between elements of each enumeration type. Sufficient additional operations shall be automatically defined so that the successor, predecessor, the position of any element, and the first and last element of the type may be computed.

*3-2C. Boolean Type.* There shall be a predefined type for Boolean values.

*3-2D. Character Types.* Character sets shall be definable as enumeration types. Character types may contain both printable and control characters. The ASCII character set shall be predefined.

## 3.3. Composite Types

*3-3A. Composite Type Definitions.* It shall be possible to define types that are Cartesian products of other types. Composite types shall include arrays (i.e., composite data with indexable components of homogeneous types) and records (i.e., composite data with labeled components of heterogeneous type).

*3-3B. Component Specifications.* For elements of composite types, the type of each component (i.e., field) must be explicitly specified in programs and determinable during translation. Components may be of any type (including array and record types). Range, precision, and scale specifications shall be required for each component of appropriate numeric type.

*3-3C.   Operations on Composite Types.*   A value accessing operation shall be automatically defined for each component of composite data elements. Assignment shall be automatically defined for components that have alterable values. A constructor operation (i.e., an operation that constructs an element of a type from its constituent parts) shall be automatically defined for each composite type. An assignable component may be used anywhere in a program that a variable of the component's type is permitted. There shall be no automatically defined equivalence operations between values of elements of a composite type.

*3-3D.   Array Specifications.*   Arrays that differ in number of dimensions or in component type shall be of different types. The range of subscript values for each dimension must be specified in programs and may be determinable at the time of array allocation. The range of each subscript value must be restricted to a contiguous sequence of integers or to a contiguous sequence from an enumeration type.

*3-3E.   Operations on Subarrays.*   There shall be built-in operations for value access, assignment, and catenation of contiguous sections of one-dimensional arrays of the same component type. The results of such access and catenation operations may be used as actual input parameter.

*3-3F.   Nonassignable Record Components.*   It shall be possible to declare constants and (unary) functions that may be thought of as record components and may be referenced using the same notation as for accessing record components. Assignment shall not be permitted to such components.

*3-3G.   Variants.*   It shall be possible to define types with alternative record structures (i.e., variants). The structure of each variant shall be determinable during translation.

*3-3H.   Tag Fields.*   Each variant must have a nonassignable tag field (i.e., a component that can be used to discriminate among the variants during execution). It shall not be possible to alter a tag field without replacing the entire variant.

*3-3I.   Indirect Types.*   It shall be possible to define types whose elements are indirectly accessed. Elements of such types may have components of their own type, may have substructure that can be altered during execution, and may be distinct while having identical component values. Such types shall be distinguishable from other composite types in their definitions. An element of an indirect type shall remain allocated as long as it can be referenced by the program. [Note that indirect types require pointers and sometimes heap storage in their implementation.]

*3-3J. Operations on Indirect Types.* Each execution of the constructor operation for an indirect type shall create a distinct element of the type. An operation that distinguishes between different elements, an operation that replaces all of the component values of an element without altering the element's identity, and an operation that produces a new element having the same component values as its argument, shall be automatically defined for each indirect type.

## 3.4. Sets

*3-4A. Bit Strings (i.e., Set Types).* It shall be possible to define types whose elements are one-dimensional Boolean arrays represented in maximally packed form (i.e., whose elements are sets).

*3-4B. Bit String Operations.* Set construction, membership (i.e., subscription) set equivalence and nonequivalence, and also complement, intersection, union, and symmetric difference (i.e., component-by-component negation, conjunction, inclusive disjunction, and exclusive disjunction, respectively) operations shall be defined automatically for each set type.

## 3.5. Encapsulated Definitions

*3-5A. Encapsulated Definitions.* It shall be possible to encapsulate definitions. An encapsulation may contain declarations of anything (including the data elements and operations comprising a type) that is definable in programs. The language shall permit multiple explicit instantiations of an encapsulation.

*3-5B. Effect of Encapsulation.* An encapsulation may be used to inhibit external access to implementation properties of the definition. In particular, it shall be possible to prevent external reference to any declaration within the encapsulation including automatically defined operations such as type conversions and equality. Definitions that are made within an encapsulation and are externally accessible may be renamed before use outside the encapsulation.

*3-5C. Own Variables.* Variables declared within an encapsulation, but not within a function, procedure, or process of the encapsulation, shall remain allocated and retain their values throughout the scope in which the encapsulation is instantiated.

## 4. Expressions

*4A. Form of Expressions.* The parsing of correct expressions shall not depend on the types of their operands or on whether the types of the operands are built into the language.

*4B. Type of Expressions.* It shall be possible to specify the type of any expression explicitly. The use of such specifications shall be required only where the type of the expression cannot be uniquely determined during translation from the context of its use (as might be the case with a literal).

*4C. Side Effects.* The language shall attempt to minimize side effects in expressions, but shall not prohibit all side effects. A side effect shall not be allowed if it would alter the value of a variable that can be accessed at the point of the expression. Side effects shall be limited to own variables of encapsulations. The language shall permit side effects that are necessary to instrument functions and to do storage management within functions. The order of side effects within an expression shall not be guaranteed. [Note that the latter implies that any program that depends on the order of side effects is erroneous.]

*4D. Allowed Usage.* Expressions of a given type shall be allowed wherever both constants and variables of the type are allowed.

*4E. Translation Time Expressions.* Expressions that can be evaluated during translation shall be permitted wherever literals of the type are permitted. Translation time expressions that include only literals and the use of translation time facilitieis (see 11C) shall be evaluated during translation.

*4F. Operator Precedence Levels.* The precedence levels (i.e., binding strengths) of all (prefix and infix) operators shall be specified in the language definition, shall not be alterable by the user, shall be few in number, and shall not depend on the types of the operands.

*4G. Effect of Parentheses.* If present, explicit parentheses shall dictate the association of operands with operators. The language shall specify where explicit parentheses are required and shall attempt to minimize the psychological ambiguity in expressions. [Note that this might be accomplished by requiring explicit parentheses to resolve the operator-operand association whenever a nonassociative operator appears to the left of an operator of the same precedence at the least-binding precedence level of any subexpression.]

## 5.  Constants, Variables, and Scopes

*5A.   Declarations of Constants.*    It shall be possible to declare constants of any type. Such constants shall include both those whose values are determined during translation and those whose value cannot be determined until allocation. Programs may not assign to constants.

*5B.   Declarations of Variables.*    Each variable must be declared explicitly. Variables may be of any type. The type of each variable must be specified as part of its declaration and must be determinable during translation [Note, "variable" throughout this document refers not only to simple variables but also to composite variables and to components of arrays and records.]

*5C.   Scope of Declarations.*    Everything (including operators) declared in a program shall have a scope (i.e., a portion of the program in which it can be referenced). Scopes shall be determinable during translation. Scopes may be nested (i.e., lexically embedded). A declaration may be made in any scope. Anything other than a variable shall be accessible within any nested scope of its definition.

*5D.   Restrictions on Values.*    Procedures, functions, types, labels, exception situations, and statements shall not be assignable to variables, be computable as values of expressions, or be usable as nongeneric parameters to procedures or functions.

*5E.   Initial Values.*    There shall be no default initial values for variables.

*5F.   Operations on Variables.*    Assignment and an implicit value access operation shall be automatically defined for each variable.

*5G.   Scope of Variables.*    The language shall distinguish between open scopes (i.e., those that are automatically included in the scope of more globally declared variables) and closed scopes (i.e., those in which nonlocal variables must be explicitly imported). Bodies of functions, procedures, and processes shall be closed scopes. Bodies of classical control structures shall be open scopes.

## 6.  Classical Control Structures

*6A.   Basic Control Facility.*   The (built-in) control mechanisms should be of minimal number and complexity. Each shall provide a single capability and shall have a distinguishing syntax. Nesting of control structures shall be allowed within the bodies of control statements. Control structures shall have only one entry point and shall exit to a single point unless exited via an explicit transfer of control (where permitted, see 6G), or the raising of an exception (see 10C).

*6B.   Sequential Control.*   There shall be a control mechanism for sequencing statements. The language shall not impose arbitrary restrictions on programming style, such as the choice between statement terminators and statement separators, unless the restriction makes programming errors less likely.

*6C.   Conditional Control.*   There shall be conditional control structures that permit selection among alternative control paths. The selected path may depend on the value of a Boolean expression, on a computed choice among labeled alternatives, or on the true condition in a set of conditions. The language shall define the control action for all values of the discriminating condition that are not specified by the program. The user may supply a single control path to be used when no other path is selected. Only the selected branch shall be compiled when the discriminating condition is a translation time expression.

*6D.   Short Circuit Evaluation.*   There shall be infix control operations for short circuit conjunction and disjunction of the controlling Boolean expression in conditional and iterative control structures.

*6E.   Iterative Control.*   There shall be an iterative control structure. The iterative control may be exited (without reentry) at an unrestricted number of places. A succession of values from an enumeration type or the integers may be associated with successive iterations and the value for the current iteration accessed as a constant throughout the loop body.

*6G.   Explicit Control Transfer.*   There shall be a mechanism for control transfer (i.e., the goto). It shall not be possible to transfer out of closed scopes, into narrower scopes, or into control structures. It shall be possible to transfer out of classical control structures. There shall be no control transfer mechanism in the form of switches, designational expressions, label variables, label parameters, or alter statements.

## 7.  Functions and Procedures

*7A.  Function and Procedure Definitions.*  Functions (which return values to expressions) and procedures (which can be called as statements) shall be definable in programs. Functions or procedures that differ in the number of types of their parameters may be denoted by the same identifier or operator (i.e., overloading shall be permitted). [Note that redefinition, as opposed to overloading, of an existing function or procedure is often error prone.]

*7B.  Recursion.*  It shall be possible to call functions and procedures recursively.

*7C.  Scope Rules.*  A reference to an identifier that is not declared in the most local scope shall refer to a program element that is lexically global, rather than to one that is global through the dynamic calling structure.

### Functions

*7D.  Function Declarations.*  The type of the result for each function must be specified in its declaration and shall be determinable during translation. The results of functions may be of any type. If a result is of a nonindirect array or record type then the number of its components must be determinable by the time of function call.

### Parameters

*7F.  Formal Parameter Classes.*  There shall be three classes of formal data parameters: (a) input parameters, which act as constants that are initialized to the value of corresponding actual parameters at the time of call, (b) input-output parameters, which enable access and assignment to the corresponding actual parameters, either throughout execution or only upon call and prior to any exit, and (c) output parameters, whose values are transferred to the corresponding actual parameter only at the time of normal exit. In the latter two cases the corresponding actual parameter shall be determined at time of call and must be a variable or an assignable component of a composite type.

*7G.  Parameter Specifications.*  The type of each formal parameter must be explicitly specified in programs and shall be determinable during translation. Parameters may be of any type. The language shall not require user specification of subtype constraints for formal parameters. If such constraints are permitted they shall be interpreted as assertions and not as additional overloading. Corresponding formal and actual parameters must be of the same type.

*7H.  Formal Array Parameters.*   The number of dimensions for formal array parameters must be specified in programs and shall be determinable during translation. Determination of the subscript range for formal array parameters may be delayed until invocation and may vary from call to call. Subscript ranges shall be accessible within function and procedure bodies without being passed as explicit parameters.

*7I.  Restrictions to Prevent Aliasing.*   The language shall attempt to prevent aliasing (i.e., multiple access paths to the same variable or record component) that is not intended, but shall not prohibit all aliasing. Aliasing shall not be permitted between output parameters nor between an input-output parameter and a nonlocal variable. Unintended aliasing shall not be permitted between input-output parameters. A restriction limiting actual input-output parameters to variables that are nowhere referenced as nonlocals within a function or routine, is not prohibited. All aliasing of components of elements of an indirect type shall be considered intentional.

## 8.  Input-Output, Formating and Configuration Control

*8A.  Low Level Input-Output.*   There shall be a few low level input-output operations that send and receive control information to and from physical channels and devices. The low level operations shall be chosen to insure that all user level input-output operations can be defined within the language.

*8B.  Low Level Input-Output.*   The language shall specify (i.e., give calling format and general semantics) a recommended set of user level input-output operations. These shall include operations to create, delete, open, close, read, write, position, and interrogate both sequential and random access files and to alter the association between logical files and physical devices.

*8C.  Input Restrictions.*   User level input shall be restricted to data whose record representations are known to the translator (i.e., data that is created and written entirely within the program or data whose representation is explicitly specified in the program).

*8D.  Operating System Independence.*   The language shall not require the presence of an operating system. [Note that on many machines it will be necessary to provide run-time procedures to implement some features of the language.]

*8E.   Resource Control.*   There shall be a few low level operations to interrogate and control physical resources (e.g., memory or processors) that are managed (e.g., allocated or scheduled) by built-in features of the language.

*8F.   Formating.*   There shall be predefined operations to convert between the symbolic and internal representation of all types that have literal forms in the language (e.g., strings of digits to integers, or an enumeration element to its symbolic form). These conversion operations shall have the same semantics as those specified for literals in programs.

## 9.   Parallel Processing

*9A.   Parallel Processing.*   It shall be possible to define parallel processes. Processes (i.e., activation instances of such a definition) may be initiated at any point within the scope of the definition. Each process (activation) must have a name. It shall not be possible to exit the scope of a process name unless the process is terminated (or uninitiated).

*9B.   Parallel Process Implementation.*   The parallel processing facility shall be designed to minimize execution time and space. Processes shall have consistent semantics whether implemented on multicomputers, multiprocessors, or with interleaved execution on a single processor.

*9C.   Shared Variables and Mutual Exclusion.*   It shall be possible to mark variables that are shared among parallel processes. An unmarked variable that is assigned on one path and used on another shall cause a warning. It shall be possible efficiently to perform mutual exclusion in programs. The language shall not require any use of mutual exclusion.

*9D.   Scheduling.*   The semantics of the built-in scheduling algorithm shall be first-in-first-out within priorities. A process may alter its own priority. If the language provides a default priority for new processes it shall be the priority of its initiating process. The built-in scheduling algorithm shall not require that simultaneosuly executed processes on different processors have the same priority. [Note that this rule gives maximum scheduling control to the user without loss of efficiency. Note also that priority specification does not impose a specific execution order among parallel paths and thus does not provide a means for mutual exclusion.]

*9E.   Real Time.*   It shall be possible to access a real time clock. There shall be translation time constants to convert between the implementation units and the program units for real time. On any control path, it shall be possible to delay until at least a specified time before continuing execution. A process may have an accessible clock giving the cumulative processing time (i.e., CPU time) for that process.

*9G.   Asynchronous Termination.*   It shall be possible to terminate another process. The terminated process may designate the sequence of statements it will execute in response to the induced termination.

*9H.   Passing Data.*   It shall be possible to pass data between processes that do not share variables. It shall be possible to delay such data transfers until both the sending and receiving processes have requested the transfer.

*9I.   Signaling.*   It shall be possible to set a signal (without waiting), and to wait for a signal (without delay, if it is already set). Setting a signal that is not already set shall cause exactly one waiting path to continue.

*9J.   Waiting.*   It shall be possible to wait for, determine, and act upon the first completed of several wait operations (including those used for data passing, signaling, and real time).

## 10.   Exception Handling

*10A.   Exception Handling Facility.*   There shall be an exception handling mechanism for responding to unplanned error situations detected in declarations and statements during execution. The exception situations shall include errors detected by hardware, software errors detected during execution, error situations in built-in operations, and user defined exceptions. Exception identifiers shall have a scope. Exceptions should add to the execution time of programs only if they are raised.

*10B.   Error Situations.*   The errors detectable during execution shall include exceeding the specified range of an array subscript, exceeding the specified range of a variable, exceeding the implemented range of a variable, attempting to access an uninitialized variable, attempting to access a field of a variant that is not present, requesting a resource (such as stack or heap storage) when an insufficient quantity remains, and failing to satisfy a program specified assertion. [Note that some are very expensive to detect unless aided by special hardware, and consequently their detection will often be suppressed (see 10G).]

*10C. Raising Exceptions.* There shall be an operation that raises an exception. Raising an exception shall cause transfer of control to the most local enclosing exception handler for that exception without completing execution of the current statement or declaration, but shall not of itself cause transfer out of a function, procedure, or process. Exceptions that are not handled within a function or procedure shall be raised again at the point of call in their callers. Exceptions that are not handled within a process shall terminate the process. Exceptions that can be raised by built-in operations shall be given in the language definition.

*10D. Exception Handling.* There shall be a control structure for discriminating among the exceptions that can occur in a specified sequence. The user may supply a single control path for all exceptions not otherwise mentioned in such a discrimination. It shall be possible to raise the exception that selected the current handler when exiting the handler.

*10E. Order of Exceptions.* The order in which exceptions in different parts of an expression are detected shall not be guaranteed by the language or by the translator.

*10F. Assertions.* It shall be possible to include assertions in programs. If an assertion is false when encountered during execution, it shall raise an exception. It shall also be possible to include assertions, such as the expected frequency for selection of a conditional path, that cannot be verified. [Note that assertions can be used to aid optimization and maintenance.]

*10G. Suppressing Exceptions.* It shall be possible during translation to suppress individually the execution time detection of exceptions within a given scope. The language shall not guarantee the integrity of the values produced when a suppressed exception occurs. [Note that suppression of an exception is not an assertion that the corresponding error will not occur.]

## 11. Representation and Other Translation Time Facilities

*11A. Data Representation.* The language shall permit but not require programs to specify a single physical representation for the elements of a type. These specifications shall be separate from the logical descriptions. Physical representation shall include object representation of enumeration elements, order of fields, width of fields, presence of "don't care" fields, positions of word boundaries, and object machine addresses. In particular, the facility shall be sufficient to specify the physical representation of any record whose format is determined by considerations that are entirely external to the program, translator, and language. The language and its translators shall not guarantee any particular choice for those aspects of physical representation that are unspecified by the program. It shall be possible to specify the association of physical resources (e.g., interrupts) to program elements (e.g., exceptions or signals).

*11C. Translation Time Facilities.* To aid conditional compilation, it shall be possible to interrogate properties that are known during translation including characteristics of the object configuration, of function and procedure calling environments, and of actual parameters. For example, it shall be possible to determine whether the caller has suppressed a given exception, the caller's optimization criteria, whether an actual parameter is a translation time expression, the type of actual generic parameters, and the values of constraints characterizing the subtype of actual parameters.

*11D. Object System Configuration.* The object system configuration must be explicitly specified in each separately translated unit. Such specifications must include the object machine model, the operating system if present, peripheral equipment, and the device configuration, and may include special hardware options and memory size. The translator will use such specifications when generating object code. [Note that programs that depend on the specific characteristics of the object machine may be made more portable by enclosing those portions in branches of conditionals on the object machine configuration.]

*11E. Interface to Other Languages.* There shall be a machine independent interface to other programming languages including assembly languages. Any program element that is referenced in both the source language program and foreign code must be identified in the interface. The source language of the foreign code must also be identified.

*11F. Optimization.* Programs may advise translators on the optimization criteria to be used in a scope. It shall be possible in programs to specify whether minimum translation costs or minimum execution costs are more important, and whether execution time or memory space is to be given preference. All such specifications shall be optional. Except for the amount of time and space required during execution, approximate values beyond the specified precision, the order in which exceptions are detected, and the occurrence of side effects within an expression, optimization shall not alter the semantics of correct programs (e.g., the semantics of parameters will be unaffected by the choice between open and closed calls).

## 12. Translation and Library Facilities

*12A. Library.* There shall be an easily accessible library of generic definitions and separately translated units. All predefined definitions shall be in the library. Library entries may include those used as input-output packages, common pools of shared declarations, application oriented software packages, encapsulations, and machine configuration specifications. The library shall be structured to allow entries to be associated with particular applications, projects, and users.

*12B. Separately Translated Units.* Separately translated units may be assembled into operational systems. It shall be possible for a separately translated unit to reference exported definitions of other units. All language imposed restrictions shall be enforced across such interfaces. Separate translation shall not change the semantics of a correct program.

*12D. Generic Definitions.* Functions, procedures, types, and encapsulations may have generic parameters. Generic parameters shall be instantiated during translation and shall be interpreted in the context of the instantiation. An actual generic parameter may be any defined identifier (including those for variables, functions, procedures, processes, and types) or the value of any expression.

## 13. Support for the Language

*13A. Defining Documents.* The language shall have a complete and unambiguous defining document. It should be possible to predict the possible actions of any syntactically correct program from the language definition. The language documentation shall include the syntax, semantics, and appropriate examples of each built-in and predefined feature. A recommended set of translation diagnostic and warning messages shall be included in the language definition.

*13B. Standards.* There will be a standard definition of the language. Procedures will be established for standard control and for certification that translators meet the standard.

*13C. Completeness of Implementations.* Translators shall implement the standard definition. Every translator shall be able to process any syntactically correct program. Every feature that is available to the user shall be defined in the standard, in an accessible library, or in the source program.

*13D.    Translator Diagnostics.*    Translators shall be responsible for reporting errors that are detectable during translation and for optimizing object code. Translators shall be responsible for the integrity of object code in affected translation units when any separately translated unit is modified, and shall ensure that shared definitions have compatible representations in all translation units. Translators shall do full syntax and type checking, shall check that all language imposed restrictions are met, and should provide warnings where constructs will be dangerous or unusually expensive in execution and shall attempt to detect exceptions during translation. If the translator determines that a call on a routine will not terminate normally, the exception shall be reported as a translation error at the point of call.

*13E.    Translator Characteristics.*    Translators for the language will be written in the language and will be able to produce code for a variety of object machines. The machine independent parts of translators should be separate from code generators. Although it is desirable, translators need not be able to execute on every object machine. The internal characteristics of the translator (i.e., the translation method) shall not be specified by the language definition or standards.

*13F.    Restrictions on Translators.*    Translators shall fail to translate otherwise correct programs only when the program requires more resources during translation than are available on the host machine or when the program calls for resources that are unavailable in the specified object system configuration. Neither the language nor its translators shall impose arbitrary restrictions on language features. For example, they shall not impose restrictions on the number of array dimensions, on the number of identifiers, on the length of identifiers, or on the number of nested parentheses levels.

*13G.    Software Tools and Application Packages.*    The language should be designed to work in conjunction with a variety of useful software tools and application support packages. These will be developed as early as possible and will include editors, interpreters, diagnostic aids, program anlayzers, documentation aids, testing aids, software maintenance tools, optimizers, and application libraries. There will be a consistent user interface for these tools. Where practical, software tools and aids will be written in the language. Support for the design, implementation, distribution, and maintenance of translators, software tools and aids, and application libraries will be provided independently of the individual projects that use them.

APPENDIX E

# Pascal Syntax
# (ISO Draft Standard)*

actual-parameter = expression | variable-access | procedure-identifier |
                 function-identifier .
actual-parameter-list = "(" actual-parameter { "," actual-parameter } ")" .
adding-operator = "+" | "−" | "or" .
apostrophe-image = "''" .
array-type = "array" "[" index-type { "," index-type } "]" "of"
              component-type .
array-variable – variable-access .
assignment-statement = ( variable-access | function-identifier ) ":"
                         expression .
base-type = ordinal-type .
block = label-declaration-part
        constant-definition-part
           type-definition-part
              variable-declaration-part
                 procedure-and-function-declaration-part
                    statement-part .
Boolean-expression = expression .
bound-identifier = identifier .
buffer-variable = file-variable "^" .

* Reprinted with the permission of the Pascal User's Group.

case-constant = constant .

case-constant-list = case-constant { "," case-constant } .

case-index = expression .

case-list-element = case-constant-list ":" statement .

case-statement = "case" case-index "of" case-list-element
{";" case-list-element } [";"] "end" .

character-string = "'" string-element {string-element} "'" .

component-type = type-denoter .

component-variable = indexed-variable | field-designator .

compound-statement = "begin" statement-sequence "end" .

conditional-statement = if-statement | case-statement .

conformant-array-parameter-specification = "var" identifier-list ":"
conformant-array-schema .

conformant-array-schema = (packed-conformant-array-schema |
unpacked-conformant-array-schema) .

constant = [sign] (unsigned-number | constant-identifier) |
character-string .

constant-definition = identifier "=" constant .

constant-definition-part = ["const" constant-definition ";"
{constant-definition ";"}] .

constant-identifier = identifier .

control-variable = entire-variable .

digit = "0" | "1" | "2" | "3" | "4" | "5" | "6" | "7" | "8" | "9" .

digit-sequence = digit {digit} .

directive = letter {letter | digit} .

domain-type = type-identifier .

else-part = "else" statement .

empty-statement = .

entire-variable = variable-identifier .

enumerated-type = "(" identifier-list ")" .

expression = simple-expression [ relational-operator simple-expression ] .

factor = variable-access | unsigned-constant | bound-identifier |
function-designator | set-constructor | "(" expression ")" |
"not" factor .

field-designator = record-variable "." field-specifier |
field-designator-identifier .

field-identifier = identifier .

field-list = [ (fixed-part [ ";" variant-part ] | variant-part) [";"]] .

field-specifier = field-identifier .

file-type = "file" "of" component-type .

file-variable = variable-access .

final-value = expression .

fixed-part = record-section { ";" record-section } .
for-statement = "for" control-variable ":=" initial-value
         ( "to" | "downto" ) final-value "do" statement .
formal-parameter-list = "(" formal-parameter-section
         {";" formal-parameter-section} ")" .
formal-parameter-section = value-parameter-specification |
         variable-parameter-specification |
         procedural-parameter-specification |
         functional-parameter-specification |
         conformant-array-parameter-specification .
function-block = block .
function-declaration = function-heading ";" directive |
         function-identification ";" function-block |
         function-heading ";" function-block .
function-designator = function-identifier [ actual-parameter-list ] .
function-heading = "function" identifier [formal-parameter-list] ":"
         result-type .
function-identification = "function" function-identifier .
function-identifier = identifier .
functional-parameter-specification = function-heading .
goto-statement = "goto" label.
identified-variable = pointer-variable "ˆ" .
identifier = letter {letter | digit} .
identifier-list = identifier { "," identifier } .
if-statement = "if" Boolean-expression "then" statement [ else-part ] .
index-expression = expression .
index-type = ordinal-type .
index-type-specification = identifier " . . " identifier ":"
         ordinal-type-identifier .
indexed-variable = array-variable "[" index-expression
         { "," index-expression } "]" .
initial-value = expression .
label = digit-sequence .
label-declaration-part = ["label" label {"," label} ";"] .
letter =

   "a" | "b" | "c" | "d" | "e" | "f" | "g" | "h" | "i " | " j " | "k" | "l" | "m" |

   "n" | "o" | "p" | "q" | "r" | "s" | "t " | "u" | "v" | "w" | "x" | "y" | " z" | .

member-designator = expression [ " . . " expression ] .
multiplying-operator = "∗" | "/" | "div" | "mod" | "and" .
new-ordinal-type = enumerated-type | subrange-type .
new-pointer-type = "ˆ" domain-type .

new-structured-type = ["packed"] unpacked-structured-type .
new-type = new-ordinal-type | new-structured-type | new-pointer-type .
ordinal-type = new-ordinal-type | integer-type | Boolean-type |
        char-type | ordinal-type-identifier .
ordinal-type-identifier = identifier .
packed-conformant-array-schema = "packed" "array" "["
        index-type-specification "]" "of"
        type-identifier .
pointer-type = new-pointer-type | pointer-type-identifier .
pointer-type-identifier = type-identifier .
pointer-variable = variable-access .
procedural-parameter-specification = procedure-heading .
procedure-and-function-declaration-part = {(procedure-declaration |
        function-declaration) ";"} .
procedure-block = block .
procedure-declaration = procedure-heading ";" directive |
        procedure-identification ";" procedure-block |
        procedure-heading ";" procedure-block .
procedure-heading = "procedure" identifier [ formal-parameter-list ] .
procedure-identification = "procedure" procedure-identifier .
procedure-identifier = identifier .
procedure-statement = procedure-identifier [ actual-parameter-list ] .
program = program-heading ";" program-block "." .
program-block = block .
program-heading = "program" identifier [ "(" program-parameters ")" ] .
program-parameters = identifier-list .
read-parameter-list = "("[file-variable ","] variable-access
        {"," variable-access} ")" .
readln-parameter-list = ["(" (file-variable | variable-access)
        {"," variable-access} ")"] .
record-section = identifier-list ":" type-denoter .
record-type = "record" field-list "end" .
record-variable = variable-access .
record-variable-list = record-variable { "," record-variable } .
relational-operator = "=" | "< >" | "<" | ">" | "<=" | ">=" | "in" .
repeat-statement = "repeat" statement-sequence "until"
        Boolean-expression .
repetitive-statement = repeat-statement | while-statement | for-statement .
result-type = simple-type-identifier | pointer-type-identifier .
scale-factor = signed-integer .
set-constructor = "[" [ member-designator { "," member-designator } ]
        "]"

set-type = "set" "of" base-type .
sign = "+" | "−" .
signed-integer = [sign] unsigned-integer .
signed-number = signed-integer | signed-real .
signed-real = [sign] unsigned-real .
simple-expression = [ sign ] term { adding-operator term } .
simple-statement = empty-statement | assignment-statement |
               procedure-statement | goto-statement .
simple-type = ordinal-type | real-type .
simple-type-identifier = type-identifier .
special-symbol = "+" | "−" | "*" | "/" | "=" | "<" | ">" | "[" | "]" |
               "." | "," | ":" | ";" | "ˆ" | "(" | ")" |
               "< >" | "<=" | ">=" | ":=" | " . . " | word-symbol .
statement = [ label ":" ] ( simple-statement | structured-statement ) .
statement-part = compound-statement .
statement-sequence = statement { ";" statement } .
string-character = one-of-a-set-of-implementation-defined-characters .
string-element = apostrophe-image | string-character .
structured-statement = compound-statement | conditional-statement |
               repetitive-statement | with-statement .
structured-type = new-structured-type | structured-type-identifier .
structured-type-identifier = type-identifier .
subrange-type = constant " . . " constant.
tag-field = identifier .
tag-type = ordinal-type-identifier .
term = factor { multiplying-operator factor } .
type-definition = identifier "=" type-denoter .
type-definition-part = ["type" type-definition ";"
               {type-definition ";"}] .
type-denoter = type-identifier | new-type .
type-identifier = identifier .
unpacked-conformant-array-schema = "array" "["
                       index-type-specification }
                       "]" "of" ( type-identifier |
                       conformant-array-schema ) .
unpacked-structured-type = array-type | record-type | set-type | file-type .
unsigned-constant = unsigned-number | character-string |
               constant-identifier | "nil" .
unsigned-integer = digit-sequence .
unsigned-number = unsigned-integer | unsigned-real .
unsigned-real = unsigned-integer "." digit-sequence ["e" scale-factor] |
               unsigned-integer "e" scale-factor .

value-parameter-specification = identifier-list ":" type-identifier .
variable-access = entire-variable | component-variable |
                 identified-variable | buffer-variable .
variable-declaration = identifier-list ":" type-denoter .
variable-declaration-part = ["var" variable-declaration ";"
                           {variable-declaration ";"}] .
variable-identifier = identifier .
variable-parameter-specification = "var" identifier-list ":"
                                  type-identifier .
variant = case-constant-list ":" "(" field-list ")" .
variant-part = "case" variant-selector "of" variant { ";" variant } .
variant-selector = [tag-field ":"] tag-type .
while-statement = "while" Boolean-expression "do" statement .
with-statement = "with" record-variable-list "do;" statement .
word-symbol = "and" | "array" | "begin" | "case" | "const" | "div" |
             "do" | "downto" | "else" | "end" | "file" | "for" |
             "function" | "goto" | "if" | "in" | "label" | "mod" |
             "nil" | "not" | "of" | "or" | "packed" | "procedure" |
             "program | "record" | "repeat" | "set" | "then" |
             "to" | "type" | "until" | "var" | "while" | "with" .
write-parameter = expression [":" expression [":" expression ]] .
write-parameter-list = "("[file-variable ","] write-parameter
                       {"," write-parameter} ")" .
writeln-parameter-list = ["(" (file-variable | write-parameter) {","
                         write-parameter}")")"] .

APPENDIX F

# User's Groups

Pascal User's Group
P.O. Box 4406
Allentown, PA 18170

UCSD p-System User's Society
P.O. Box 1148
La Jolla, CA 92038

# Pascal Standards Organizations

*American ANSI Standard*

ANSI/X3J9
X3 Secretariat
CBEMA
311 First St., N.W.
Washington, D.C. 20001

*International Standard*

A. M. Addyman
(Convener ISO/TC97/SC5/WG4)
Department of Computer Science
University of Manchester
Oxford Road
Manchester, M13 9PL,
United Kingdom

# Bibliography*

A. M. Addyman, On the Suitability of a Pascal Compiler in an Undergraduate Environment, *Pascal Newsletter* **6**, 35–36 (November 1976).

A. M. Addyman et al., The BSI/ISO Working Draft of Standard Pascal by the BSI DPS/13/4 Working Group, *Pascal News* **14** (entire issue) (January 1979).

A. M. Addyman et al., A Draft Description of Pascal, *S-P&E* **9**, 381–424 (1979).

A. M. Addyman, A Draft Proposal for Pascal, *SIGPLAN Notices* **15**(4), 1–66 (1980), and *Pascal News* **18**, 2–70 (May 1980).

A. M. Addyman, Pascal Standardisation, *SIGPLAN Notices* **15**(4), 67–69 (1980).

L. Aiello, M. Aiello, and R. W. Weyhrauch, *The Semantics of Pascal in LCF*, Stanford University (August 1974).

S. Alagic and M. A. Arbib, *The Design of Well Structured and Correct Programs*, Springer-Verlag, New York, 1978.

S. Alagic and A. Kulenovic, Relational Pascal Database Interface, *Computer Journal* **24**(2), 112–117 (1981).

P. F. Albrecht et al., Source-to-source Translations: Ada to Pascal and Pascal to Ada, *Sigplan Notices* **15**(11), 183–193 (1980).

I. I. Alonso-Velez and J. G. Bourque, "The Pascal/64000 Compiler, *Hewlett-Packard Journal* **31**(10), 23–28 (1980).

A. L. Ambler and C. G. Hoch, A Study of Protection in Programming Languages, *SIGPLAN Notices* **12**(3), 25–40 (1977).

U. Ammann, The Method of Structured Programming Applied to the Development of a Compiler, in *International Computing Symposium 1973*, Gunther et al., eds., 93–99, North-Holland, Amsterdam, 1974.

U. Ammann, On Code Generation in a Pascal Compiler, *S-P&E* **7**, 391–423 (1977).

* Courtesy of David V. Moffat, North Carolina State University, Raleigh, North Carolina.
© 1981, David V. Moffat. Reprinted by permission.

U. Ammann, Error Recovery in Recursive Descent Parsers, ETH Zurich, Berichte des Instituts fur Informatik, No. 25 (May 1978).

B. Appelbe and M. Kroening, Concurrent Programming on Microcomputers, *SIGSmall Newsletter* **5**(2), 20–27 (1979).

K. R. Apt, Equivalence of Operational and Denotational Semantics for a Fragment of Pascal, *Proceedings of the IFIP Working Conference on Formal Descriptions of Programming Concepts, St. Andrews, Canada, August, 1977*, 139–163, North-Holland, Amsterdam, 1978.

K. R. Apt, A Sound and Complete Hoare-like System for a Fragment of Pascal, *Stichting Mathematics Centrum*, Amsterdam, Netherlands (July 1978).

K. R. Apt and J. W. De Bakker, Semantics and Proof Theory of Pascal Procedures, (Preprint), *Mathematics Center*, Department of Computer Science, Amsterdam, 1977.

J. Q- Arnold, A Novel Approach to Compiler Design, *Pascal News* **11**, 34–36 (February 1978).

L. Atkinson, A Contribution to Minimal Subranges, *Pascal News* **15**, 60–61 (September 1979).

L. V. Atkinson, Know the State You Are in, *Pascal News* **13**, 66–69 (December 1978).

L. V. Atkinson, Pascal Scalars as State Indicators, *S-P&E* **9**, 427–431 (1979).

L. V. Atkinson, *Pascal Programming*, Wiley, New York, 1980.

J. W. Atwood and T. M. Pham, A Concurrent Pascal Interpreter for the Texas Instruments 980B, *Proceedings of the International Symposium on Mini and Micro Computers, Montreal, Canada, November, 1977*, IEEE, 41–48 (1978).

B. Austermuehl and H.-J. Hoffman, Generic Routines and Variable Types in Pascal, *Pascal News* **9 & 10**, 43–46 (September 1977).

H. G. Baker, Jr., A Source of Redundant Identifiers in Pascal Programs, *SIGPLAN Notices* **15**(2), 14–16 (1980).

T. P. Baker and A. C. Fleck, Does Scope-Block in Pascal?, *Pascal News* **17**, 60–61 (March 1980).

T. P. Baker and A. C. Fleck, A Note on Pascal Scopes, *Pascal News* **17**, 62 (March 1980).

M. S. Ball, *Pascal 1100: An Implementation of the Pascal Language for Univac 1100 Series Computers*, Naval Ocean Systems Center, San Diego, CA (July 1978).

D. Bar, A Methodology for Simultaneously Developing and Verifying Pascal Programs, *Constructing Quality Software, Novsibirsk, USSR, May, 1977*, 419–448, North-Holland, Amsterdam, Netherlands (1978).

W. Barabesh, C. R. Hill, and R. B. Kieburtz, A Proposal for Increased Security in the Use of Variant Records, *Pascal Newsletter* **8**, 15 (May 1977).

D. Barron, On Programming Style, and Pascal, *Computer Bulletin* **2**, 21 (September 1979).

D. W. Barron and J. M. Mullins, What To Do After a While, *Pascal News* **11**, 48–50 (February 1978).

D. W. Barron and J. M. Mullins, Life, Liberty and the Pursuit of Unformatted Input, *Pascal Newsletter* **7**, 8–9 (February 1977).

D. W. Barron and J. Mullins (eds.), Pascal, The Language and Its Implementation, *Proceedings of the Southampton Symposium*, University of Southampton, 24–25 March 1977 (1977).

D. W. Barron (ed.), *Pascal: The Language and Its Implementation*, Wiley, New York, 1981.

F. Baskett, Pascal and Virtual Memory in a Z8000 or MC68000 Based Design Station, *Compcon Spring '80, VLSI: New Architectural Horizons*, San Francisco, IEEE, 456–459 (1980).

D. Bates, Letter to the Editor (on formatting Pascal programs), *SIGPLAN Notices* **13**(3), 12–15 (1978).

D. Bates and R. Cailliau, Experience with Pascal Compilers on Mini-Computers, *SIGPLAN Notices* **12**(11), 10–22 (1977).

R. M. Bates, A Pascal Prettyprinter with a Different Purpose, *SIGPLAN Notices* **16**(3), 10–17 (1981).

D. M. Berry, Pascal or Algol-68?, *Research Directions in Software Technology*, P. Wegner, ed., pp. 641–646, MIT Press, Cambridge, MA, 1979.

R. E. Berry, Experience with the Pascal P-Compiler, *S-P&E* **8**, 617–627 (1978).

A. Biedl, An Extension of Programming Languages for Numerical Computation in Science and Engineering with Special Reference to Pascal, *SIGPLAN Notices* **12**(4), 31–33 (1977).

C. Bishop, Some Comments on Pascal I/O, *Pascal Newsletter* **8**, 18 (May 1977).

C. Bishop, Pascal: Standards and Extensions, *Pascal News* **11**, 54–56 (February 1978).

J. M. Bishop, Subranges and Conditional Loops, *Pascal News* **12**, 37–38 (June 1978).

J. M. Bishop, On Publication Pascal, *S-P&E* **9**, 711–717 (1979).

J. M. Bishop, Implementing Strings in Pascal, *S-P&E* **9**, 779–788 (1979).

R. Bond, Another Note on Pascal Indention, *SIGPLAN Notices* **14**(12), 47–49 (1979).

T. M. Bonham, "Minor" Problems in Pascal, *Pascal Newsletter* **5**, 20–22 (September 1976).

H. J. Boom and E. DeJong, A Critical Comparison of Several Programming Languages, *S-P&E* **10**, 435–473 (1980).

M. Boot, Comparable Computer Languages for Linguistic and Literary Data Processing, II: SIMULA and Pascal, *Association for Literary and Linguistic Computing Bulletin* **7**(2), 137–146 (1979).

F. D. Boswell and J. W. Welch, *Pascal Reference Manual and Waterloo Pascal User's Guide*, Watfac Publications Ltd., Waterloo, Ontario, 1980.

K. L. Bowles, *Microcomputer Problem Solving Using Pascal*, Springer-Verlag, New York, 1977).

K. L. Bowles, Update on UCSD Pascal Activities, *Pascal Newsletter* **8**, 16–18 (May 1977).

K. L. Bowles, An Introduction to the UCSD Pascal System, *Behavioral Research Methods and Instruments* **10**(4), 531–534 (1978).

K. L. Bowles, Status of UCSD Project, *Pascal News* **11**, 36–40 (February 1978).

K. L. Bowles, *Beginner's Guide for the UCSD Pascal System*, BYTE/McGraw-Hill, New York, 1979.

K. I. Bowles, A (Nearly) Machine Independent Software System for Micro and Mini Computers, *SIGPC Notes* **1**(1), 6–15 (1978).

P. Brinch Hansen, Universal Types in Concurrent Pascal, *Information Processing Letters* **3**, 165–166 (1975).

P. Brinch Hansen, Concurrent Pascal, A Programming Language for Operating Systems Design, *Technical Report* **10**, *Information Science*, California Institute of Technology (April 1974).

P. Brinch Hansen, The Purpose of Concurrent Pascal, *SIGPLAN Notices* **10**(6), 305–309 (1975).

P. Brinch Hansen, The Programming Language Concurrent Pascal, *IEEE TSE* **1**(2), 199–207 (1975).

P. Brinch Hansen, Experience with Modular Concurrent Programming, *IEEE TSE* **3**(2), 156–159 (1977).

P. Brinch Hansen, *The Architecture of Concurrent Programs*, Prentice-Hall, Englewood Cliffs, NJ, 1977.

P. Brinch Hansen, Concurrent Pascal Machine, *Information Science*, California Institute of Technology (1975).

P. Brinch Hansen, The SOLO Operating System: A Concurrent Pascal Program, *S-P&E* **6**, 141–149 (1976).

P. Brinch Hansen and A. C. Hartman, Sequential Pascal Report, *Technical Report*, Information Science, California Institute of Technology (1975).

P. Brinch Hansen, Microcomputer Comparisons, *S-P&E* **9**, 211–217 (1979).

P. Brinch Hansen and J. Fellows, The TRIO Operating System, *S-P&E* **10**, 943–948 (1980).

C. Bron and W. de Vries, A Pascal Compiler for PDP-11 Minicomputers, *S-P&E* **6**(1), 109–116 (1976).

C. Bron and E. J. Dijkstra, A Discipline for the Programming of Interactive I/O in Pascal, *SIGPLAN Notices* **14**(12), 59–61 (1979).

D. M. Bulman, Stack Computers, *Computer* (May 1977).

D. W. Bustard, *Pascal-Plus User's Manual*, Queen's University of Belfast (1978).

D. W. Bustard, An Introduction to Pascal-Plus, in *On the Construction of Programs*, R. M. Macnaghten and A. M. McKeag, eds., pp. 1–57, Cambridge, 1980.

J. L. Byrnes, *NPS-Pascal: A Pascal Implementation for Microprocessor Based Computer Systems*, Naval Postgraduate School, Monterey, California (1979).

R. H. Campbell and R. B. Kolstad, Path Expressions in Pascal, *Proceedings of the 4th International Conference of Software Engineering, Munich, Germany*, IEEE, New York (1979).

A. Celentano, P. Della Vigna, C. Ghezzi, and D. Mandrioli, Modularization of Block-Structured Languages: The Case of Pascal, *Proceedings of the Workshop on Reliable Software, Bonn, Germany*, 167–179, Carl Hasser Verlag, Munich (1979).

A. Celentano, P. Della Vigna, C. Ghezzi, and D. Mandrioli, Separate Compilation and Partial Specification in Pascal, *IEEE TSE, SE-6* **4**, 320–328 (1980).

A. Celentano, P. Della Vigna, C. Ghezzi, and D. Mandrioli, SIMPLE: A Program Development System, *Computer Languages* 5(2), 103–114, (1980).

S. Chernicoff, *Pascal Language Manual*, Science Research Associates, Inc., 1978.

G. W. Cherry, *Pascal Programming Structures: An Introduction to Systematic Programming*, Reston, Virginia, 1980.

P. M. Chirlian, *Pascal*, Matrix Publishers, Portland, OR, 1980.

T. Chusho, A Good Program = A Structured Program + Optimization Commands, *Information Processing* **80**, North-Holland, Amsterdam, 269–274 (1980).

R. Cichelli, Pascal-I—Interactive Conversational Pascal-S, *Pascal News* **15**, 63–67 (September 1979), and *SIGPLAN Notices* 15(1), 34–44 (1980).

R. J. Cichelli, Pascal Potpourri, *Pascal Newsletter* **6**, 36–41 (November 1976).

R. J. Cichelli, Fixing Pascal's I/O, *SIGPLAN Notices* 15(5), 19 (1980), and *Pascal News* **17**, 65 (March 1980).

R. J. Cichelli (ed.), Pascal-S: Compiler and Interpreter for a Subset of Pascal, *Pascal News* **19**, 30–40 (September 1980).

R. J. Cichelli, Notes on System Dependent Code in Pascal-S and Pascal-I, *Pascal News* **19**, 41–43 (September 1980).

R. G. Clark, Interactive Input In Pascal, *SIGPLAN Notices* 14(2), 9–13 (1979).

R. G. Clark, Input in Pascal, *SIGPLAN Notices* 14(11), 7–8 (1979).

D. Coleman, R. M. Gallimore, J. W. Hughes, and M. S. Powell, An Assessment of Concurrent Pascal, *S-P&E* **9**, 827–837 (1979).

D. Coleman, J. W. Hughes, and M. S. Powell, Developing a Programming Methodology for Multiprograms, *Department of Computation Report No. 218*, UMIST (1978).

D. Coleman, Concurrent Pascal—An Appraisal, in *On the Construction of Programs*, R. M. Macnaghten and A. M. McKeag, eds., 213–227, Cambridge, 1980.

D. Comer, MAP: A Pascal Macro Preprocessor for Large Program Development, *S-P&E* **9**, 203–209 (1979).

M. N. Condict, The Pascal Dynamic Array Controversy and a Method for Enforcing Global Assertions, *SIGPLAN Notices* 12(11), 23–27 (1977).

R. Conradi, Further Critical Comments on Pascal, Particularly as a Systems Programming Language, *SIGPLAN Notices* 11(11), 8–25 (1976).

R. Conway, J. Archer, and R. Conway, *Programming for Poets: A Gentle Introduction Using Pascal*, Winthrop, Cambridge, MA, 1980.

R. Conway, D. Gries, and E. C. Zimmerman, *A Primer on Pascal*, Winthrop, Cambridge, MA, 1976 (2nd ed., 1981).

J. W. Cooper, *Introduction to Pascal for Scientists,* Wiley, New York, 1981.

B. J. Cornelius, D. J. Robson, and M. I. Thomas, Modification of the Pascal-P Compiler for a Single-Accumulator One-Address Minicomputer, *S-P&E* **10**, 241–246 (1980).

J. E. Crider, Structured Formatting of Pascal Programs, *SIGPLAN Notices* **13**(11), 15–22 (1978).

J. Crider, Why Use Structured Formatting, *Pascal News* **15**, 68–70 (September 1979).

H. Davis, *Pascal Notebook: Vol. I: Introduction to Pascal,* Matrix Publishers, Beaverton, OR, 1981.

J. Deminet and J. Wisniewska, SIMPASCAL, *Pascal News* **17**, 66–68 (March 1980).

P. Desjardins, A Pascal Compiler for the Xerox Sigma 6, *SIGPLAN Notices* **8**(6), 34–36 (1973).

P. Desjardins, Type Compatibility Checking in Pascal Compilers, *Pascal News* **11**, 33–34 (February 1978).

R. S. Deverill and A. C. Hartmann, Interpretive Pascal for the IBM 370, *Information Science Technical Report No. 6,* California Institute of Technology (1973).

J. L. Diaz-Herrera and R. C. Flude, Pascal/HSD: A Graphical Programming System, *Computer Software and Applications Conference, Chicago,* IEEE, 723–728 (1980).

J. E. Donahue, Complementary Definitions of Programming Language Semantics, *Lecture Notes in Computer Science* **42**, Springer-Verlag, New York, 1976.

V. A. Dyck, J. A. Smith, J. D. Lawson, and R. J. Beach, *Computing: An Introduction to Structured Problem Solving Using Pascal,* Reston, VA, 1981.

R. Edwards, Is Pascal a Logical Subset of Algol 68 or Not?, *SIGPLAN Notices* **12**(6), 184–191 (1977).

S. Eisenbach and C. Sadler, *Pascal for Programmers,* Springer-Verlag, New York, 1981.

J. Eisenberg, In Defense of Formatted Input, *Pascal Newsletter* **5**, 14–15 (September 1976).

H. Erkio, J. Sajanienu, and A. Salava, An Implementation of Pascal on the Burroughs B6700, *Report A-1977-1,* Department of Computer Science, University of Helsinki, Finland (1977).

R. N. Faiman and A. A. Kortesoja, An Optimizing Pascal Compiler, *Proceedings of COMPSAC* (IEEE Third International Computer Software and Applications Conference), IEEE, 624–628 (1979), and *IEEE TSE* **SE-6**(6), 512–519 (1980).

L. Feiereisen, Implementation of Pascal on the PDP-11/45, *DECUS Conference, Zurich,* pp. 259 (1974).

E. E. Ferguson and G. T. Ligler, The TI Pascal System: Run-Time Support, *Proceedings of the Eleventh Hawaii International Conference on System Sciences, Part III,* pp. 69–84, Western Periodicals Co., North Hollywood, CA, 1978.

W. Findlay, The Performance of Pascal Programs on the MULTUM, *Report No. 6,* Computing Department, University of Glasgow, Scotland (July 1974).

W. Findlay and D. F. Watt, *Pascal: An Introduction to Methodical Programming*, Pittman, London, 1978.

C. N. Fischer and R. J. LeBlanc, Efficient Implementation and Optimisation of Run-Time Checking in Pascal, *SIGPLAN Notices* **12**(3), 19–24 (1977).

C. N. Fischer and R. J. LeBlanc, A Diagnostic Compiler for the Programming Language Pascal, *USE Fall Conference Technical Papers*, Lake Buena Vista, FL (October 1976).

C. N. Fischer and R. J. LeBlanc, The Implementation of Run-Time Diagnostics in Pascal, *IEEE TSE* **SE-6**(4), 313–319 (1980).

C. N. Fischer and J. Mauney, On the Role of Error Productions in Syntactic Error Corrections, *Computer Languages* **5**(3&4), 131–139 (1980).

V. S. Foster, Performance Measurement of a Pascal Compiler, *SIGPLAN Notices* **15**(6), 34–38 (1980).

R. A. Fraley, Suggested Extensions to Pascal, *Pascal News* **11**, 41–48 (February 1978).

R. A. Fraley, SYSPAL: A Pascal-Based Language for Operating System Implementations, *Proceedings of Spring Compcon 78, San Francisco*, IEEE, 32–35 (1978).

G. Friesland, C.-O. Grosse-Lindemann, F. W. Lorenz, H.-H. Nagel, and P. J. Stirl, A Pascal Compiler Bootstrapped on a DEC-System 10, *Lecture Notes in Computer Science* **7**, Springer-Verlag, 101–113 (1974).

A. J. Gerber, Pascal at Sydney University, *Pascal News* **9&10**, 39–40 (September 1977).

S. M. German, An Extended Semantic Definition of Pascal for Proving the Absence of Common Runtime Errors, *STAN-CS-80-811*, Department of Computer Science, Stanford University (1980).

B. J. Gerovac, An Implementation of NEW and DISPOSE Using Boundary Tags, *Pascal News* **19**, 49–59 (September 1980).

J. C. Gracida and R. R. Stilwell, *NPS-Pascal. A Partial Implementation of Pascal Language for a Microprocessor-Based Computer System*, AD-A061040/2 Naval Postgraduate School (June 1978).

N. Graef, H. Kretschmar, K. P. Loehr, and B. Morawetz, How to Design and Implement Small Time-sharing Systems Using Concurrent Pascal, *S-P&E* **9**, 17–24 (1979).

N. Graham, *Introduction to Pascal*, West, St. Paul, MN, 1980.

D. Gries and N. Gehani, Some Ideas on Data Types in High Level Languages, *CACM* **20**(6), 414–420 (1977).

G. R. Grinton, Converting an Application Program from OMSI Pascal 1.1F to AAEC Pascal 8000/1.2, *Pascal News* **17**, 59 (March 1980).

P. Grogono, On Layout, Identifiers and Semicolons in Pascal Programs, *SIGPLAN Notices* **14**(4), 35–40 (1976).

P. Grogono, *Programming in Pascal*, Addison-Wesley, Reading, MA, 1978 (revised 1980).

P. Grogono, *Programming in Pascal 1000*, Addison-Wesley, Reading, MA, 1980.

C. O. Grosse-Lindemann and H.-H. Nagel, Postlude to a Pascal-Compiler Boot-strapped on a DEC-System 10, *S-P&E* **6**, 29–42 (1976).

G. G. Gustafson, Some Practical Experiences Formatting Pascal Programs, *SIGPLAN Notices* **14**(9), 42–49 (1979).

G. G. Gustafson and T. A. Johnson, (Letter about capitalizing keywords), *SIGPLAN Notices* **14**(5), 7 (1979).

G. G. Gustafson, T. A. Johnson, and G. S. Key, Some Practical Experiences with the Pascal Language, *AFIPS Conference Proceedings, 1980 NCC, Anaheim, Ca.* 741–746 (1980).

A. N. Habermann, Critical Comments on the Programming Language Pascal, *ACTA Information* **3**, 47–57 (1973).

M. P. Hagerty, The Case for Extending Pascal's I/O, *Pascal Newsletter* **6**, 42–45 (November 1976).

G. J. Hansen and C. E. Lindahl, *Preliminary Specifications of Real-time Pascal.* Florida University (July 1976).

G. J. Hansen, G. A. Shoults, and J. D. Cointment, Construction of a Transportable, Multi-Pass Compiler for Extended Pascal, *SIGPLAN Notices* **14**(8), 117–126 (1979).

S. Hanson, R. Jullig, P. Jackson, P. Levy, and T. Pittman, Summary of the Characteristics of Several "Modern" Programming Languages, SIGPLAN Notices **14**(5), 28–45 (1979).

A. C. Hartman, A Concurrent Pascal Compiler for Minicomputers, *Lecture Notes in Computer Science* **50**, Springer-Verlag (1977).

D. Heimbigner, Writing Device Drivers in Concurrent Pascal, *SIGOPS* **11** (1978).

D. L. Heiserman, *Pascal* ("Tiny" Pascal), Tab Books, Blue Ridge Summit, PA, 1980.

E. Heistad, Pascal—Cyber Version, *Teknisk Notat S-305 Forsvarets Forskningsinsti-tutt*, Norwegian Defense Research Establishment, Kjeller, Norway (June 1973).

F. W. v. Henke and D. C. Luckham, *Automatic Program Verification III: A Method ology for Verifying Programs*, Stanford University (December 1974).

T. Hikita and K. Ishihata, An Extended Pascal and Its Implementation Using a Trunk, *Report of the Computer Centre* **5**, 23–51, University of Tokyo, (1976).

C. A. R. Hoare and N. Wirth, An Axiomatic Definition of the Programming Language Pascal, *ACTA Informatica* **2**, 335–355 (1973).

R. C. Holt and J. N. P. Hume, *Programming Standard Pascal*, Reston, Virginia, 1980.

J. Hueras and H. Ledgard, An Automatic Formatting Program for Pascal, *SIGPLAN Notices* **12**(7), 82–84 (1977).

J. W. Hughes, Pascal—Data, *Advanced Techniques for Microprocessor Systems*, Peter Peregrinus, Stevenage, England, 78–83 (1980).

J. W. Hughes, Pascal—Program and Control Structures, *Advanced Techniques for Microprocessor Systems*, pp. 84–92, Peter Peregrinus, Stevenage, England, 1980.

A. J. Hurst, Pascal-P, Program Structure and Program Behaviour, *S-P&E* **10**, 1029–36 (1980).

M. Iglewski, J. Madey, and S. Matwin, A Contribution to an Improvement of Pascal, *SIGPLAN Notices* **13**(1), 48–58 (1978).

D. C. Ince and M. Keynes, Paged Input/Output in Some High Level Languages, *SIGPLAN Notices* **15**(7 & 8), 52–57 (1980).

T. Irish, What to Do After a While . . . Longer, *Pascal News* **13**, 65 (December 1978). 1978).

K. Ishihata and T. Hikita, *Bootstrapping Pascal Using a Trunk*, Department of Information Science, Faculty of Science, University of Tokyo (1976).

M. Jackel, A Formatting Parser for Pascal Programs, *SIGPLAN Notices* **15**(7 & 8), 58–63 (1980).

Ch. Jacobi, Dynamic Array Parameters, *Pascal Newsletter* **5**, 23–25 (September 1976).

K. Jensen, and N. Wirth, Pascal—User Manual and Report, *Lecture Notes in Computer Science* **18**, Springer-Verlag, New York, 1974.

K. Jensen and N. Wirth, *Pascal—User Manual and Report,* Springer-Verlag, New York, 1974 (corrected printing 1978).

G. Jin, *A Pascal Cross-compiler for a Microcomputer* (M.S. thesis), Department of Computer Science, University of North Carolina, Chapel Hill (1979).

O. G. Johnson, A Generalized Instrumentation Procedure for Concurrent Pascal Systems, *Proceedings of the 1979 International Conference on Parallel Processing*, IEEE, 205–207 (1979).

D. B. Johnston and A. M. Lister, An Experiment in Software Science, *Language Design and Programming Methodology, Lecture Notes in Computer Science*, Vol. 79, pp. 195–215, Springer-Verlag, New York, 1979.

J. Jones, Towards a HLL-oriented Microprocessor Instruction Set, *Euromicro Journal* **6**(3), 158–160 (1980).

D. A. Joslin, A Case for Acquiring Pascal, *S-P&E* **9**, 691–692 (1979).

T. Kagimasa, T. Araki, and N. Tokura, "A Pascal Compiler for Separate Compilation, *Transactions of the Institute for Electronic and Communications Engineering, Jpn. Sect. E.* **E63**(2), Japan, 171–172 (1980).

H. Katzan, Jr., *Invitation to Pascal*, Petrocelli Books, Princeton, NJ, 1981.

W. H. Kaubisch, R. H. Perrott, and C. A. R. Hoare, Quasiparallel Programming, *S-P&E* **6**, 341–356 (1976).

D. R. Kaye, Interactive Pascal Input, *SIGPLAN Notices* **15**(1), 66–68 (1980).

W. Kempton, Suggestions for Pascal Implementations, *Pascal News* **11**, 40–41 (February 1978).

B. W. Kernighan and P. J. Plauger, *Software Tools in Pascal,* Addison-Wesley, New York, 1981.

R. Kieburtz, *Structured Programming and Problem Solving with Pascal*, Prentice-Hall, Englewood Cliffs, NJ 1977.

R. B. Kieburtz, W. Barabash, and C. R. Hill, A Typechecking Program Linkage System for Pascal, *Proceedings of the Third International Conference on Software Engineering*, Atlanta, GA, May 10–12 (1978).

E. N. Kittlitz, Block Statements and Synonyms for Pascal, *SIGPLAN Notices* **11**(10), 32–35 (1976).

E. N. Kittlitz, Another Proposal for Variable Size Arrays in Pascal, *SIGPLAN Notices* **12**(1), 82–86 (1977).

B. Knobe and G. Yuval, Some Steps Toward a Better Pascal, *Journal of Computer Languages* **1**, 277–286 (1976).

S. Knudsen, Indexed Files, *Pascal Newsletter* **6**, 33 (November 1976).

E. B. Koffman, *Problem Solving and Structured Programming in Pascal*, Addison-Wesley Reading, MA, 1981.

G. A. Korn, Programming Continuous-System Simulation in Pascal, *Mathematics and Computers in Simulation* **21**, 276–281 (November 1979).

P. Kornerup, B. B. Kristensen, and O. L. Madsen, Interpretation and Code Generation Based on Intermediate Languages, *S-P&E* **10**, 635–658 (1980).

V. A. Kostin, Some Features of Interactive Pascal, *Programming and Computer Software* **5**(4), 280–284 (1979).

B. B. Kristensen, O. L. Madsen, and B. B. Jensen, A Pascal Environment Machine (P-Code), *Daimi PB-28*, University of Aarhus, Denmark (April 1974).

J. Kriz and H. Sandmayr, Extension of Pascal by Coroutines and Its Application to Quasi-parallel Programming and Simulation, *S-P&E* **10**, 773–789 (1980).

C. Lakos and A. H. J. Sale, Is Disciplined Programming Transferable, and Is It Insightful?, *Australian Computer Journal* **10**(3), 87–97 (1978).

W. R. Lalonde, The Zero Oversight, *SIGPLAN Notices* **14**(7), 3–4 (1979).

S. P. Lapin and R. C. Whiffen, Device Drivers in Micro Concurrent Pascal, *Proceedings of the MicroDelcon '80, The Delaware Bay Microcomputer Conference*, IEEE, 74–79 (1980).

A. R. Lawrence and D. Schofield, SFS—A File System Supporting Pascal Files, Design and Implementation, *NPL Report NAC 88*, National Physics Laboratory (February 1978).

R. J. LeBlanc, Extensions to Pascal for Separate Compilation, *SIGPLAN Notices* **13**(9), 30–33 (1978).

R. J. LeBlanc and J. J. Coda, *A Guide to Pascal Textbooks*, School of Information and Computer Science, Georgia Institute of Technology, Atlanta, GA.

O. Lecarme, Structured Programming, Programming Teaching and the Language Pascal, *SIGPLAN Notices* **9**(7), 15–21 (1974).

O. Lecarme, Development of a Pascal Compiler for the CII IRIS 50. A Partial History, *Pascal Newsletter* **8**, 8–11 (May 1977).

O. Lecarme, Is Algol 68 a Logical Subset of Pascal or Not?, *SIGPLAN Notices* **12**(12), 33–35 (1977).

O. Lecarme and P. Desjardins, More Comments on the Programming Language Pascal, *ACTA Informatica* **4**, 231–244 (1975).

O. Lecarme and P. Desjardins, Reply to a Paper by A. N. Habermann on the Programming Language Pascal, *SIGPLAN Notices* **9**, 21–27 (1974).

O. Lecarme and M-C. Peyrolle-Thomas, Self Compiling Compilers: An Appraisal of Their Implementation and Portability, *S-P&E* **8**, 149–170 (1978).

H. F. Ledgard, J. F. Hueras, and P. A. Nagin, *Pascal with Style*, Hayden Rochelle Park, NJ, 1979.

T. G. Lewis, *Pascal Programming for the Apple*, Reston, VA, 1980.

L. A. Liddiard, Yet Another Look at Code Generation for Pascal on CDC 600 and Cyber Machines, *Pascal Newsletter* **7**, 17–23 (February 1977).

B. W. Liffick (ed.), *The BYTE Book of Pascal*, McGraw-Hill, New York, 1979.

S. Ljungkvist, Pascal and Existing FORTRAN Files, *SIGPLAN Notices* **15**(5), 54–55 (1980).

K. P. Loehr, Beyond Concurrent Pascal, *Proceedings of the Sixth ACM Symposium on Operating System Principles*, 173–180 (1977).

D. C. Luckham, S. M. German, F. W. v. Henke, R. A. Karp, and P. W. Milne, *Stanford Pascal Verifier User Manual*, STAN-CS-79-731, Department of Computer Science, Stanford University, CA (1979).

D. C. Luckham and N. Suzuki, Verification of Array, Record, and Pointer Operations in Pascal, *ACM TOPLAS* **1**(2), 226–244 (1979).

W. I. MacGregor, An Alternative Approach to Type Equivalence, *Pascal News* **17**, 63–65 (March 1980).

M. Machura, Implementation of a Special-Purpose Language Using Pascal Implementation Methodology, *S-P&E* **9**, 931–945 (1979).

B. J. MacLennan, A Note on Dynamic Arrays in Pascal, *SIGPLAN Notices* **10**(9), 39–40 (1975).

N. Magnenat-Thalmann and D. Thalmann, A Graphical Pascal Extension Based on Graphical Types, *S-P&E* **11**, 53–62 (1981).

D. Marca, Some Pascal Style Guidelines, *SIGPLAN Notices* **16**(4), 70–80 (1981).

C. D. Marlin, A Model for Data Control in the Programming Language Pascal, *Proceedings of the Australian Colleges of Advanced Education Computing Conference, August 1977*, A. K. Duncan, ed., 293–306 (1977).

C. D. Marlin, A Heap-based Implementation of the Programming Language Pascal, *S-P&E* **9**, 101–119 (1979).

E. Marmier, A Program Verifier for Pascal, in *Information Processing*, Vol. *74* (IFIP Congress 1974), North-Holland, Amsterdam, 1974.

P. Mateti, Pascal Versus C: A Subjective Comparison, in *Lecture Notes in Computer Science*, Vol. *79*, pp. 37–70, Springer-Verlag, New York, 1979.

S. E. Mattsson, Implementation of Concurrent Pascal on LSI-11, *S-P&E* **10**, 205–217 (1980).

S. Matwin and M. Missala, A Simple, Machine Independent Tool for Obtaining Rough Measures of Pascal Programs, *SIGPLAN Notices* **11**(8), 42–45 (1976).

B. A. E. Meekings, A Further Defence of Formatted Input, *Pascal Newsletter* **8**, 11 (May 1977).

S. M. Merritt, On the Importance of Teaching Pascal in the IS Curriculum, *SIGCSE Bulletin* **12**(1), 88–91 (1980).

R. E. Merwin, *Performance Optimization of the Pascal to DEC VAX 11/780 Microcode Compiler*, AD-A089424/6, School of Engineering and Applied Science, George Washington University, Washington DC (1980).

S. J. Metz (Letter about enumerations), *SIGPLAN Notices* **16**(5), 10 (1981).

A. Mickel, *Pascal Newsletter*, University of Minnesota Computer Center, Minneapolis: No. 5 (September 1976), No. 6 (November 1976), No. 7 (February 1977), No. 8 (May 1977). *Pascal News* (change of name): No. 9 and 10 (September 1977), No. 11 (February 1978), No. 12 (June 1978), No. 13 (December 1978), No. 14 (January 1979), No. 15 (September 1979), No. 16 (October 1979). (See also G. Richmond and R. Shaw.)

A. Mickel, Pascal for Personal Computers *SIGPC Notes* **1**(1), 3 (1978).

A. Miller, *Pascal Programs for Scientists and Engineers*, Sybex, Berkeley, CA, 1981.

D. D. Miller, Adapting Pascal for the PDP 11/45, *Pascal News* **11**, 51–53 (February 1978).

J. Miner, Overlays: A Proposal, *Pascal Newsletter*, **5**, 16–19 (September 1976).

D. V. Moffat, A Pascal Bibliography (June, 1980), *Pascal News* **19**, 12–22 (September 1980).

D. V. Moffat, A Categorized Pascal Bibliography (June, 1980), *SIGPLAN Notices* **15**(10), 63–75 (1980), and *Technical Report TR80-06*, Department of Computer Science, North Carolina State University, Raleigh (1980).

D. V. Moffat, Enumerations in Pascal, Ada, and Beyond, *SIGPLAN Notices* **16**(2), 77–82 (1981).

P. R. Mohilner, Prettyprinting Pascal Programs, *SIGPLAN Notices* **13**(7), 34–40 (1978).

P. R. Mohilner, Using Pascal in a FORTRAN Environment, *S-P&E* **7**, 357–362 (1977).

T. Molster and V. Sundvor, Unit Pascal System for the Univac 1108 Computer, *Teknisk Notat 1/74*, Institutt for Databehandling, Univeritettet 1 Trondheim, Norway (February 1974).

L. Moore, *Foundations of Programming with Pascal*, Halsted Press (John Wiley & Sons), New York, 1980.

H. H. Nagel and W. F. Burger, An Introduction to Pascal on the DEC-10, *Report TR-22B*, Department of Computer Sciences, University of Texas at Austin (March 1975).

H.-H. Nagel, Pascal for the DEC-System 10, Experiences and Further Plans, *Mitteilung Nr. 21*, Institut fur Informatik, Universitat Hamburg (November 1975).

J. Nagle, A Few Proposed Deletions, *Pascal News* **12**, 39 (June 1978).

K. T. Narayana, V. R. Prasad, and M. Joseph, Some Aspects of Concurrent Programming in CCNPASCAL, *S-P&E* **9**(9), 749–770 (1979).

D. Neal and V. Wallentine, Experiences with the Portability of Concurrent Pascal, *S-P&E* **8**, 341–353 (1978).

P. A. Nelson, A Comparison of Pascal Intermediate Languages, *SIGPLAN Notices* **14**(8), 208–213 (1979).

J. Nielsen, Comments on Global Enumeration Types, *SIGPLAN Notices* **16**(5), 9 (1981).

T. Noodt, Pascal Environment Interface, *Pascal News* **12**, 35–37 (June 1978).

T. Noodt and D. Belsnes, A Simple Extension to Pascal for Quasi-Parallel Processing, *SIGPLAN Notices* **15**(5), 56–65 (1980), and *Pascal News* **19**, 60–66 (September 1980).

K. V. Nori, U. Ammann, K. Jensen, H. H. Nageli, and Ch. Jacobi, *The Pascal "P" Compiler: Implementation Notes (Revised Edition)*, Berichte Nr. 10, Institut für Informatik, Eidgenossische Technische Hochschule, Zurich, Switzerland, 1976.

K. V. Nori, U. Ammann, K. Jensen, H. H. Nageli, and Ch. Jacobi, *Corrections to the "Pascal Compiler: Implementation Notes,"* Berichte Nr. 10, Institut für Informatik, Eidgenossische Technische Hochschule, Zurich, Switzerland, 1976.

G. J. Nutt, A Comparison of Pascal and FORTRAN as Introductory Programming Languages, *SIGPLAN Notices* **13**(2), 57–62 (1978).

H. L. Ogushwitz, Pascal Programming Language, June 1970–June 1980, (Citations from the Engineering Index Data Base) and . . . (Citations from the NTIS Data Base), *PB80-853229* and *PB80-853211*, New England Research Application Center, Storrs, CT (1980).

M. Overgaard, UCSD Pascal: A Portable Software Environment for Small Computers, *AFIPS Conference Proceedings, 1980 NCC, Anaheim, Ca.*, 747–754 (1980).

J. S. Parry, The Pascal String Library Notes, *Information Science Student Report*, University of Tasmania (1978).

A. L. Parsons, A Microcomputer Pascal Cross Compiler, *Proceedings of Spring Compcon 78, San Francisco, February-March, 1978*, IEEE, 146–150 (1978).

M. Pasturel, What Makes Pascal a Modern Test Language, *Digest of Papers, 1980 Test Conference, Philadelphia, Pa.*, IEEE, 326–330 (1980).

H. D. Peckham and A. Luehrmann, *Apple Pascal: A Hands-on Approach*, McGraw-Hill, New York, 1981.

S. Pemberton, Comments on an Error-recovery Scheme by Hartmann, *S-P&E* **10**, 231–240 (1980).

D. R. Perkins and R. L. Sites, Machine-Independent Pascal Code Optimization, *SIGPLAN Notices* **14**(8), 201–207 (1979).

H. Perkins, Lazy I/O Is Not the Answer, *SIGPLAN Notices* **16**(4), 81–88 (1981).

R. H. Perrott and P. S. Dhillon, An Experiment with FORTRAN and Pascal, *S-P&E* **11**, 491–496 (1981).

G. Persch and G. Winterstein, Symbolic Interpretation and Tracing of Pascal Programs, *3rd International Conference on Software Engineering, Atlanta, Georgia, May, 1978*, IEEE, 312–319 (1978).

J. L. Peterson, On the Formatting of Pascal Programs, *SIGPLAN Notices* **12**(12), 83–86 (1977).

D. Pfleger, Pascal and Its Suitability to Microprocessor Software Development, *Pro-

*ceedings of Microprocessor Applications in the '80s, Arizona Technical Symposium,* IEEE, 85–90 (1980).

S. Pokrovsky, Formal Types and Their Application to Dynamic Arrays in Pascal, *SIGPLAN Notices* **11**(10), 36–42 (1976).

M. S. Powell, Experience of Transporting and Using the SOLO Operating System, *S-P&E* **9**(7), 561–569 (1979).

T. W. Pratt, Control Computations and the Design of Loop Control Structures, *IEEE TSE* **SE-4**, 2 (1978).

W. C. Price, What is a Textfile?, *Pascal News* **9 & 10**, 42 (September 1977).

J. Pugh and D. Simpson, Pascal Errors—Empirical Evidence, *Computer Bulletin* **2**(19), 26–28 (March 1979).

J. Ramsdell, Prettyprinting Structured Programs with Connector Lines, *SIGPLAN Notices* **14**(9), 74–75 (1979).

R. R. Ransom, Pascal Survey, *Pascal News* **17**, 57–58 (March 1980).

B. W. Ravenel, Toward a Pascal Standard, *IEEE Computer* **12**(4), 68–82 (1979).

B. W. Ravenel, Will Pascal be the Next Standard Language?, *COMPCON 79 Digest of Papers,* IEEE, 144–146 (1979).

W. Remmele, Design and Implementation of a Programming System to Support the Development of Reliable Pascal Programs, *Proceedings of the Workshop on Reliable Software, Bonn, Germany,* 73–87, Carl Hanser Verlag, Munich (1979).

F. Richard and H. F. Ledgard, A Reminder for Language Designers, *SIGPLAN Notices* **12**(12), 73–82 (1977).

G. H. Richmond, Proposals for Pascal, *Pascal Newsletter* **8**, 12–14 (May 1977).

G. Richmond (ed.), *Pascal Newsletter,* University of Colorado Computing Center, Boulder: No. 1 (January 1974), *SIGPLAN Notices* **9**(3), 21–28 (1974); No. 2 (May 1974), *SIGPLAN Notices* **9**(11), 11–17 (1974); No. 3 (February 1975), *SIGPLAN Notices* **11**(2), 33–48 (1976); No. 4 (July 1976). (See also A. Mickel and R. Shaw.)

M. Roberts and R. Macdonald, A Resolution of the Boolean-Evaluation Question—or—*if not* Partial Evaluation *then* Conditional Expressions, *Pascal News* **13**, 63–65 (December 1978).

K. Robinson, The Design of a Successor to Pascal, *Lecture Notes in Computer Science* **79**, Springer-Verlag, 151–168 (1979).

J. S. Rohl and H. J. Barrett, *Programming via Pascal,* Cambridge University Press, Cambridge, MA, 1980.

J. H. Roth, Jr., A Comment on Ada Enumerations, *SIGPLAN Notices* **16**(5), 12 (1981).

P. Roy, Linear Flowchart Generator for a Structured Language, *SIGPLAN Notices* **11**(11), 58–64 (1976).

H. Rubenstein, Pascal Printer Plotter, *Pascal Newsletter* **7**, 9–16 (February 1977).

A. Rudmik, Compiler Design for Efficient Code Generation and Program Optimization, *SIGPLAN Notices* **14**(8), 127–38 (1979).

C. Runciman, Scarcely Variabled Programming and Pascal, *SIGPLAN Notices* **14**(11), 97–106 (1979).

A. Sale, The Pascal Validation Suite—Aims and Methods, *Pascal News* **16**, 5–9 (October 1979).

A. Sale, Scope and Pascal, *SIGPLAN Notices* **14**(9), 61–63 (1979).

A. Sale, General Thoughts on Pascal Arising out of Correspondence Between Southampton and Tasmania, *Pascal Newsletter* **6**, 45–47 (November 1976).

A. Sale, Pascal Stylistics and Reserved Words, *S-P&E* **9**, 821–825 (1979).

A. Sale, Uppercase Letter Conventions, *SIGPLAN Notices* **14**(2), 3–4 (1979).

A. Sale, Some Observations on Pascal and Personal Style, *Pascal News* **17**, 68–71 (March 1980).

A. Sale, Counterview in Favor of Strict Type Compatibility, *SIGPLAN Notices* **15**(12), 53–55 (1980).

A. H. J. Sale, Stylistics in Languages with Compound Statements, *Australian Computer Journal* **10**, 2 (1978).

A. H. J. Sale, Strings and the Sequence Abstraction in Pascal, *S-P&E* **9**, 671–683 (1979).

A. H. J. Sale, Implementing Strings in Pascal—Again, *S-P&E* **9**, 839–841 (1979).

A. H. J. Sale, A Note on Scope, One-Pass Compilers, and Pascal, *Australian Computer Sciences Communications* **1**(1), 80–82 (1979), and *Pascal News,* **15**, 62–63 (September 1979).

A. H. J. Sale, Conformant Arrays in Pascal, *Pascal News* **17**, 54–56 (March 1980).

A. H. J. Sale, Pascal—Riding on the Micro Wave (Programming Languages), *Proceedings of the IREE Australia* **41**(1), 4–10 (1980).

A. H. J. Sale, Forward-Declared Procedures, Parameter Lists and Scope, *S-P&E* **11**, 123–130 (1981).

A. H. J. Sale, Proposal for Extension to Pascal, *SIGPLAN Notices* **16**(4), 98–103 (1981).

V. Santhanam, A Hardware-Independent Virtual Architecture for Pascal, *AFIPS Conference Proceedings* **48**, 637–648 (1979).

V. Santhanam, Translating Non-standard Extensions to Standard Pascal, *AFIPS Conference Proceedings, 1980 NCC, Anaheim, Ca.,* 877–882 (1980).

J. B. Saxe and A. Hisgen, Lazy Evaluation of the File Buffer for Interactive I/O, *Pascal News* **13** (December 1979).

S. Schach, Tracing the Heap, *Pascal News* **15**, 67–68 (September 1979).

S. R. Schach, A Portable Trace for the Pascal Heap, *S-P&E* **10**, 421–426 (1980).

H. Schauer, Micropascal—A Portable Language Processor for Microprogramming Education, *Euromicro J. (Netherlands)* **5**(2), 89–92 (1979).

R. Schild, Implementation of the Programming Language Pascal, *Lecture Notes in Economics and Mathematical Systems* **75** (1972).

J. W. Schmidt, Some High Level Language Constructs for Data of Type Relation, *ACM Transactions on Database Systems* **2**(3), 247–261 (1977).

F. B. Schneider and A. J. Bernstein, Scheduling in Concurrent Pascal, *Operating Systems Review* **12**(2), 15–20 (1978).

G. M. Schneider, The Need for Hierarchy and Structure in Language Management, *Pascal Newsletter* **6**, 34 (November 1976).

G. M. Schneider, Pascal: An Overview, *IEEE Computer* **12**(4), 61–65 (1979).

G. M. Schneider, S. W. Weingart, and D. M. Perlman, *An Introduction to Programming and Problem Solving with Pascal*, Wiley, New York, 1978.

M. J. R. Shave, The Programming of Structural Relationships in Dynamic Environments, *S-P&E* **8**, 199–211 (1978).

R. Shaw (ed.), *Pascal News*, Digital Equipment Corp., Atlanta, GA: No. 17 (March 1980), No. 18 (May 1980), No. 19 (September 1980), No. 20 (December 1980). (See also A. Mickel and G. Richmond.)

K. A. Shillington and G. M. Ackland (eds.), *UCSD Pascal Version 1.5*, Institute for Information Systems, University of California, San Diego (1978).

M. Shimasaki, S. Fukaya, K. Ikeda, and T. Kiyono, An Analysis of Pascal Programs in Compiler Writing, *S-P&E* **10**, 149–157 (1980).

S. K. Shrivastava, Sequential Pascal with Recovery Blocks, *S-P&E* **8**, 177–185 (1978).

S. K. Shrivastava, Concurrent Pascal with Backward Error Recovery: Language Features and Examples. *S-P&E* **9**, 1001–1020 (1979).

S. K. Shrivastava, Concurrent Pascal with Backward Error Recovery: Implementation, *S-P&E* **9**, 1021–1033 (1979).

A. Silberschatz, On the Safety of the I/O Primitive in Concurrent Pascal, *Computer Journal 22*, 142–145 (May 1979).

A. Silberschatz, R. B. Kieburtz, and A. J. Bernstein, Extending Concurrent Pascal to Allow Dynamic Resource Management, IEEE TSE, SE-3 **3** (May 1977).

D. Simpson, Structured Programming and the Teaching of Computing: Experience with Pascal, Department of Computer Studies, Sheffield City Polytechnic, Sheffield, England (1979).

A. Singer, J. Hueras, and H. Ledgard, A Basis for Executing Pascal Programmers, *SIGPLAN Notices* **12**(7), 101–105 (1977).

R. L. Sites, Programming Tools: Statement Counts and Procedure Timings, *SIGPLAN Notices* **13**(12), 98–101 (1978).

R. L. Sites, Moving a Large Pascal Program from an LSI-11 to a Cray-1, *Pascal News* **13**, 59–60 (December 1978).

R. L. Sites and D. R. Perkins, *Universal P-code Definition, Version (0.2)*, California University, San Diego (January 1979).

G. Smith and R. Anderson, LSI-11 Writable Control Store Enhancements to UCSD Pascal, *UCRL-81808, NTIS UCID-18046*, Lawrence Livermore Labs (1978).

N. Solntseff, McMaster Modifications to the Pascal 6000 3.4 System, *Computer Science Technical Note 74-CS-2*, McMaster University, Ontario, Canada (November 1974).

N. Solntseff and D. Wood, Pyramids: A Data Type for Matrix Representation in Pascal, *BIT*, **17**(3), 344–350 (1977).

A. Springer, A Comparison of Language C and Pascal, *IBM Technical Report No. G320-2128*, IBM Cambridge Scientific Center, Cambridge, MA (August 1979).

J. Steensgaard-Madsen, More on Dynamic Arrays in Pascal, *SIGPLAN Notices* **11**(5), 63–64 (1976).

J. Steensgaard-Madsen, Pascal—Clarifications and Recommended Extensions, *ACTA Informatica* **12**, 73–94 (1979).

N. Suzuki and K. Ishihata, Implementation of an Array Bound Checker, *Internal Report of the Department of Computer Science*, Carnegie-Mellon University (1976).

M. Takeichi, *Pascal Compiler for the FACOM 230 OS2/VS*, University of Tokyo (1975).

K. Tanabe and M. Yamamoto, Single Chip Pascal Processor: Its Architecture and Performance Evaluation, *Proceedings of Distributed Computing, COMPCON 80, Twenty-First IEEE International Conference, Washington, D.C.*, 395–399 (1980).

A. Tanenbaum, (Letter about conformant arrays), SIGPLAN Notices **15**(6), 10–11 (1980).

A. S. Tanenbaum, A Comparison of Pascal and Algol 68, *The Computer Journal* **21**(4), 316–323 (1978).

R. D. Tennent, Another Look at Type Compatibility in Pascal, *S-P&E* **8**, 429–437 (1978).

R. D. Tennent, A Denotational Definition of the Programming Language Pascal, *Technical Report 77-47*, Computing and Information Science, Queen's University, Canada (1977).

R. D. Tennent, Language Design Methods Based on Semantic Principles, *ACTA Informatica* **8**(2), 97–112 (1977).

R. D. Tennent, A Note on Files in Pascal, *BIT* **17**(3), 362–366 (1977).

R. D. Tennent, *Principles of Programming Languages*, Prentice-Hall, Englewood Cliffs, NJ, 1981.

N. Thalmann and D. Thalmann, The Use of Pascal as a Teaching Tool in Introductory, Intermediate, and Advanced Computer Science Courses, *Proceedings of the SIGCSE/CSA Technical Symposium, Detroit*, 277–281 (1978).

D. Thibault and P. Mancel, Implementation of a Pascal Compiler for the CII Iris 80 Computer, *SIGPLAN Notices* **8**(6), 89–90 (1973).

J. Tiberghien, *The Pascal Handbook*, Sybex, Berkeley, CA, 1980.

A. M. van Tilborg and L. D. Wittie, A Concurrent Pascal Operating System for a Network Computer, *Computer Software and Applications Conference, Chicago*, IEEE, 757–763 (1980).

J.-P. Tremblay, R. B. Bunt, and L. M. Opseth, *Structured Pascal*, McGraw-Hill, New York, 1980.

D. H. Uyeno and W. Vaessen, PASSIM: A Discrete-event Stimulation Package for Pascal, *Simulation* **35**(6), 183–190 (1980).

R. D. Vavra, What Are Pascal's Design Goals?, *Pascal News* **12**, 34–35 (June 1978).

T. Venema and J. des Rivieres, Euclid and Pascal, *SIGPLAN Notices* **13**(3), 57–69 (1978).

W. de Vries, An Implementation of the Language Pascal for the PDP 11 Series, Based on a Portable Pascal Compiler, *Technische Hogeschool Twente*, Enschede (March 1975).

S. P. Wagstaff, Disposing of Dispose, *Pascal News* **9** & **10**, 40–41 (September 1977).

M. Waite and D. Fox, *Pascal Primer*, Howard W. Sams & Co., Indianapolis, 1981.

J. F. Wakerly, Pascal Extensions for Describing Computer Instruction Sets, *Computer Architecture News* **8**(7), 15–23 (1980).

B. Wallace, More on Interactive Input in Pascal, *SIGPLAN Notices* **14**(9), 76 (1979).

A. I. Wasserman, Testing and Verification Aspects of Pascal-like Languages, *Computer Languages* **4**, 155–169 (1979).

D. A. Watt, An Extended Attribute Grammar for Pascal, *SIGPLAN Notices* **14**(2), 60–74 (1979).

C. A. G. Webster, *Introduction to Pascal*, Heyden, London, 1976.

J. Welsh, Economic Range Checks in Pascal, *S-P&E* **8**, 85–97 (1978).

J. Welsh and D. W. Bustard, Pascal-Plus—Another Language for Modular Multiprogramming, *S-P&E* **9**, 947–957 (1979).

J. Welsh and J. Elder, *Introduction to Pascal*, Prentice-Hall International, London, 1979.

J. Welsh and R. M. McKeag, *Structured System Programming*, Prentice-Hall, Englewood Cliffs, NJ, 1980.

J. Welsh and C. Quinn, A Pascal Compiler for the ICL 1900 Series Computers, *S-P&E* **2**, 73–77 (1972).

J. Welsh, W. J. Sneeringer, and C. A. R. Hoare, Ambiguities and Insecurities in Pascal, *S-P&E* **7**, 685–696 (1977).

M. Whitebread, *Microprocessor Software, Topics in Microprocessing, Book 2*, Castle House Publications, Ltd., Tunbridge Wells, England, 1980.

B. A. Wichmann and A. H. J. Sale, A Pascal Processor Validation Suite, *Pascal News* **16**, 12–24 (October 1979), and *REPORT NPL-CSU-7/80*, National Physics Laboratory, Teddington, England (1980).

K. Wickman, Pascal is a Natural, *IEEE Spectrum* (March 1979).

J. Wilander, An Interface Programming System for Pascal, *BIT* **20**(2), 163–174 (1980).

R. Wilsker, On the Article "What to do After a While," *Pascal News* **13**, 61–62 (December 1978).

I. R. Wilson, Teaching Pascal to Large Student Groups, *IUCC Conference on Teaching Pascal and Algol 68*, Norwich (1978).

I. R. Wilson, Pascal for School and Hobby Use, *S-P&E* **10**, 659–671 (1980).

I. R. Wilson and A. M. Addyman, *A Practical Introduction to Pascal*, Springer-Verlag, New York, 1979.

N. Wirth, The Design of a Pascal Compiler, *S-P&E* **1**, 309–333 (1971).

N. Wirth, The Programming Language Pascal and Its Design Criteria, *High Level Languages*, Infotech State of the Art Report 7 (1972).

N. Wirth, *Pascal-S: A Subset and Its Implementation*, Berichte Nr. 12, Institut für Informatik, Eidgenossische Technische Hochschule, Zurich, Switzerland, 1975.

N. Wirth, The Programming Language Pascal, *ACTA Informatica* **1**, 35–63 (1971).

N. Wirth, The Programming Language Pascal (Revised Report), *Berichte der Fachgruppe Computer-Wissenschaften* **5**, Zurich, 49 (November 1972).

N. Wirth, Comment on a Note on Dynamic Arrays in Pascal, *SIGPLAN Notices* **11**(1), 37–38 (1976).

N. Wirth, An Assessment of the Programming Language Pascal, *SIGPLAN Notices* **10**(6), 23–30 (1975).

N. Wirth, *Algorithms + Data Structures = Programs,* Prentice-Hall, Englewood Cliffs, NJ, 1976.

N. Wirth, *Systematic Programming: An Introduction,* Prentice-Hall, Englewood Cliffs, NJ, 1973.

H. Wupper, Some Remarks on "A Case for Acquiring Pascal," *S-P&E* **10**, 247–48 (1980).

M. Yasumura, Evolution of Loop Statements, *SIGPLAN Notices* **12**(9), 124–129 (1977).

R. Zaks, *An Introduction to Pascal (Including UCSD Pascal),* Sybex, Berkeley, CA, 1980.

R. Zaks and R. Langer, *Fifty Pascal Programs,* Sybex, Berkeley, CA, 1981.

# Glossary

**Access type.**   An access type is a type whose objects are created by execution of an *allocator*. An *access value* designates such an object.

**Aggregate.**   An aggregate is a written form denoting a *composite value*. An *array aggregate* denotes a value of an array type; a *record aggregate* denotes a value of a record type. The components of an aggregate may be specified using either *positional* or *named* association.

**Allocator.**   An allocator creates a new object of an access *type*, and returns an *access value* designating the created object.

**Attribute.**   An attribute is a predefined characteristic of a named entity.

**Body.**   A body is a program unit defining the execution of a subprogram, package, or task. A *body stub* is a replacement for a body that is compiled separately.

**Collection.**   A collection is the entire set of allocated objects of an *access type*.

**Compilation unit.**   A compilation unit is a *program unit* presented for compilation as an independent text. It is preceded by a *context specification*, naming the other compilation units on which it depends. A compilation unit may be the specification or body of a subprogram or package.

**Component.**   A component denotes a part of a composite object. An *indexed component* is a name containing expressions denoting indices, and names a component in an array or an entry in an entry family. A *selected component* is the identifier of the component, prefixed by the name of the entity of which it is a component.

**Composite type.**   An object of a composite type comprises several components. An *array type* is a composite type, all of whose components are of the same type and subtype; the individual components are selected by their *indices*. A *record type* is a composite type whose components may be of different types; the individual components are selected by their identifiers.

**Constraint.**   A constraint is a restriction on the set of possible values of a type. A *range constraint* specifies lower and upper bounds of the values

326

of a scalar type. An *accuracy constraint* specifies the relative or absolute error bound of values of a real type. An *index constraint* specifies lower and upper bounds of an array index. A *discriminant constraint* specifies particular values of the discriminants of a record or private type.

**Context specification.**   A context specification, prefixed to a compilation unit, defines the other compilation units upon which it depends.

**Declarative part.**   A declarative part is a sequence of declarations and related information such as subprogram bodies and representation specifications that apply over a region of a program text.

**Derived type.**   A derived type is a type whose operations and values are taken from those of an existing type.

**Discrete type.**   A discrete type has an ordered set of distinct values. The discrete types are the enumeration and integer types. Discrete types may be used for indexing and iteration, and for choices in case statements and record variants.

**Discriminant.**   A discriminant is a syntactically distinguished component of a record. The presence of some record components (other than discriminants) may depend on the value of a discriminant.

**Elaboration.**   Elaboration is the process by which a declaration achieves its effect. For example, it can associate a name with a program entity or initialize a newly declared variable.

**Entity.**   An entity is anything that can be named or denoted in a program. Objects, types, values, program units, are all entities.

**Entry.**   An entry is used for communication between tasks. Externally an entry is called just as a subprogram is called; its internal behavior is specified by one or more accept statements specifying the actions to be performed when the entry is called.

**Enumeration type.**   An enumeration type is a discrete type whose values are given explicitly in the type declaration. These values may be either identifiers or character literals.

**Exception.**   An exception is an event that causes suspension of normal program execution. Bringing an exception to attention is called *raising* the exception. An *exception handler* is a piece of program text specifying a response to the exception. Execution of such a program text is called *handling* the exception.

**Expression.**   An expression is a part of a program that computes a value.

**Generic program unit.**   A generic program unit is a subprogram or package specified with a generic clause. A *generic clause* contains the declaration of generic parameters. A generic program unit may be thought of as a possibly parameterized model of program units. Instances (that is, filled-in copies) of the model can be obtained by *generic instantiation*. Such instantiated program units define subprograms and packages that can be used directly in a program.

**Introduce.** An identifier is introduced by its declaration at the point of its first occurrence.

**Lexical unit.** A lexical unit is one of the basic syntactic elements making up a program. A lexical unit is an identifier, a number, a character literal, a string, a delimiter, or a comment.

**Literal.** A literal denotes an explicit value of a given type, for example a number, an enumeration value, a character, or a string.

**Model number.** A model number is an exactly representable value of a real numeric type. Operations of a real type are defined in terms of operations on the model numbers of the type. The properties of the model numbers and of the operations are the minimal properties preserved by all implementations of the real type.

**Object.** An object is a variable or a constant. An object can denote any kind of data element, whether a scalar value, a composite value, or a value in an access type.

**Overloading.** Overloading is the property of literals, identifiers, and operators that can have several alternative meanings within the same scope. For example, an overloaded enumeration literal is a literal appearing in two or more enumeration types; an overloaded subprogram is a subprogram whose designator can denote one of several subprograms, depending upon the kind of its parameters and returned value.

**Package.** A package is a program unit specifying a collection of related entities such as constants, variables, types, and subprograms. The *visible part* of a package contains the entities that may be used from outside the package. The *private part* of a package contains structural details that are irrelevant to the user of the package but that complete the specification of the visible entities. The *body* of a package contains implementations of subprograms or tasks (possibly other packages) specified in the visible part.

**Parameter.** A parameter is one of the named entities associated with a subprogram, entry, or generic program unit. A *formal parameter* is an identifier used to denote the named entity in the unit body. An *actual* parameter is the particular entity associated with the corresponding formal parameter in a subprogram call, entry call, or generic instantiation. A *parameter mode* specifies whether the parameter is used for input, output, or input-output of data. A *positional parameter* is an actual parameter passed in positional order. A *named parameter* is an actual parameter passed by naming the corresponding formal parameter.

**Pragma.**  A pragma is an instruction to the compiler, and may be language defined or implementation defined.

**Private type.**  A private type is a type whose structure and set of values are clearly defined, but not known to the user of the type. A private type is known only by its discriminants and by the set of operations defined for it. A private type and its applicable operations are defined in the visible part of a package. Assignment and comparison for equality or inequality are also defined for private types, unless the private type is marked as *limited.*

**Qualified expression.**  A qualified expression is an expression qualified by the name of a type or subtype. It can be used to state the type or subtype of an expression, for example, for an overloaded literal.

**Range.**  A word range is a contiguous set of values of a scalar type. A range is specified by giving the lower and upper bounds for the values.

**Rendezvous.**  A rendezvous is the interaction that occurs between two parallel tasks when one task has called an entry of the other task, and a corresponding accept statement is being executed by the other task on behalf of the calling task.

**Representation specification.**  Representation specifications specify the mapping between data types and features of the underlying machine that execute a program. In some cases, they completely specify the mapping, in other cases they provide criteria for choosing a mapping.

**Scalar types.**  A scalar type is a type whose values have no components. Scalar types comprise discrete types (that is, enumeration and integer types) and real types.

**Scope.**  The scope of a declaration is the region of text over which the declaration has an effect.

**Static expression.**  A static expression is one whose value does not depend on any dynamically computed values of variables.

**Subprograms.**  A subprogram is an executable program unit, possibly with parameters for communication between the subprogram and its point of call. A *subprogram declaration* specifies the name of the subprogram and its parameters; a *subprogram body* specifies its execution. A subprogram may be a *procedure*, which performs an action, or a *function*, which returns a result.

**Subtype.**  A subtype of a type is obtained from the type by constraining the set of possible values of the type. The operations over a subtype are the same as those of the type from which the subtype is obtained.

**Task.**   A task is a program unit that may operate in parallel with other program units. A *task specification* establishes the name of the task and the names and parameters of its entries; a *task body* defines its execution. A *task type* is a specification that permits the subsequent declaration of any number of similar tasks.

**Type.**   A type characterizes a set of values and a set of operations applicable to those values and a set of operations applicable to those values. A *type definition* is a language construct introducing a type. A *type declaration* associates a name with a type introduced by a type definition.

**Use clause.**   A use clause opens the visibility to declarations given in the visible part of a package.

**Variant.**   A variant part of a record specifies alternative record components, depending on a discriminant of the record. Each value of the discriminant establishes a particular alternative of the variant part.

**Visibility.**   At a given point in a program text, the declaration of an entity with a certain identifier is said to be *visible* if the entity is an acceptable meaning for an occurrence at that point of the identifier.

# Index

Daniel R. McGlynn is the author of *Personal Computing: Home, Professional, and Small Business Applications, 2nd Ed.* (Wiley, 1982), *Distributed Processing and Data Communications* (Wiley, 1978) and other works in computer technology. He has lectured extensively to university and industrial audiences in the U.S. and abroad and has also appeared on radio and television. Dr. McGlynn has received awards from Honeywell Corporation, the National Science Foundation, and the Ford Foundation and holds patents for a number of computer applications. He received his Ph.D. in physics from New York University.